Transforming the Finance Function

In an increasingly competitive world, we believe it's quality of thinking that will give you the edge – an idea that opens new doors, a technique that solves a problem, or an insight that simply makes sense of it all. The more you know, the smarter and faster you can go.

That's why we work with the best minds in business and finance to bring cutting-edge thinking and best learning practice to a global market.

Under a range of leading imprints, including *Financial Times Prentice Hall*, we create world-class print publications and electronic products bringing our readers knowledge, skills and understanding which can be applied whether studying or at work.

To find out more about our business publications, or tell us about the books you'd like to find, you can visit us at www.business-minds.com

For other Pearson Education publications, visit www.pearsoned-ema.com

Transforming the Finance Function

Adding company-wide value in a web-enabled environment

Second Edition

MARGARET MAY

An imprint of Pearson Education

London ■ New York ■ Toronto ■ Sydney ■ Tokyo ■ Singapore ■ Hong Kong ■ Cape Town
New Delhi ■ Madrid ■ Paris ■ Amsterdam ■ Munich ■ Milan ■ Stockholm

PEARSON EDUCATION LIMITED

Head Office:
Edinburgh Gate
Harlow CM20 2JE
Tel: +44 (0)1279 623623
Fax: +44 (0)1279 431059

London Office:
128 Long Acre
London WC2E 9AN
Tel: +44 (0)20 7447 2000
Fax: +44 (0)20 7240 5771
Website: www.briefingzone.com

Second edition published in Great Britain in 2002

© Pearson Education Limited 2002

The right of Margaret May to be identified as Author
of this Work has been asserted by her in accordance with
the Copyright, Designs and Patents Act 1988.

ISBN 0 273 65666 X

First edition 0 273 64313 0

British Library Cataloguing in Publication Data
A CIP catalogue record for this book can be obtained from the British Library.

All rights reserved; no part of this publication may be reproduced, stored
in a retrieval system, or transmitted in any form or by any means, electronic,
mechanical, photocopying, recording, or otherwise without either the prior
written permission of the Publishers or a licence permitting restricted copying
in the United Kingdom issued by the Copyright Licensing Agency Ltd,
90 Tottenham Court Road, London W1P 0LP. This book may not be lent,
resold, hired out or otherwise disposed of by way of trade in any form
of binding or cover other than that in which it is published, without the
prior consent of the Publishers.

10 9 8 7 6 5 4 3 2 1

Typeset by Monolith – www.monolith.uk.com
Printed and bound in Great Britain by Ashford Colour Press Ltd, Gosport, Hants.

The Publishers' policy is to use paper manufactured from sustainable forests.

About the author

Margaret May FCMA is a managing director of a firm of consulting CIMA (Chartered Institute of Management Accountants) members, Management Accountants in Practice, known as MAP, based near Gatwick. MAP specializes in advanced management techniques designed to prepare organizations to change the present and manage the future.

Following a career in finance and administration in both the private and public sectors, working for, among others, British Steel, North West Securities (Bank of Scotland), Cheshire Police, Southern Electricity and Bowthorpe Holdings, she moved into general management, running the Thermoplastic Sheet Division of Doeflex plc. She entered consultancy, forming MAP with other CIMA practising members, in the early 1990s and has specialized in the development of process/activity-based techniques, performance management, performance improvement, information and change management, concentrating particularly on the practical aspects of implementation.

In addition to her training and consultancy work, Margaret is a regular seminar and conference presenter, visiting university lecturer and a member of CIMA Council since 1994. She currently sits on the CIMA Executive, International and Technical Committees. Her recent publications include articles in *Management Accounting/Financial Management*, *Real Finance* and *Finance Today*; a chapter in the Gee/CIMA *Handbook of Management Accounting*; and IFAC-published research entitled *Preparing Organisations to Manage the Future*. This current book is supplemented by a second book by the author, entitled *Business Process Management: Integration in a web-enabled environment*, also published by Pearson as part of their Financial Times Prentice Hall Executive Briefing series.

The author runs seminars through MAP – both public and tailored in-house – on the subject matter of these books and she can be contacted directly at mmay@m-a-p.co.uk or mobile 07973 500539 or via the MAP office on 01293 618323.

Contents

List of figures — xi

Foreword — xiii

Introduction — xv

Acknowledgements — xviii

PART 1 THE TWENTY-FIRST-CENTURY FINANCE FUNCTION — 1

1 Finance in the twenty-first-century organization — 3

1.1 Development of technology-driven finance from manual to 'lights out' — 5
1.2 The challenges of the changing business environment — 7
1.3 Changing roles of the twenty-first-century finance professionals — 10
1.4 The finance function as facilitator of change, adding company-wide value — 14
1.5 Case studies – Leading twenty-first-century organizations — 15

2 The process of transforming the finance function — 19

2.1 Introduction — 21
2.2 Establishing the transformation project — 22
2.3 Analyze the present finance function activities/processes — 23
2.4 Develop the vision for the future of the finance function — 26
2.5 Create the change strategy — 30
2.6 Align staff skills and competencies — 31
2.7 Implement the transformation — 33
2.8 Monitor the success and results of implementation — 33
2.9 Case studies – Worldwide excellence in finance — 34

PART 2 THE TECHNOLOGY-DRIVEN FINANCE FUNCTION — 37

3 Shared service centres — 39

3.1 Introduction — 41
3.2 Which processes are best suited to an SSC? — 42

3.3	Checklist of technical considerations in establishing an SSC	43
3.4	Phases in the implementation of an SSC	45
3.5	Benefits of the SSC approach	47
3.6	Case study – SSCs at Ciba Speciality Chemicals	47

4 Outsourcing 49

4.1	Introduction	51
4.2	IT outsourcing – risks, problems and lessons learnt	51
4.3	Outsourcing the finance function	53
4.4	Application service providers	58
4.5	Outsourcing partnerships	59
4.6	Case study – Outsourced shared services at the BBC	60

5 Information management delivering business intelligence 67

5.1	Introduction	69
5.2	Defining the business requirement	70
5.3	Technological developments	72
5.4	Formulating a company-wide information strategy	73
5.5	Knowledge management	75
5.6	Decision support and business intelligence tools	77
5.7	Case study – Data warehousing at Nationwide	82

PART 3 VALUE-BASED MANAGEMENT 87

6 Delivering shareholder value/best value 89

6.1	Introduction	91
6.2	Rappaport's theory	92
6.3	Shareholder value calculation models	93
6.4	EVA exercise	95
6.5	EVA example	96
6.6	SVA options matrix	97
6.7	Best Value	97
6.8	Embedded value-based management	99
6.9	Characteristics of VBM organizations	101
6.10	Inter-business unit charging and service level agreements	101

6.11	Case study – Creating corporate value at Wienerberger	102
6.12	Case study – Value-based management at British Aerospace	103

7 Valuing intangible assets/intellectual capital 111

7.1	Introduction	113
7.2	Customer (relational) capital	113
7.3	Organizational (structural) capital	115
7.4	Human capital	116
7.5	Corporate reputation	117
7.6	Enterprise risk management (ERM)	118
7.7	Ethical, environmental and social reporting	122
7.8	Case studies – Managing intangibles	123

PART 4 BEYOND TRADITIONAL BUDGETING 125

8 Scenario planning, forecasting and resource allocation 127

8.1	Resource allocation	129
8.2	Empowered organizational culture	129
8.3	Beyond traditional budgeting	132
8.4	Scenario planning	136
8.5	Forecasting	138
8.6	Case studies – Beyond traditional budgeting	140

9 The balanced scorecard 145

9.1	Introduction	147
9.2	Measures that drive performance	148
9.3	The strategy-focused organization	149
9.4	Weighting the balanced scorecard	153
9.5	The ten commandments of implementation	155
9.6	Links to quality frameworks	156
9.7	Case studies – e-BSC	158
9.8	Case study – Manchester Housing's information strategy	160

10 Benchmarking 167

10.1	Introduction	169
10.2	Types of benchmarking	169

10.3	Data-gathering methods	171
10.4	Phases of the benchmarking process	172
10.5	The Benchmarking Code of Conduct	175
10.6	Benefits of benchmarking	177
10.7	Case study – Tower Hamlets benchmarking project	177

PART 5 EXECUTIVE SUMMARY 181

References 193

Index 198

Figures

1.1	The development of technology-driven finance	5
1.2	The web-enabled organization	7
1.3	Forward-looking finance	9
1.4	Transformation of the finance function	11
1.5	Finance in the twenty-first-century organization	13
2.1	Activity/process analysis	24
2.2	Sales invoicing process	25
2.3	Finance function transformation process	31
3.1	Business process, web-enabled shared services	41
3.2	Possible phases in the implementation of SSC	45
3.3	Stages of an SSC project	46
4.1	The stages in an outsourcing award	56
4.2	The stages in an outsourcing implementation	56
4.3	BBC – Overview of the arrangements	61
4.4	BBC – MedAS delivers all components of finance and IT services	62
4.5	BBC – Service delivery models	62
4.6	BBC – Examples of in-house v outsourced service delivery	63
4.7	BBC – Outsourcing service delivery models	64
4.8	BBC – Outsourcing contracts can be complex	65
4.9	BBC – Different (and conflicting) agendas within an organization	65
5.1	Web-enabled information management	72
5.2	From information to business intelligence	76
5.3	Advantages of data warehousing	78
5.4	DSS and ERP alliances	80
5.5	Nationwide – Balanced scorecard	84
6.1	EVA published example	96
6.2	SVA options matrix	97
6.3	VBM integrates management processes	100
6.4	BAe – Jetspares	105
6.5	BAe – Value driver map yielding performance indicators	105
6.6	BAe – Value impact of a 1% movement in top 10 KPIs	106

6.7	BAe – Characteristics of KPIs	106
6.8	BAe – Identification of KPIs	107
6.9	BAe – The initial management view of movability on KPIs	107
6.10	BAe – Potential value creation	108
7.1	Corporate valuation	117
7.2	Materiality of risk	121
8.1	The 'top-down' control cycle	130
8.2	Stifling innovation memorandum	131
8.3	The 'bottom-up' empowerment cycle	132
8.4	Barriers to strategic implementation	134
8.5	The BBRT model	135
8.6	Continuous planning process	140
8.7	Borealis – Performance measurement and reporting	141
9.1	Integrated performance management	147
9.2	The balanced scorecard	149
9.3	Defining the cause and effect relationships between perspectives	150
9.4	Strategy map of a retailer	152
9.5	Balanced scorecard of a retailer	152
9.6	The EFQM Business Excellence model	156
9.7	The Malcolm Baldrige National Quality Award	157
9.8	MH – Balanced scorecard outcomes	162
9.9	MH – Housing demand and rehousing	163
9.10	MH – Graphical trends	164
9.11	MH – Geographic 'drill down'	164
9.12	MH – Balanced scorecard functional perspectives	165
10.1	Fishbone diagram	173
10.2	Z chart	174
10.3	Forcefield analysis	174
10.4	Process enablers' hierarchy	175
10.5	Tower Hamlets – Phase 1 list of processes and published reports	178

The author and publisher have made every effort to seek permission for the figures used in this book.

Foreword

Ian Kleinman, Finance Director, Global Sales and Operations, Reuters

The turn of the millennium is cause for reflection on the past and quite a few predictions about the future. We see this almost daily in articles and television programmes. Two common themes that are discussed are the final arrival of the global village, already heralded by Marshall McLuhan some thirty years ago, and the ever increasing rate of change. Both of these trends are directly influenced by technology. The global village can only exist because of the current all-pervasive nature of electronic mail and the internet. Similarly, the increased rate of change reflects, to a large extent, the impact of new industrial technologies, as well as commercial technologies, such as electronic commerce. Just think of their influence on products, costs, processes and even ways of doing business.

A similar process of reflection and review is taking place in business. The more forward-looking companies took the opportunity of Y2K reviews to re-think their underlying business strategies and what impact any resulting changes will have on their structures and operations. There are also other factors that are adding even more urgency to such reviews. First, many firms are increasingly finding themselves in a very competitive global or, in some cases at least, regional marketplace. The fall of the Iron Curtain, the creation of the Eurozone, NAFTA and other regional trading zones, are offering companies larger marketing opportunities than ever before, and at lower cost. Combined with this, there has been a dramatic acceleration in the deregulation of markets and industries. This is often driven by the needs of governments both to improve their financial position by selling off state-owned assets, and to ensure that their economies remain competitive internationally. Similarly, the growing presence of international markets, particularly financial markets, as well as multinational companies means that capital and human resources are flowing more freely than ever to where the best returns can be found. The pressure for best returns is also being directly influenced by ever more active shareholders.

But probably the most important driver for change in business is the impact of technology. Technology is not only breaking down barriers to entry, it is also fundamentally changing the rules of the competitive game. There is no longer any need to have fully owned integrated operations. Companies can have almost complete freedom of location and can provide immediate responsiveness to customer demand. One only has to look at some well-documented case studies in the use of electronic commerce technologies to see the actual impact achieved. Take Dell Computer, for example. Its factory in Limerick, on the West Coast of Ireland, supplies custom-built PCs all over Europe. It takes some $15 million daily of customer orders over its own website and call centres, and then passes on details, of which components it needs and when, to suppliers through its extranet. Both customers and suppliers are plugged into the whole process. The results from such a transparent and electronic process are clear: more accurate and timely hand-offs between customers, the company and its suppliers, lower costs for all and therefore increased satisfaction for all. A truly win-win-win situation.

So what does all this mean for the finance function? Margaret May's book is a timely reminder to us all that the finance function, like all other functions, has to react to the opportunities as well as the challenges posed by the changes already mentioned. So profound are the changes that no less than a transformation is required. 'From what to what?' you may ask. In simple terms, I would say from a specialist control function with its focus on historical financial data to one of a business partner focused on the future, using its skills to take a holistic view of the business, both internally and externally.

The next question is how to achieve this transformation. Margaret May provides us with a practical blueprint. First, she explains what finance in the twenty-first century has become – looking at the development of technology, the pressures for change, organization and roles – and takes us through the implementation of a transformation of the finance function. It is apparent that finance needs to reposition itself within the organization – to re-tool itself – and Margaret May introduces the latest ideas and techniques being applied in leading-edge organizations by finance departments. In the second part she examines the impact of technology on finance – shared service centres, outsourcing and business intelligence in a web-enabled environment. The third section looks at ways of ensuring that value is being added for stakeholders, including the valuation of intellectual property, and the final part makes the case for integrated performance management techniques, moving beyond traditional budgeting.

If you are currently working in a finance department, consider this. Assume that you are at a funfair but there is only one attraction, a carousel. You have three options – to watch, to jump on, or to wait until the carousel is moving and then try to jump on. Once you are on, the experience is exhilarating and rewarding. If you try to get on once it's moving, it is not only difficult but also dangerous. The longer you wait to get on, the faster the carousel goes, and the more dangerous it gets. Or alternatively, you could stand on the sidelines and watch the world go by. Which option would you take?

Introduction

This second edition, although published less than three years after the original, has been substantially updated – with three completely new chapters (on finance in the twenty-first century, valuing intangible assets/intellectual capital and scenario planning, forecasting and resource allocation). All chapters have been amended and the book has been restructured into four parts, each containing two to three chapters:

- *The twenty-first century finance function* – looking at the organization and roles, as well as the process of transforming the finance function.

- *The technology-driven finance function* – with chapters on shared service centres, outsourcing and information management delivering business intelligence.

- *Value-based management* – examining the delivery of shareholder value/Best Value and the need to value intangible assets, have an integrated risk management policy and environmental, ethical and social reporting.

- *Beyond traditional budgeting* – looking at the case for replacing the budget, with chapters on resource allocation, forecasting, scenario planning, the balanced scorecard and benchmarking.

The new edition reflects the amount and speed of change that is taking place within the finance function as we begin the new millennium, driven primarily by web-enabled technological developments. Organizations are choosing to manage their non core activities by processes that reach beyond company boundaries to partners, suppliers customers and employees using web-technology.

Whilst updating this book, it became apparent that a further book was needed to cover *Business Process Management: Integration in a web-enabled environment*. This book, also published by Financial Times Prentice Hall Executive Briefings, looks at both business community integration (BCI) – including supply chain management (SCM), customer relationship management (CRM), enterprise resource planning (ERP) and internet technology. And business process management (BPM) including the analysis, re-engineering and change management as well as the performance measurement aspects of these integrated processes. It includes case studies from Unilever, RNLI, Anglian Water and Averi Brown Boveri (ABB).

In the twenty-first century it is no longer acceptable to spend over 80% of the finance function's resources on transaction processing and control activities, utilizing outdated financial computer systems and budgeting, without adding significant company-wide value. Transaction processing is fast becoming a 'lights out' activity with information managed to deliver business intelligence at the push of a button. This has freed up skilled finance professionals for retraining and redeployment, demonstrating their ability to add value throughout the organization in new, customer-focused roles that include as much strategic and non-financial performance management as financial content.

Stephen Hodge, Director of Finance at the Shell Group, has written:

Shell recognised that the concept of a finance function with the right to exist was obsolete – finance would need to earn and maintain its standing as a supplier to the business leading Shell's digitisation by enabling e-business process design across the whole value chain. The goal was to become the 'top performer of first choice' through Shell Financial Services, whose mission is to provide specialist financial management and decision support skills to the operating businesses, organised as a virtual business in a few global locations and in competition with external providers.[1]

'Maximising shareholder value' stood out as the number-one priority of CFOs worldwide in research carried out by Price Waterhouse in 1997. Equally, the achievement of delivering Best Value is a statutory duty for those involved in the public sector. The challenge is to link strategy successfully to operational goals and set measures and targets that ensure that added value is delivered. Performance-management frameworks must incorporate far more than measures; they need to incorporate processes that ensure that the necessary change occurs to execute the strategy successfully.

Although most organizations have switched to a bottom-up empowered culture, finance functions have been reluctant to 'bin the budget', which still supports the command-and-control culture of a top-down organization and stifles innovation. There is now a sense of urgency about the need to replace traditional budgeting techniques. New methods of planning, control and allocating/attracting resources must be introduced before permanent, long-term damage is done to the health of businesses. They include enterprise-wide business intelligence, value-based management, forecasts, balanced scorecards, benchmarking and process-based management.

The finance function must be transformed to take the lead role in building and running such a framework that links, in a meaningful way, strategy, operations, resource allocation and performance measurement, in addition to facilitating the necessary changes. It is ideally placed to undertake this challenge because it is the only part of the organization that holds the key pivotal role linking stakeholder demands with business strategy and operational performance.

As a practising consultant and trainer since the early 1990s, I have specialized in the practical aspects of implementation of these value-adding tools and techniques. In this book I have attempted to convey not only why change must be inevitable for survival of the finance function and how to make the necessary transformation, but what value-adding tools and techniques you will need to adopt to effect the change company-wide. My approach, as always, is pragmatic, explaining the techniques, their origins and uses and illustrating with examples and up-to-date case studies.

As a member of the Chartered Institute of Management Accountants (CIMA) Council, I believe that the finance function and finance professionals can achieve the change required to remain in a pivotal position within the organization. For those students training to become accountants in business, CIMA, together with the other accountancy bodies, has changed its syllabus, training and membership criteria to cater for this new role. For those qualified accountants working in business, in both the private and public sectors, the responsibility must rest with you, as none of the professional accountancy bodies presently imposes continuing professional development on members in business. You will need to be proactive in facilitating and driving these changes to ensure that the management accountancy profession remains in demand worldwide for at least another 100 years.

Acknowledgements

The author would like to thank the following for their help, advice and contributions in the form of case studies, all of which she gratefully acknowledges:

- Management Accountants in Practice Limited (MAP), her employers, who have kindly consented to the use of seminar material being used extensively in this publication, whilst retaining the intellectual property rights.

- Richard Hartt of MedAS and Penny Lawson from the BBC for contributing the outsourced shared services at the BBC case study in Chapter 4.

- Abhai Rajguru for writing the Nationwide case study on data warehousing, originally published by IFAC in 1997, in Chapter 5.

- Tony Bryan and Rogan Dixon for their contribution of the British Aerospace case study on value-based management in Chapter 6.

- Hilary Vaughan and the Departmental Management Team at Manchester City Council Housing Department for approving the use of their balanced scorecard client case study in Chapter 9.

- Mike Howes for writing the case study on the Tower Hamlets benchmarking project, originally published by IFAC in 1997, in Chapter 10.

- The editorial and production team at Pearson for their assistance in finalizing the book for publication.

Any mistakes or shortcomings are, of course, the author's responsibility.

Part 1

The twenty-first-century finance function

- 1 Finance in the twenty-first-century organization 3
- 2 The process of transforming the finance function 19

Finance in the twenty-first-century organization

- 1.1 Development of technology-driven finance from manual to 'lights out' 5
- 1.2 The challenges of the changing business environment 7
- 1.3 Changing roles of the twenty-first-century finance professionals 10
- 1.4 The finance function as facilitator of change, adding company-wide value 14
- 1.5 Case studies – Leading twenty-first-century organizations 15

1.1 DEVELOPMENT OF TECHNOLOGY-DRIVEN FINANCE FROM MANUAL TO 'LIGHTS OUT'

Following the invention of accounting, manual techniques were developed. Up until the 1970s separate manual, loose-leaf ledgers – financial and cost – were kept, with reports being typed. Calculations were carried out by slide rule, mechanical calculators and comptometer operators, whilst Hollerith punch-card technology allowed some mechanical sorting of data – all very labour intensive. Then in the late 1960s and early 1970s very large big-box first-generation computers were introduced, processing data for centralized finance departments and outputting tons of standard printouts. In the 1980s the advent of the PC and lower-cost local technology and the invention of spreadsheet software heralded the start of devolved finance departments. These operated within each business unit, and were in addition to a head office finance function whose main role was one of consolidation. Reporting was still paper-based, with a standard monthly pack of management accounts and ad hoc reports on request. Fig. 1.1 shows how the function has evolved.

Fig. 1.1 Development of technology-driven finance

Organization	Manual based finance	Centralized finance	Devolved finance	Shared service centres	Web-enabled shared services	Virtual
Technology	Manual financial and cost ledgers	Big-box computers	Local servers, PCs	Global ERP	Fully integrated end-to-end processes	Lights out processing
Reporting	Typed reports	Standard printout	Spreadsheet reporting packs	Electronic reporting	Decision support systems	Business intelligence systems
	Pre 1970s →	1970s →	1980s →	1990s →	2000s →	2010s →

By the 1990s developments in technology enabled flexible client-server systems to operate centralized shared service centres (SSCs), which could be located in the most advantageous geographic location in terms of cost-effective operation, e.g. India. These operations made significant savings in transaction processing costs through standardization, rationalization and economies of scale in processing. In addition, their focus is upon providing flexible, economic and appropriate services to their customers in a demonstrable, measured environment through service level agreements. By now reporting was delivered electronically and accessible from any location, with SSCs generating standard reports and decision support tools for additional analysis.

By the turn of the millennium the development of web technology had facilitated the full integration of business processes, including direct electronic links to suppliers, partners and customers. Web-enabled SSCs managed all non-core processes with enterprise resource planning (ERP) linking to supply chain management (SCM) and customer relationship management (CRM) systems. Data can now be input into a data warehouse and information, performance measures and business intelligence made available through personalized internet portals, the intranet and enterprise information systems (EIS) – *see* Fig. 5.1 in Chapter 5 (p. 72).

Continued developments are moving towards complete 'lights out' processing, which would use some of the following:

- optical readers, scanners, mobiles (m-commerce), WAP (wireless application protocol) and other automated input devices, removing the need for manual inputting;

- web-enabled, self service applications that facilitate data entry and query resolution to be carried out entirely at source by employees (business-to-employees: B2E), by customers (business-to-customers: B2C) and by suppliers (business-to-business: B2B).

- workflow, document management, computer and telephone integration (CTI), electronic data interchange (EDI), and other automated, collaborative computing tools (c-commerce), facilitating the free exchange of transactions, documents and information automatically between any geographic location inside or outside the organization;

- EAI middleware and internet standards like XML to integrate intelligently different systems from within and outside the organization, enabling automated end-to-end processes covering the whole business environment, removing the need for any re-keying of data;

- sophisticated interactive business intelligence tools, which, for example, can carry out analysis in real time and decide what information to display to a customer, partner, supplier or employee, based on analysis of their previous history of transactions, through their own personalized portal.

The eventual outcome will be virtual finance and the complete elimination of transaction processing, which will be replaced by web-based systems maintenance and audit (*see* Fig. 1.2). Web technology, business community integration, end-to-end business processes, SCM, CRM and ERP are dealt with in detail in another

FT Executive Briefing by the same author, entitled *Business Process Management: Integration in a web-enabled environment.*[1]

Fig. 1.2 The web-enabled organization

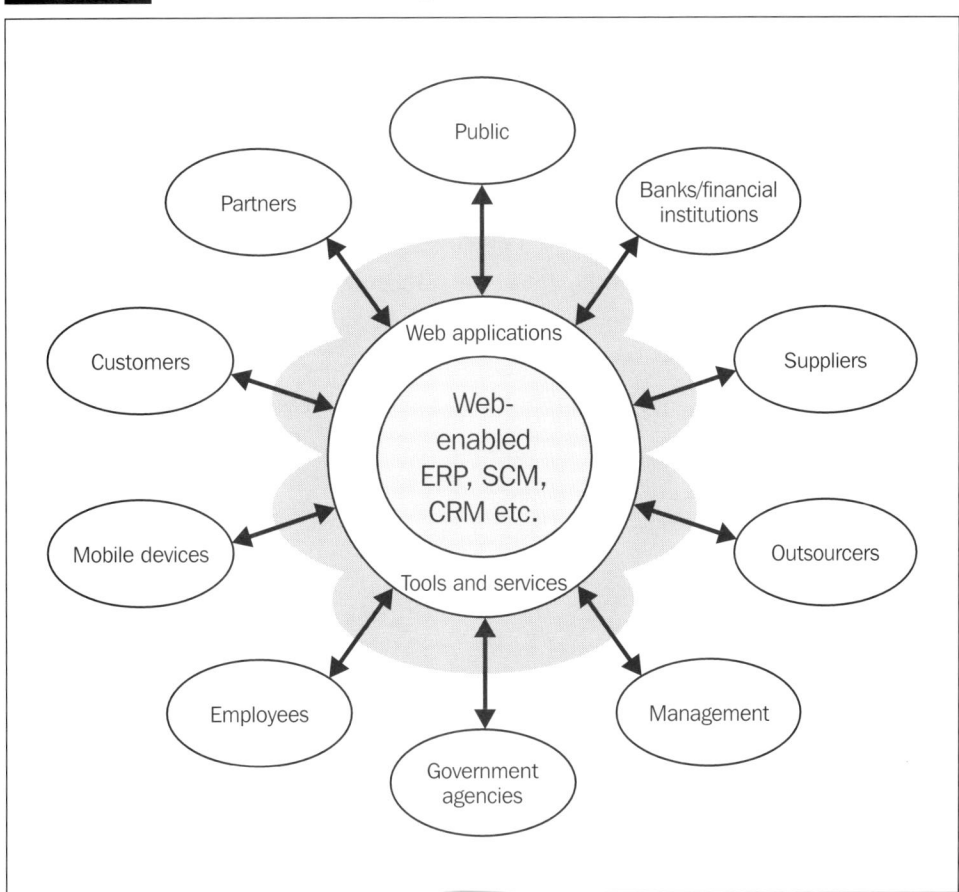

1.2 THE CHALLENGES OF THE CHANGING BUSINESS ENVIRONMENT

In addition to the considerable impact that technological developments have had on organizations, over the last 10–15 years all businesses have experienced exceptional levels of change, attributed to new challenges, including:

- *The increase in power of shareholders* – shareholders' power to influence boardroom decisions forces organizations to focus their attentions on delivering shareholder value. It is no longer sufficient to calculate the traditional profit and loss and balance sheet statements; it is equally important to address the drivers of economic value creation through shareholder value calculations, which reveal economic profit or loss. Part of this calculation in a twenty-first-century organization is the need to include the intrinsic value of intangible assets, which are essential when addressing an organization with an e-business strategy. Corporate reputation, which is made up of the combination of intellectual capital and financial assets, must be protected by building an integrated enterprise risk-management system. The organization needs to recognize and mitigate all risks that could be regarded as a liability, and to evaluate, for the benefit of shareholders, those risks that could be regarded as assets. The Turnbull Report, effective from the beginning of 2000, has introduced rules on how companies listed on the London Stock Exchange manage and report on business risks.

- *Growth in environmental, ethical and social awareness* – as of the beginning of 2000, companies are required to have an embedded internal control system that monitors important threats, including environmental, ethical and social risks. With almost £4 billion being invested in ethical stocks in 2000, companies can no longer afford to ignore the implications. This is particularly unavoidable now that pension trustees are obliged under the Pensions Act 2000 to disclose the extent to which they take social, environmental and ethical decisions into account when making investment decisions. In the year 2000, 37 of the FTSE 100 companies already published environmental reports, and a further 22 have pledged to do so in 2001, whilst pressure is being exerted on others by the Department of Environment, Transport and the Regions on behalf of the Government.

- *Legislation requiring the public sector to deliver value* – in the last two decades the public sector has been subjected to unprecedented transformation and change. The Chancellor of the Exchequer has reiterated his commitment to a continuing programme of radical improvement in the way that the public sector manages itself. He has stated:

  > *Only by taking a progressively more business-like approach can the Government continue to bear down on cost to the taxpayer of delivering public services whilst improving service standards through the Citizens' Charter ... The proposals are probably the most important reform of the Civil Service accounting and budgeting arrangements this century ... To implement the changes successfully will require the development of new skills, and commitment and leadership from managers at all levels in the Civil Service.*[2]

  The change continues and the local government Best Value initiative became effective in 2000, changing the compulsory competitive tendering (CCT) regime to one that requires demonstration of best value.

- *Changes in organizational culture* – including the focus on quality and the changing of culture from a command and control, top-down organization to an empowered, innovative, bottom-up structure. In the modern organization, all departments have had to adapt to the idea of providing a service (often through a service level agreement – SLA) to their internal customers, and all too often the finance function has lagged behind in making this cultural leap. A critical part of this change has to be replacing the conventional budgeting process with scenario planning, rolling forecasts, balanced scorecards (which link strategy to operations) and benchmarking, complemented by the provision of business intelligence and integrated performance management systems (*see* Fig. 1.3).

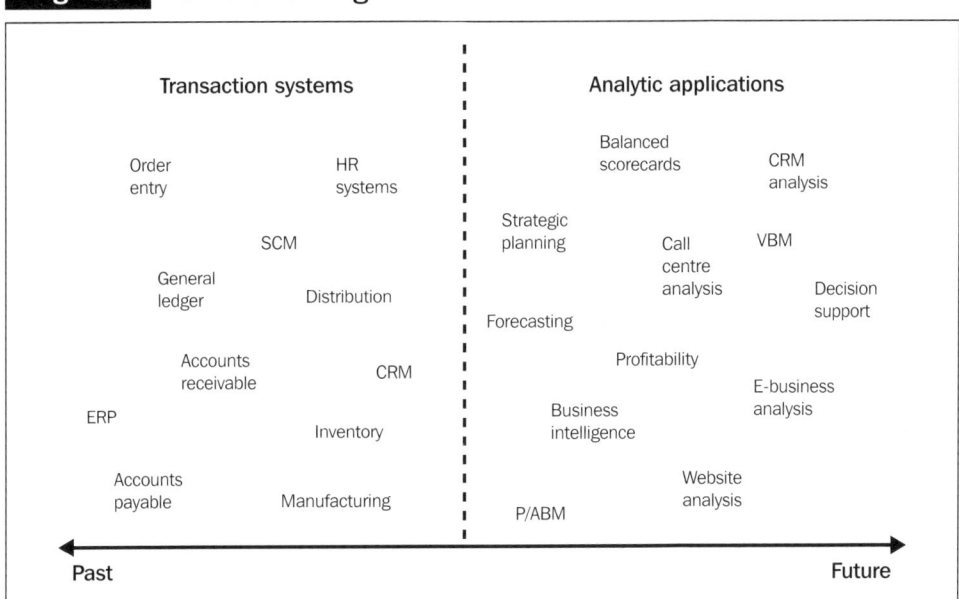

Fig. 1.3 Forward-looking finance

Equally challenging for finance is the change in emphasis from gatekeeper to opportunity seeker.

- *Changes in organization structure* – typical structures see support areas managed by process rather than the traditional functional approach, often in shared service centres (SSCs) and operational areas divided into autonomous strategic business units (SBUs), motivated to deliver value. Switching to business process management requires the re-engineering of working practices and systems and the utilization of process management techniques like priority-based budgeting (PBB). In many organizations, outsourcing partnerships of all non-core activities like finance and IT and even manufacturing in certain industries like electronics, is becoming commonplace.

- *Globalisation of business and financial centres* – leading to a growth in strategic alliances and partnerships, changing patterns of customer demand and increasing customers' bargaining power. The new alliances require new policies for control and risk management, based around the web-based systems that drive them.

- *Government legislation* – affecting not just the public sector and the regulated industries but also all businesses through such policies as the introduction of the euro and the climate change levy.

As organizations look to respond to these challenges and become truly 'world class' they inevitably place new demands on their finance functions. The challenge for finance is to become more cost effective, embedded within the business processes, and more customer focused and service oriented, adding company-wide value and reacting quickly when responding to ever-changing needs. This can only be achieved by transformation. The question is not whether the organization's SBUs will each have a new style 'business analyst' as part of their core management team, but whether that person will be a finance professional or from another management discipline with some acquired financial skills. The pure financial content of this new role will form less than 50%, whilst the requirement for the new strategic value-adding skills will dominate the choice of individuals selected for these roles. This is a challenge not only to every finance professional but also to the accountancy bodies responsible for their training.

In the new millennium, all parts of the organization must be able to demonstrate visibly that they are using best-practice methodology, delivering best value and are cost effective and efficient. All parts of the organization that are responsible for delivering services, like the finance function, must develop a service-oriented culture, focusing on the customer's requirements, utilizing internal service-level agreements (SLAs) wherever practicable. The finance function should, as part of its new transformed role, be driving this initiative throughout the business and therefore should be leading the way by example, by undergoing the change before the rest of the organization. This change is not just one of introducing and learning new techniques and utilizing new tools, but involves a complete change of culture, requiring a flexible and responsive approach, with newly developed skills in selling as well as delivering services.

1.3 CHANGING ROLES OF TWENTY-FIRST-CENTURY FINANCE PROFESSIONALS

Transformation of the finance function

The introduction of web-enabled, integrated, enterprise-wide computer systems often operating from geographically distant shared service centres (SSCs) is transforming the finance function by reducing time-consuming, transaction-processing activities by up to two-thirds. This will allow at least some of the resultant freed-up financial resources to be redeployed on company-wide value-adding activities.

Figure 1.4 illustrates the change that is taking place, with decision support and other value-adding activities making up 50% of the new slimline finance function. Traditional financing and stewardship activities are also being redesigned, utilizing web-based technology to reduce costs to half their previous average levels. According to the Hackett Benchmarking Solutions ongoing study of the finance function, the range between the lowest and the highest finance function cost has reduced in Europe from 0.61–6.93% in 1998 to 0.51–4.79% in 2000, as a percentage of total revenues.[3] This benchmark is based on 75 European organizations with average annual revenues of $1 billion and indicates that this change is already well underway in the finance function. As Gregory Hackett of the Hackett Group has said:

By the year 2005, the finance function as we know it will have changed beyond recognition.

At least 50% of the effort of the 21st-century web-enabled, finance function is focused on active participation in the organization's on-going pursuit of competitive excellence. Such a change involves huge amounts of upheaval for traditional finance professionals, many of whom have been content spending most of their time on processing and technical issues, not needing to venture far from the safety of their offices. Realigning and retraining of the existing finance professionals is one of the biggest challenges in the transformation journey.

Fig. 1.4 Transformation of the finance function

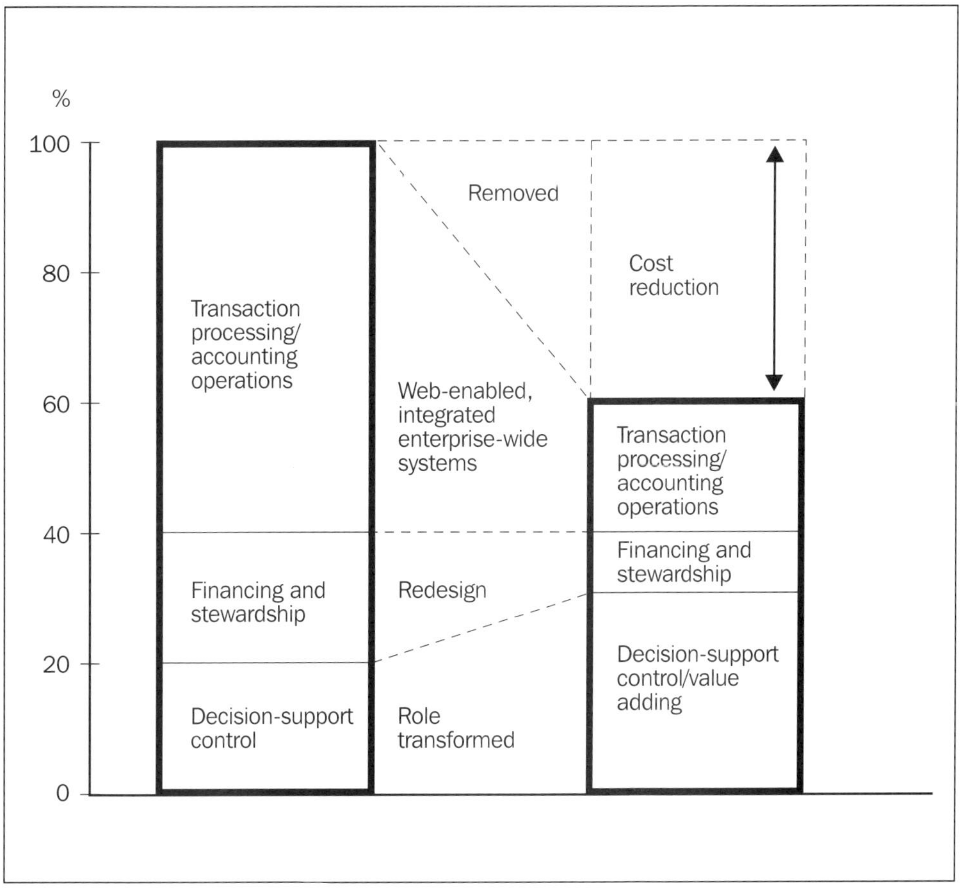

The new roles for finance professionals

SMAC (the Society of Management Accountants of Canada), in its publication *Redesigning the Finance Function*,[4] believes that the new finance function requires the skills to:

- deliver analytically, strategically and value-added oriented services;
- act as a consultative business partner and adviser;
- become a participant and leader in the decision-making process;
- foster company-wide continual performance enhancement.

Finance professionals of the transformed function will typically fall into three categories, to which, wherever possible, existing staff will be deployed based on their strengths, maximizing the potential for successful retraining. These three new job roles, and the activities they will carry out, are:

- Business consultants – usually a core of shared-service corporate staff, who specialize in specific processes, models or initiatives, providing advice and support to the strategic business units (SBUs). They act as information managers, project managers and facilitators on company-wide projects to deliver continuous improvement and value, e.g. enterprise-wide business intelligence, web-enabling end-to-end processes, scenario planning, value-based management (VBM), the balanced scorecard (BSC), benchmarking, business process re-engineering (BPR) and priority-based budgeting (PBB) (all are explained in detail later in this book or in *Business Process Management*).[1] The need to deliver new best-practice procedures and controls around global web-enabled, end-to-end process management is crucial to success. Other tasks include global economic and business monitoring, new ventures and other strategic analyses.

- Business analysts – generally operating from within the business units as the financial specialist on the management team. They replace the traditional roles of the SBU financial controller or management accountant – scorekeeping and budgetary control – with tasks that include project leader, information provider, business partner, analyst, performance measurement, SBU reporting and competitor analysis. The business analysts, who spend at least 50% of their time on non-financial performance and strategic work, are an integral part of the SBU management team. They operate at the sharp end of delivering the new decision-support business intelligence and tools and techniques explained in this book, demonstrably adding value through their skills and knowledge of the business.

- Technical specialists – experts in finance and accounting, who provide the traditional transaction-processing, financing and stewardship activities, using the new systems with improved reporting and control services at much reduced costs, e.g. moving towards the virtual close. Their roles include all of the traditional tasks as far as they continue to exist, including systems audit and implementation, general ledger, audit, tax, legal, compliance, accounts receivable, accounts payable and treasury. The move to web-enablement not only provides opportunities to move to a virtual treasury function but also to reduce the need for working capital in the business cycle. The speed and efficiency of the new ways of operating considerably reduce the requirement for working capital to run the business and, as case studies like Dell and Cisco demonstrate, they operate with either a nil requirement or in some cases a positive working capital. These professionals are often located centrally in SSCs or at head office and are far fewer in number than in the traditional finance function. For example, in the BBC MedAS SSC case study in Chapter 4 (page 60), the number of qualified accountants has been reduced to just five.

These new, dynamic finance professionals will become leaders of multi-disciplined teams engaged in strategic and tactical planning, taking equal responsibility for the future success of the company.

Figure 1.5 shows what roles finance-trained professionals are holding within the new web-enabled organizational structures of the twenty-first century, which are based in geographically beneficial locations. The roles that finance-trained professionals are ideally suited to hold include:

- Traditional roles – Treasurer, Company Secretary and Technical Specialists.
- Wider business roles – Chief Operations Officer (COO), Chief Information Officer (CIO), Chief Finance Officer (CFO), Chief Executive Officer (CEO) and Business Consultants.
- Commercial roles – SBU CEOs, Commercial Managers and Business Analysts

Fig. 1.5 Finance in the twenty-first-century organization

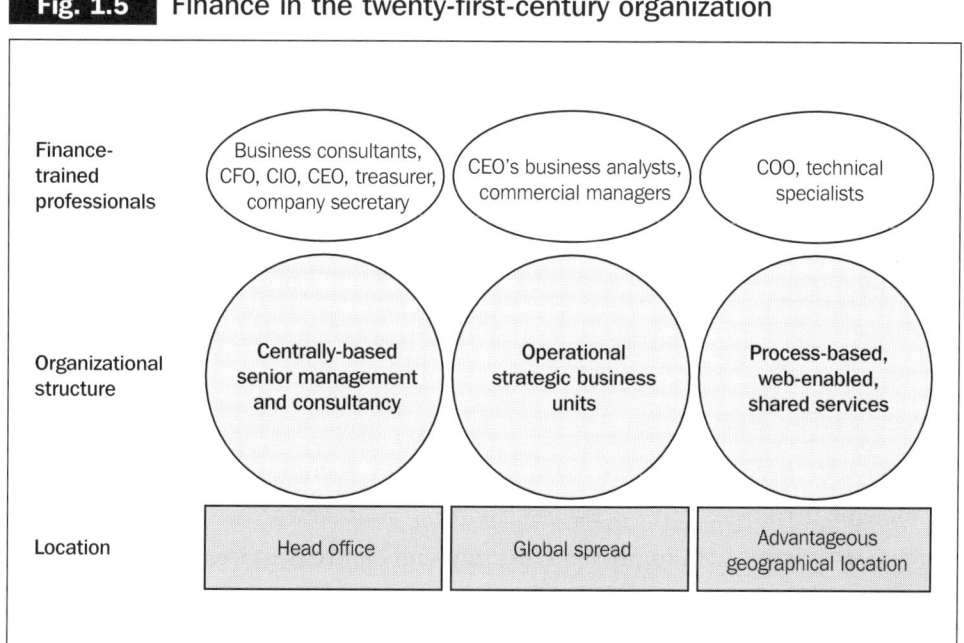

The pertinent point is that none of these roles require the same mix of skills that a traditionally trained accountant would have held and most incorporate a high proportion of non-financial work and face stiff competition from other professionals in the organization. It cannot be taken for granted that the finance function will be allowed automatically to take on this new value-adding company-wide role. There will be other disciplines that believe that they are equally well qualified for these broader roles, which encompasse as much non-financial as financial content. Susan Jee, Head of Finance for the Magnox Business Group of British Nuclear Fuels, warns:

We have to earn the right to be taken seriously by the business generally. We have to prove that we can provide more than just the numbers while recognising that these numbers are still of critical importance. It is arrogant for us to believe that if we find the time to look over a new business proposal we will automatically add value. People within the business have been doing this very well without us for a long time.[5]

1.4 THE FINANCE FUNCTION AS FACILITATOR OF CHANGE, ADDING COMPANY-WIDE VALUE

If we accept that the key accountabilities of finance are to:

- ensure the delivery of value to shareholders/stakeholders;
- challenge and assist business managers to generate value and monitor their success in doing so;
- manage financial risk and maintain financial control;

then the transformed finance function has a key role to play in facilitating performance improvement and company-wide change, ensuring that finances and resources are used as efficiently and effectively as possible throughout the whole business. It then follows that the implementation of web-enabled end-to-end processes and other value-adding tools and techniques must be driven by finance.

Wilson and Chua's[6] definition of management accounting:

encompassing techniques and processes that are intended to provide financial and non-financial information to people within an organization to make better decisions and thereby achieve organizational control and enhance organizational effectiveness emphasizes this role. Equally, the ultimate test of successful management accounting is whether or not it motivates and assists managers in achieving organizational control and enhancing organizational effectiveness.

While finance no longer owns the information it provides within the business, it has clear roles to fulfil, which include:

- To train, to ensure understanding of the advantages and opportunities offered by the internet and all the value-adding tools and techniques throughout the business.
- To collect, analyze and present information. This must include design and implementation of web-enabled processes, models and enterprise-wide business intelligence and performance management systems.
- To act as a catalyst for change and improvement, facilitating cross-functional workshops and panels, project managing and driving web-enablement of end-to-end processes and value-adding tools, throughout the business.
- To bring a financial perspective to assessing improvement ideas and proposals coming out of these processes and to encourage and nurture new business opportunities for generating value.
- To assist in planning, forecasting, performance measurement and monitoring and move beyond the annual budgeting process to support the empowered organization.
- To validate all information. This is an audit role that finance is best qualified to carry out and should include the dissemination of best-practice procedures and controls right across the web-enabled organization.

The subject of change management and business process re-engineering (BPR) is covered in detail in *Business Process Management*.[1]

1.5 Case studies

Leading twenty-first-century organizations

Microsoft UK[7]

Microsoft UK has a finance team of just 12 because most of its day-to-day finances are outsourced, according to Steve Harvey, Microsoft UK Director of People, Profit and Loyalty. Accounts payable are looked after by Microsoft's manufacturing plant in Ireland, while accounts receivable, facilities and employee benefits management are all outsourced to third parties. Andersen carries out both the company's statutory accountancy and tax work. Harvey says,

> We are lucky because the systems do most of the donkey-work for us so the finance guys go out supporting the sales guys ... You have to be out there living and breathing the business day in, day out.

Intel[8]

Intel, the $26-billion US chip giant, had already started to improve the effectiveness of the accounts payable, which handles 60% of the firm's transactions (about one million a year) and 75% of the value of payments for Intel, by implementing the latest EDI and imaging technology. Richard Taylor, Corporate Controller, wanted further improvements and put forward a plan to move the whole operation to a single low-cost centre such as India – he gave his team three months to come up with a better alternative.

Jeff Lupinacci, head of the business process re-engineering (BPR) project, decided that this was not radical enough as a solution and proposed 'lights out' accounting. The process could be reduced to confirmation of a purchase order and confirmation of receipt – the invoice was superfluous and could be eliminated. The aim was to automate those two mechanisms by using web-enabled IT solutions. Under the new system, when Intel staff want to buy something, they access their firm's web portal – which contains catalogues from authorized suppliers that list prices, availability and contract terms – and place their order online. Once goods are received, they enter a confirmation on to the system, which automatically triggers a payment. The average cost per transaction reduced from $8 in 1999 to $1 in 2001.

There are four main types of payment – direct materials, manufacturing support products, services, and consultants and temporary staff. Fortunately, the team was able to 'piggy-back' on existing projects like e-procurement and EDI. Internal controls were built in for controlling access to accounts payable data and ensuring that security was robust enough to guarantee that payments were made only when goods were received. Hard copies of invoices are kept for use in countries where it is obligatory.

CISCO[9]

Cisco Systems employs 40,000 people worldwide with revenues in 2000 of $18 billion. Mike Tierney, Cisco's UK Finance Director, says that Cisco's technology, and more importantly its management ethos, allows it to close its books in 24 hours – a virtual close. It was management's determination to get better information faster to give the company competitive advantage that forced the changes. It helps that 90% of Cisco's orders are received electronically and filtered through an Amsterdam office that acts like a European SSC for revenue purposes and that it sells indirectly through a few hundred partners.

When an order is received for, say, a 'lower end router', it will go electronically into the master scheduler in the database in San Jose; it can then go on to the production line at an outsourced company in Scotland and be shipped to the customer – and never physically go near Cisco. Cisco owns only two of its 40 manufacturing operations – the rest are run by partners, who participate in Cisco's supply chain. Less than a quarter of all orders actually touch Cisco – most are fulfilled directly by partners. Cisco owns the designs and software that controls its products; the rest is in the hands of its manufacturing partners and resellers. This makes Cisco as near as you get to a virtual corporation, yet it is the third most valuable company in the world today.

Cisco has an EIS that operates like corporate telemetry. Key data is available on Cisco's intranet the next day and accessible for managers throughout the company to drill down, and the sales people forecast on a weekly basis. Part of the sales team's remuneration is based on minimal divergence from linearity, which discourages tail-end bunching and all the advantages that having evenly spread orders brings. A large part of Tierney's time is spent working with the sales team on the preparation of bids, adding value as a crucial member of the team.

MOD[10]

The MOD (Ministry of Defence) used PWC and Deloitte Consulting to help it solve the problems posed by the Government's White Paper *Better accounting for the taxpayers' money* (June 1995), which sought to make the armed forces more accountable and efficient. The MOD wanted a system that measured what it took to achieve a front-line objective (an output), e.g. stabilizing East Timor at short notice or long-term peacekeeping in Bosnia, and that would cost the process accordingly so that ministers could make short- and long-term planning decisions. The project involved 550 consultants running 150 different projects, with 2,500 users and over 100 accounting systems.

Project CAPITAL has tackled five main areas:

- Systems – new accounting processes will run on commercial off-the-shelf packages (Oracle Financials, Sun Accounts and CLIME).
- Management structures (roles and responsibilities) – a new finance function will be established, and financial management at board level will be greatly enhanced and new financial management skills will be learned.
- Decision making – in line with the MOD's new management strategy, decision making will be delegated to the organization's lower levels and longer-term thinking will be required.
- Performance measurement – management activity will have a new focus: outputs will be agreed within and between budget holders and performance indicators set accordingly.
- Planning – long- and short-term planning will become separate activities; a top-down, ten-year plan will be operated in conjunction with a four-year short-term plan.

2

The process of transforming the finance function

- 2.1 Introduction   21
- 2.2 Establishing the transformation project   22
- 2.3 Analyze the present finance function activities/processes   23
- 2.4 Develop the vision for the future of the finance function   26
- 2.5 Create the change strategy   30
- 2.6 Align staff skills and competencies   31
- 2.7 Implement the transformation   33
- 2.8 Monitor the success and results of implementation   33
- 2.9 Case studies – Worldwide excellence in finance   34

2.1 INTRODUCTION

From the previous chapter it can seen that the finance function of the twenty-first century has changed dramatically – driven by technology and the need to add company-wide value. This chapter provides a practical blueprint for re-engineering your finance function to ensure it heeds the warning of Hugh Collum, CFO of SmithKline Beecham, that:

> *Accountants could go the way of coal miners! A mighty industry that once employed three-quarters of a million and helped bring down a government today employs fewer than SmithKline Beecham. I believe that accountants in industry could go the same way if they do not realise the fundamental changes they need to make.*[1]

Instead consider the words and vision of Stephen Hodge, Director of Finance at the Shell Group:

> *Shell recognised that the concept of a finance function with the right to exist was obsolete – finance would need to earn and maintain its standing as a supplier to the business leading Shell's digitisation by enabling e-business process design across the whole value chain. The goal was to become the 'top performer of first choice' through Shell Financial Services, whose mission is to provide specialist finance management and decision support skills to the operating businesses, organised as a virtual business in a few global locations and in competition with external providers. Existing developments include:*
>
> - *Continuing to build up SSCs, which are outsourced and will eventually become virtual. The need for transaction processing will be eliminated and replaced by web-based systems maintenance and audit.*
> - *Corporate finance M & A.*
> - *Risk management associated with global customer reach, access to new suppliers, credit risks associated with auctions versus catalogue channels to market.*
> - *Web-based information portals underpinned with ERP and finance-led technological development in CRM and logistics.*[2]

Figure 1.4 (page 11) illustrates the change that must take place, not only converting half of the function's activities to 'value-adding', decision-support activities, but also reducing costs significantly overall by the introduction of the latest web-enabled technology.

In this chapter, the generic process that needs to be undertaken is detailed, including analysis of the present finance function activities, developing future vision for finance, assessing current staff skills and competencies, creating strategy for change and implementing changes to monitor actions and results. This is followed by three brief case studies of transformed finance functions in action.

2.2 ESTABLISHING THE TRANSFORMATION PROJECT

Put together a business case

The senior management team needs to be committed to this project, which, although focusing primarily on the finance function, will encroach on the whole of the rest of the business at various stages of the project. Whatever the organization, private or public sector, the case for change is compelling.

Appoint a steering group

A steering group should be formed comprising the finance director, the project manager, a consultant (if used), the head of IT and, ideally, at least three other senior managers from within the business, including the chief executive. This group needs to agree the objectives, timescales, resources and methodology of the project and review its progress regularly.

Appoint a project team

Because of the obvious sensitivity of the nature of the investigation and the inherent barriers to change from within finance itself, care must be taken in choosing the 'best' people to carry out the investigation. The success of the operation will depend largely on the team selected. It is worth considering who within the finance function is capable of carrying out this analysis in a constructive, sensitive and unbiased manner. Consider whether the team can be supplemented by staff from other departments who are trained in carrying out this kind of analysis, and indeed whether you need to include outsiders, possibly consultants, who can take an impartial view and have knowledge of the running of other organizations' finance functions. Whatever the eventual make-up, the project team must be able to address strategic, operational and technological issues. It is probable that some members of the team will change as the project progresses.

Identify customers and suppliers of the finance function to consult

Although not full-time members of the project team, representatives of the internal suppliers to and customers of the finance function need to be identified and some of their time earmarked for the project. Without their views the analysis will be worthless. Be sure to get a wide range of opinions – critics as well as fans.

Identify benchmarking partners

The identification of appropriate finance function 'benchmarks' will be invaluable as the transformation process progresses. Identifying two or three partners who wish to benchmark directly and who are willing to exchange information freely would be the ideal scenario. External benchmark databases that focus on the finance function, for example Hackett and PWC's Global Benchmark Alliance, are useful alternatives, providing their shortcomings are appreciated. An analysis of methodologies that can be used is discussed in detail in Chapter 10 (p. 167).

Set up communication media

It is important to communicate objectives, timescales, progress and other news about the project on an on-going basis, both within the finance function and company wide.

2.3 ANALYZE THE PRESENT FINANCE FUNCTION ACTIVITIES/PROCESSES

Once the project is properly established, the first stage in the transformation must be an analysis of what the finance function currently does. Utilizing some of the process/activity tools and techniques described in *Business Process Management*,[3] a systematic analysis of the activities performed must be undertaken.

Documentation and costing of the finance activities and processes

Even if activities and processes are already documented, it will be necessary to carry out a detailed activity analysis update and costing of all the activities undertaken by the finance function (*see* Fig. 2.1).

Fig. 2.1 Activity/process analysis

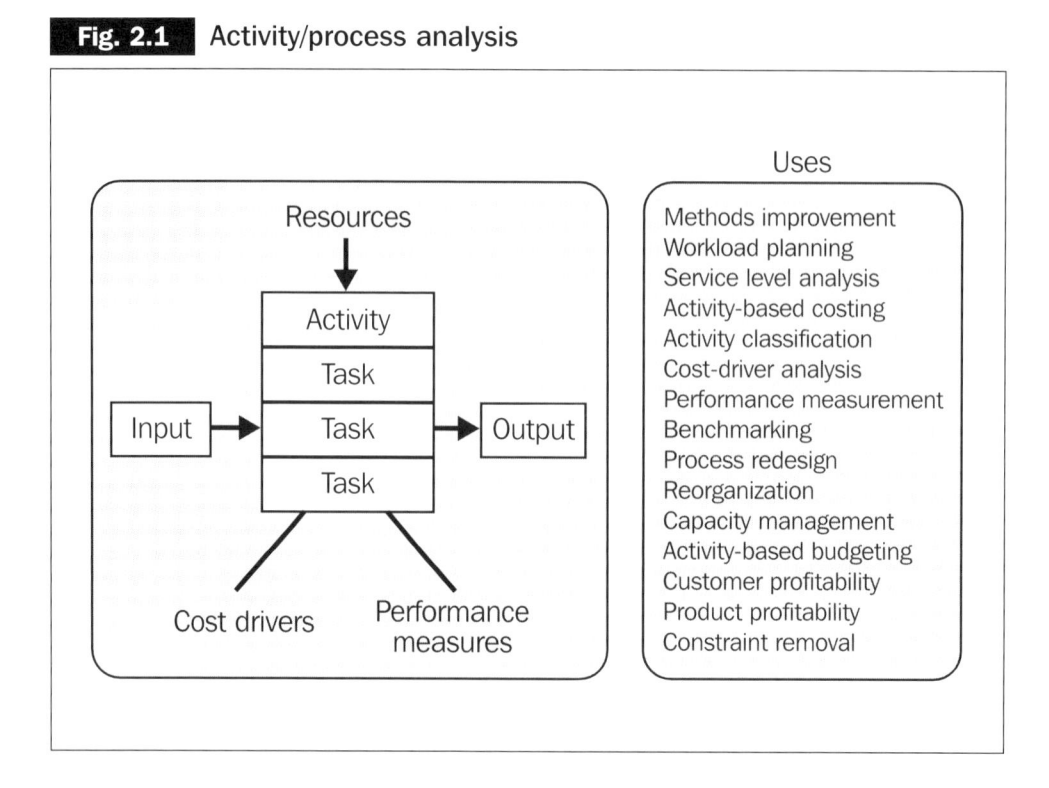

```
                    Resources
                        |
                        v
                  +-----------+
                  | Activity  |
                  +-----------+
                  |   Task    |
   Input -------> |   Task    | -------> Output
                  |   Task    |
                  +-----------+
                   /         \
                  /           \
           Cost drivers    Performance
                            measures
```

Uses
- Methods improvement
- Workload planning
- Service level analysis
- Activity-based costing
- Activity classification
- Cost-driver analysis
- Performance measurement
- Benchmarking
- Process redesign
- Reorganization
- Capacity management
- Activity-based budgeting
- Customer profitability
- Product profitability
- Constraint removal

It will be necessary to understand all attributes of the activities/processes to provide:

- activity analysis, costings and end-to-end process maps;
- objectives and responsibilities of all parts of the function processes;
- understanding of all the outputs, levels of service and the reasons for them;
- understanding of the interrelationships with other departments and those extending beyond the organisation to suppliers, partners and customers;
- identification of any financial or non-financial performance measures and key performance indicators (KPIs), including time and quality that already exist, often informally, and knowledge of any existing service level agreements (SLAs);
- understanding of all relevant systems and technological interfaces, including stretching outside the company and to all geographical locations;
- method of generating ideas for improvement; system and process constraints; and any unnecessary diversionary activity.

Finance process map example

Figure 2.2 is an actual client example of a finance function process that has been documented not only in finance but throughout the business, where it can be seen that considerable activity took place, both in operational and support areas. The process map shows that invoices are raised manually and then typed on a word processor by the operational teams where direct contact with the customers takes place; the processing is then carried out in finance, transferring the information on to Oracle Financials. Out-of-pocket (OOP) expenses are added to customer invoices, resulting in an expensive process of mainly manual collection and analysis of OOP.

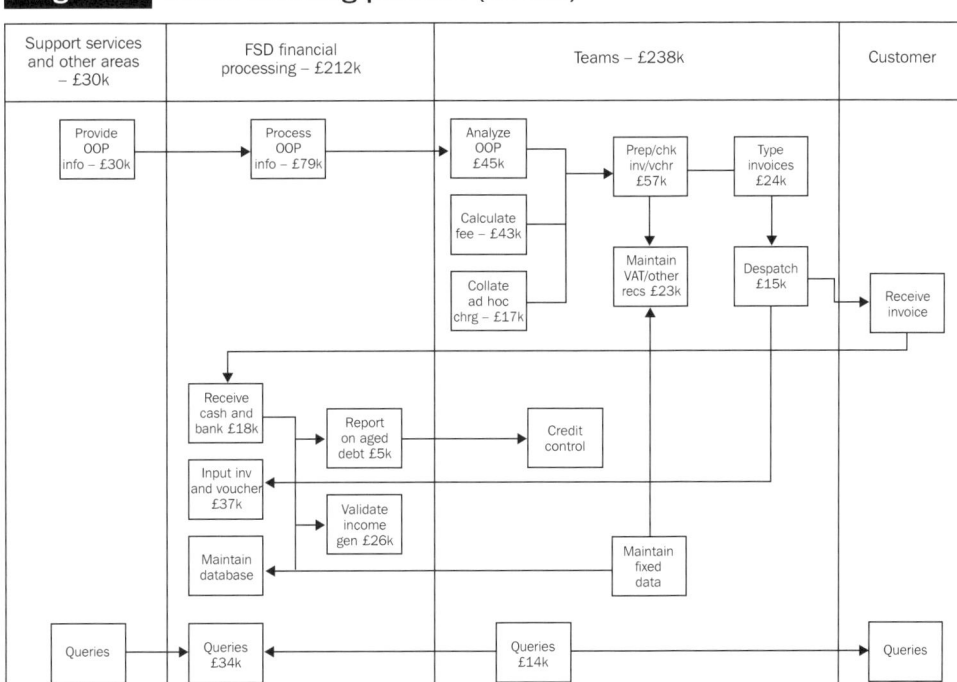

Fig. 2.2 Sales invoicing process (£480k)

Support services and other areas – £30k	FSD financial processing – £212k	Teams – £238k		Customer
Provide OOP info – £30k →	Process OOP info – £79k →	Analyze OOP £45k →	Prep/chk inv/vchr £57k → Type invoices £24k	
		Calculate fee – £43k	Maintain VAT/other recs £23k ← Despatch £15k →	Receive invoice
		Collate ad hoc chrg – £17k		
	Receive cash and bank £18k			
	Input inv and voucher £37k	Report on aged debt £5k → Credit control		
	Maintain database ←	Validate income gen £26k	Maintain fixed data	
Queries →	Queries £34k ←	Queries £14k ←		Queries

It is also necessary to note that this example service company had about 500 customers, a high proportion of whom have a minimum fee charge of £2,000 per annum, with the process being applied to all customers in the same way. Until the process analysis was carried out, the organization had no appreciation of the total true cost of the process, which was approximately £1,000 a customer. It is not difficult once presented with this information to find ways of simplifying the process and reducing costs, including possibilities for:

- inputting invoices directly into Oracle;
- transferring minimum-charge customers on to a fixed fee inclusive of OOP, rendering this expensive process unnecessary in these cases (invoices needing to be raised and paid only once a year);
- automating the collection of OOP data through use of the operational systems, which not only reduced considerable manual effort in the support, finance and operational areas, but provided improved customer billing information and considerably reduced the number of queries being raised;
- removing duplication of maintenance of customer information;
- eventual plans to automate the process fully.

Validate the data collected

Once analyzed, the data collected needs to be verified to ensure that it is correct and amendments made as necessary.

2.4 DEVELOP THE VISION FOR THE FUTURE OF THE FINANCE FUNCTION

Once the present finance function activities are fully understood, it is time to start collecting comparable information on best practices in finance and building the future vision, in consultation with colleagues throughout the business.

Collect benchmark data

In addition to a complete picture of what finance is currently doing, it is necessary at this point to collect benchmark and best-practice data from other organizations. The aim of this exercise is to compare all aspects of finance activities, both quantitative and qualitative, against what is regarded as best practice and to measure where the gaps exist and how efficiency and effectiveness can be improved. As discussed in Chapter 10, the ideal situation would enable discussion to take place between the partners to understand fully the reasons for the differences.

Some organizations find self-assessment against one of the quality frameworks (*see* Section 9.6, page 156) to be a beneficial measure of necessary quality improvements. One such company is Sun Life Assurance, which is quoted as measuring itself against the EFQM criteria and, according to Keith Brassington, Business Improvement Manager, finding that:

> *the results highlighted the fact that finance was not customer focused, didn't really understand processes and was weak in areas of people strategies and leadership.*[4]

Hold brainstorming sessions throughout the organization and wider business community

The analyses collected on the current finance activities and the best-practice finance data, together with the senior management team's view on the requirements of the business from the finance function, are presented for discussion both by the finance function itself and by its customers and suppliers throughout the business. The content of this book provides a good indication of the likely outline change that will be needed. Process simplification and rationalization is unlikely to be sufficient to deliver the radical change demanded of a twenty-first-century finance function.

This book concentrates on the need for and the direction the change must take. That view is confirmed by Christine Gattenio of the Hackett Group,[5] who outlines how finance professionals from the traditional finance function are perceived by their peers as:

- hard workers
- historical reporters
- data manipulators
- transaction processors
- reactors and followers
- corporate cops.

Compare this to the role that they can be expected to play in the new transformed finance function:

- focus on better information
- provide insightful direction
- be concerned with planning for the future
- help build relationships
- become change agents
- take a global perspective
- reduce costs.

The finance function of one company, EDS, has its own vision, mission and value statements and key goals, which are typical of those organizations leading the way:

> *Vision:*
> *To create a world-class financial team.*
>
> *Mission:*
> *To provide global financial leadership and expertise to EDS.*
>
> *Value statement:*
> *The controller organisation will enable EDS to achieve its vision by providing leadership with a broad and unique business perspective and relevant information through efficient business processes.*
>
> *Goals:*
> - *Develop business leaders.*
> - *Drive strategy formulation and decision making.*
> - *Provide actionable information.*[4]

Define and agree the transformed finance function specification

Once the process has reached this stage, a clear vision should have emerged through consensus throughout the company. The specification that is then drawn up must spell out how the transformed finance function is going to deliver added value.

What services is finance going to deliver in future?

- Financing, internal audit and stewardship services (*see* Chapter 1).
- Operational services – through a process-oriented shared service centre (SSC) and/or 'lights out', possibly outsourced (*see* Chapters 3 and 4).
- Facilitators of company-wide information management, delivering business intelligence (*see* Chapter 5).
- Facilitators of company-wide value generation (VBM and best value) (*see* Chapter 6).
- Valuers of intellectual capital (IC) (*see* Chapter 7).
- Facilitators of enterprise risk management (ERM) (*see* Chapter 7).
- Compilers and publishers of ethical, environmental and social reports (*see* Chapter 7).
- Strategic and operational decision support, resource allocation/attraction, forecasting and scenario planning (*see* Chapter 8).
- Facilitators of integrated performance management, moving beyond traditional budgeting, incorporating balanced scorecards (BSCs) and benchmarking linked from strategy through to operational measures (*see* Chapters 9 and 10).
- Provision of costing, pricing and customer profitability data (ABC).
- Facilitators of company-wide performance improvement (BPR).
- Deliverers of the new enterprise digitization programmes through web-enabled end-to-end processes and business community integration, including web technology, process analysis, redesign and implementation.
- Effective business process management (BPM), including alternate service levels and priority-based budgeting (PBB).

These final four points are covered in *Business Process Management*.[3]

What efficiencies need to be achieved in delivering services?

- BPR applied to all processes.
- Specifics as identified.
- Benchmark gaps.
- Continuous improvement culture.
- Flexibility and responsiveness.

- Elimination of 'diversionary' activities.
- Customer-focus and service-orientation.

What technological advances will be harnessed to effect that delivery?

(*See* Chapter 5 and *Business Process Management*.)

- Enterprise-wide systems, e.g. ERP.
- 'Lights out' processing.
- Business community integration and enterprise application integration (EAI) middleware.
- Desktop personal tools and B2E self service, wireless devices.
- Business intelligence tools:
  - data warehousing, on-line analytical processing (OLAP) and decision-support systems (DSS)
  - enterprise portals.
- Web technology, including standards and security.
- Integrated end-to-end processes, e.g. SCM, CRM.
- Collaborative computing:
  - workflow systems, e.g. POP routing
  - document management, e.g. imaging
  - computer and telephone integration (CTI)
  - groupware, e.g. Lotus Notes
  - mobile devices and telecommunications.

What combination of competencies and skills are required?

(*See* section 1.3, page 10 and section 2.6, page 31.)

- Business consultants.
- Business analysts.
- Technical specialists.
- Job and person specifications.
- Training and development programmes.
- Non-financial staff.
- IT.

What organization structure will be appropriate?

(*See* Chapter 1 and Fig. 1.5, page 13.)

- Outsourcing or application service provision (ASP) (*see* Chapter 4).
- Shared service centres (SSCs), 'lights out' processing (*see* Chapters 1 and 3).
- Devolvement to business units.
- Centralized services.
- Virtual, digitized, web-enabled finance function.
- Incorporation of non-financial staff.
- Customer-focus and service-oriented.
- Clearly defined accountability, authority and responsibility lines.

What control and measurement of the finance function will be maintained?

(*See* Part 4.)

- Qualitative, EFQM.
- Quantitative, financial.
- Cultural.
- Customer satisfaction, service-level agreements setting and monitoring.
- Staff satisfaction and requirements for training and development.
- Balanced scorecard – drilled-down and weighted.
- Integrated performance management, linking compensation to performance.
- Continuous benchmarking.
- Demonstration of added value.

2.5 CREATE THE CHANGE STRATEGY

It will be necessary to prepare a detailed plan at this stage, setting out the following.

Project plan

Depending on the radical nature of the changes that have been agreed, it could take up to two years to complete the transformation fully (*see* Fig. 2.3 for a summary of the process). This will depend on the scale of the changes and whether they involve the implementation of IT solutions, such as ERP, SCM, CRM and EIS (enterprise information system), or the setting-up of a global, web-enabled, shared service centre. It will be possible to schedule other changes during that period and a detailed project plan, clearly showing interdependencies, will need to be drawn up without delay. If too many ideas were forthcoming from the visioning exercise, then it may be necessary to prioritize and phase the improvements and changes at this point. Do not underestimate the resources required to make the changes successfully.

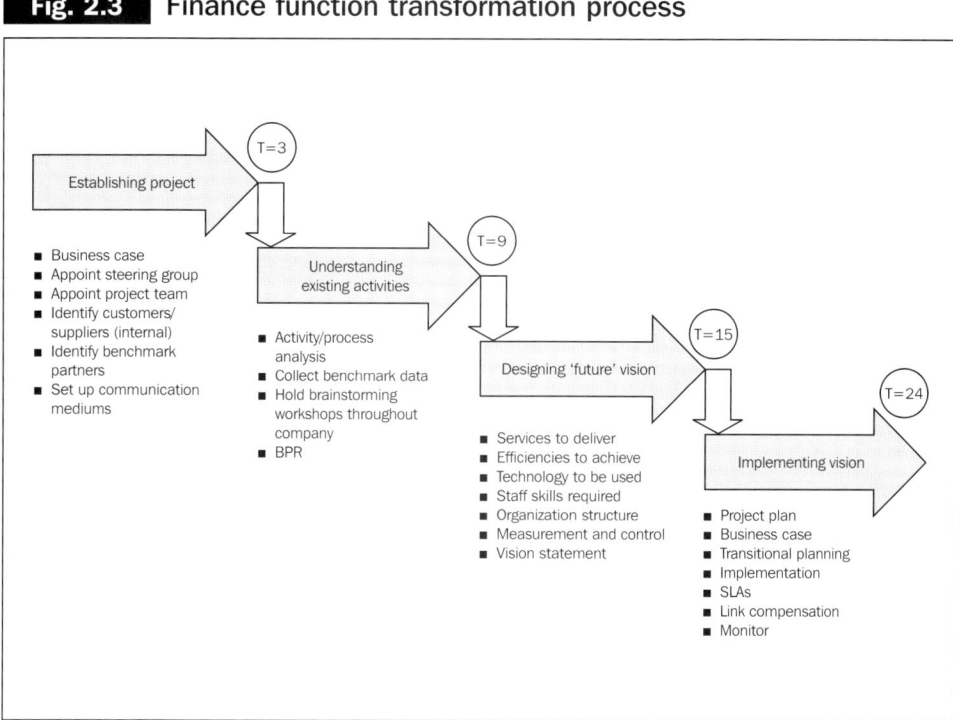

Fig. 2.3 Finance function transformation process

```
Establishing project (T=3)
■ Business case
■ Appoint steering group
■ Appoint project team
■ Identify customers/
  suppliers (internal)
■ Identify benchmark
  partners
■ Set up communication
  mediums

Understanding existing activities (T=9)
■ Activity/process analysis
■ Collect benchmark data
■ Hold brainstorming workshops throughout company
■ BPR

Designing 'future' vision (T=15)
■ Services to deliver
■ Efficiencies to achieve
■ Technology to be used
■ Staff skills required
■ Organization structure
■ Measurement and control
■ Vision statement

Implementing vision (T=24)
■ Project plan
■ Business case
■ Transitional planning
■ Implementation
■ SLAs
■ Link compensation
■ Monitor
```

Business case

Once the detailed plan has been produced and fully costed, it needs to be incorporated into a business case to gain official board approval. This should be a formality at this stage, as all the senior management team (SMT) members will have been involved in the discussions to formulate the new strategy. The end vision should be so compelling – both in terms of reduced costs and improved services – that no opposition should emerge.

2.6 ALIGN STAFF SKILLS AND COMPETENCIES

As we saw in Fig. 1.5 (page 13), the roles in the finance function of the twenty-first-century are very different from previous decades. In the main they contain as much non-financial as financial content and they lead to a large variety of senior management posts in a non-departmental structure. Whilst this presents huge opportunities for finance-trained professionals to move into exciting new roles it also offers opportunities to other professionals to move into what would once have been considered traditional finance territory.

According to Price Waterhouse's CFO 2000 survey,[6] by far the biggest barrier to improving finance's role is the current level of competencies among finance staff. CIMA research on *Changing Work Patterns*[7] discovered that accountants in business rank current and future required skills and knowledge in order of importance as:

- business acumen/commercial awareness
- interpersonal/communication skills
- managing people
- strategic thinking (second in future analysis)
- information technology
- management accountancy (traditional).

These are very different to the technical skills and competencies of traditional finance function personnel.

Assess existing staff for new posts

The company human resources (HR) specialists will be involved in this process, which may consist of the following steps.

- *Draw up job and people specifications to match the transformed finance function specification.* These will be in line with those described in section 1.3 (page 10), and include business consultants, business analysts and technical specialists, as well as traditional, wider business and commercial roles.

- *Compare requirements against existing staff profiles:*
  - Compare the established requirements to the current staff skills and competencies profiles.
  - Identify any matches, near matches and mismatches and draw up plans, without delay, for slotting existing personnel into jobs.
  - Consider if any staff from other departments might be suitable for the business analyst or consultant roles and raise internal job advertisements.
  - If a downsizing is resulting from, for example, setting up an SSC in another country, then take great care to keep those staff who will become redundant until the transfer is complete, possibly utilizing termination bonuses. In some cases it will be crucial to keep key staff and their retention needs to be treated as a priority.
  - Assess whether new staff, with different skills, need to be recruited from outside the company and begin the process of recruitment.

- *Draw up staff training and development plans.* Begin to arrange the necessary additional training and development that will be required for staff. All staff will undoubtedly require customer-focus training, even if they are going to fulfil one of the technical roles for which they are a good skills match. Many will need more extensive new skills training and support, particularly in creative problem solving, communication skills, business and commercial understanding and company-wide value-adding skills.

- *Communicate the results of the exercise as quickly and as sensitively as possible.* Undue delay in this process causes anxiety, demotivation and uncertainty, and can result in the best staff departing.

2.7 IMPLEMENT THE TRANSFORMATION

- Successful implementation will require considerable efforts, not just in terms of good project planning but in effective leadership, company-wide communication, project selling and management of the change process. This will take time, so be sure to build it into your plans.

- Transition planning must be rigorous to ensure that customers do not suffer unduly during the changes. It is often prudent to make changes and minor improvements in existing systems immediately, to gain the support of the customer and ease the transition.

- Take care to agree service-level agreements and project plans with every customer individually, getting each business unit's 'buy-in' to the transformation. If new costing and decision-support systems are being built, remember that finance is facilitating this process for the operational managers and not the other way around.

- Ensure that all staff, particularly finance staff, are communicated with regularly during the implementation process. This must include progress reviews of training and development programmes.

2.8 MONITOR THE SUCCESS AND RESULTS OF IMPLEMENTATION

- The success of the implementation against plan should be monitored regularly by the steering group. This will include monitoring of timescales, resource utilization, expenditure, staff retention and recruitment.

- Once complete, each stage of the project must then be monitored against the set objectives to ensure that they are being met in full, including customer satisfaction and culture changes.

- Continue to monitor staff requirements for additional training, development and support.

- Continue to benchmark against 'best practice' and 'best value' to ensure that the company maintains upper-quartile performance.

- Regularly review service level agreements (SLAs) with customers.
- Produce a balanced scorecard monthly for senior management to monitor progress.
- Link compensation to performance and achievement of corporate objectives.
- Communicate success company wide.

2.9 Case studies

Worldwide excellence in finance

Adidas-Salomon[8]

In five years the German footwear and apparel manufacturer Adidas-Salomon has pulled back from bankruptcy, gone public and seen its stock price triple. Once a classic case of mismanagement, the company is striving to become a decentralized, virtual enterprise with multicultural management. Robert Louis-Dreyfus, who took over as CEO in 1993, launched a company-wide campaign to reduce its cycle times, increase on-time delivery, manage seasonal inventory and respond quickly to changes in consumer tastes.

The CFO, Australian Dean Hawkins, set about establishing closer relationships between his department and operating areas. The tenets of the company's formal finance mission statement stress that the finance function's primary duty is to support the decision-making process of senior management and operating divisions. Hawkins made it his main goal to demonstrate to business heads that finance could do more than manage the books. He said:

> *I want to effect this change through trust-building measures. Trust-building measures result when members of the finance function provide value-added analysis before it is requested. Ideally, the finance function is not to be viewed as a necessary evil but rather as a partner.*

The drive to 'add value at every point where the work of finance touches the rest of the business' runs like a leitmotif through Hawkins' strategy. In his short tenure as CFO he has effectively 'changed the status quo of what was previously acceptable for the CFO to do'. He has employed the 'right mix' of people (including new recruits who do not have accounting backgrounds), improved analysis, and fostered better understanding, more trust and fewer political agendas.

Dell Computer[9]

Dell Computer Corporation boosted its return on invested capital from 37% in 1995 to 186% in 1998, due to a single-minded focus on financial and operating discipline, according to Tom Meredith, CFO. The company combines a clear understanding of its business model, a company-wide determination to boost return on invested capital, a fierce appetite for information and a rigorous analysis of both financial and operating performance. At Dell, say Tom Meredith and Michael Dell, Chairman and CEO, financial understanding is not the province of the finance department only but permeates the atmosphere.

The thrust of the changes was as follows:

- *Finding a common data model*, which was a global financial initiative to develop a common architecture, system and practice.
- *Balancing liquidity, profitability and growth*, reducing inventories down to seven days, by reducing the numbers of suppliers.
- *Changing focus and behaviour* by educating employees about the increasing emphasis on ROCE (return on capital employed) – which included tying a significant portion of employee compensation to that measure.
- *Creating value for customers profitably*.
- Maintaining a focus on people development. In addition to reinvigorating finance's recruiting and development efforts, Meredith now spends more of his own time educating financial managers. He says:

> *I don't believe finance is a support function, We are either integral partners or we are rented units. The quest to improve the finance team's knowledge is never ending. If I have a real heartache it is that we're not yet able to spend more time analysing, and a whole lot less time compiling, information. We're starting to move from information to knowledge. Eventually, I hope we'll move from knowledge to wisdom.*

SmithKline Beecham[1]

SmithKline Beecham's R&D division has been transforming its finance function from scorekeeper to business partner by focusing on:

- *Streamlining transaction processing* – from the individual businesses to company and country-wide shared service centres.
- *Establishing decision-support tools and processes* – finance has built up a team with skills to support decisions.
- *Developing skills and technologies*.
- *Building the finance discipline* – a central team maintains the finance discipline within R&D; its role includes the continual development of processes, tools and systems, adopting best practice wherever possible.

Part 2

The technology-driven finance function

- 3 Shared service centres 39
- 4 Outsourcing 49
- 5 Information management delivering business intelligence 67

3

Shared service centres

- 3.1 Introduction   41
- 3.2 Which processes are best suited to an SSC?   42
- 3.3 Checklist of technical considerations in establishing an SSC   43
- 3.4 Phases in the implementation of an SSC   45
- 3.5 Benefits of the SSC approach   47
- 3.6 Case study – SSCs at Ciba Speciality Chemicals   47

3.1 INTRODUCTION

From Fig. 1.1 (page 5), it can be seen that during the 1990s organizations implementing enterprise resource planning (ERP) systems found it cost effective to establish a centralized shared service centre (SSC) in a geographically beneficial location, initially to handle high-volume transaction-based activities, then whole processes and now – in the web-enabled environment – end-to-end processes linking to customers, suppliers, partners and employees. Figure 3.1 shows how a twenty-first-century SSC might look.

Fig. 3.1 Business process, web-enabled shared services

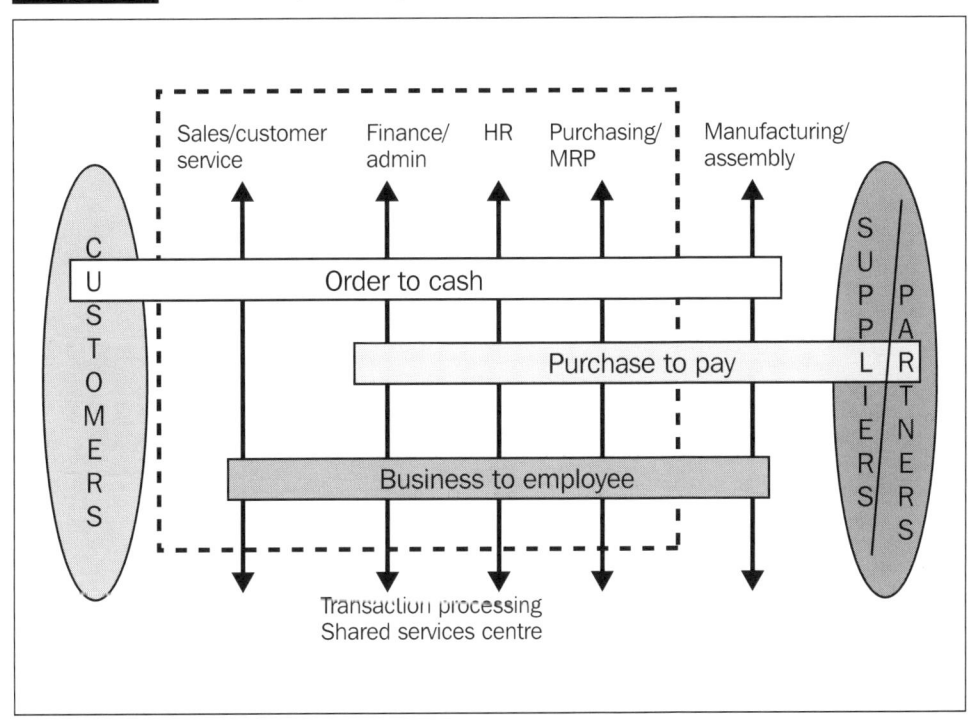

Shared service centres are a type of 'internal outsourcing', the focus being to provide non-core services to individual business units, and often they are set up and run in conjunction with an external outsourcing partner. An SSC can contain one or several support processes, from high-volume, transaction-based processes like purchase order processing (POP) to specialist services like legal.

The move towards profit/value-accountable strategic business units (SBUs) trading internally with other SBUs including finance, has forced the adoption of a more customer-focused, service-oriented culture. If finance and other SBUs do not provide a cost-efficient, effective, flexible, responsive and appropriate service to their internal customers, then the customers will look to outsource, not least because their bonuses are usually linked to their profit/value-added targets. Cost savings achieved through utilizing SSC-based approaches are quoted as high as 50% in the USA and 30–40% in Europe.

PwC research in 1998[1] indicates that when most business processes are stripped down to their basics, about 70% of these processes are generic. The processes are operated differently in different countries, mostly because of history, tradition and culture. PwC's SSC five-year benchmarking study[2] looked at more than 80 companies and 1,600 business sites across 50 countries and revealed the following dramatic improved efficiencies:

- Procurement – cost savings of 30% have been realized through new supplier agreements.
- Customer invoicing – processing changes have led to cost reductions approaching 40%, primarily in the area of lower personnel costs.
- Accounts payable – SSCs require 60% less personnel.
- Accounts receivable – 100% improvement in processing efficiency and 34% reductions in processing costs have been achieved.
- General accounting – the required staffing levels have been reduced by 50%.

Costs are not the only factor. When PwC was setting up an SSC in Europe in co-operation with BP and Mobil, Rotterdam was chosen because of its ability to provide the necessary multilingual staff, which, on this occasion, gave the Netherlands comparative and competitive advantage. Others choosing Holland include DHL, Cisco and Reebok. Another important consideration in Europe is the potential tax savings that can be achieved. Some countries, like Belgium and the Netherlands, have introduced specific tax regimes to encourage SSCs being located in their countries. Equally, other factors must be considered, including relocation of staff, process re-engineering, legal implications, IT and individual country statutory requirements. For example, in Sweden it is a criminal offence not to hold computerized accounting records on a computer physically located in Sweden. Moreover, as the trend to SSC gained momentum in the second half of the 1990s, it was recognized that greater savings could be achieved by locating further afield in lesser-developed economies, where running costs are significantly cheaper, for example, India and Eastern Europe have become popular.

3.2 WHICH PROCESSES ARE BEST SUITED TO AN SSC?

With the move to profit-accountable business units, with ever greater autonomy, it is more important than ever to ensure that support functions are as efficient as possible. The difficulties involved in negotiating the sale of centralized services to profit-oriented business units are great. If it is found (through benchmarking and market testing) that the services are not provided as efficiently as can be bought in from outside, what do you do? Generally speaking, ground rules are introduced to protect in-house services, at least in the short term. However, it is incumbent on all support functions to ensure that in the medium term they provide the most customer-oriented, appropriate, flexible, effective and cost-efficient services, which can compete with outside providers.

So considerable soul searching is needed in examining all support activities, including those that are partly or completely contained within the individual business units, such as some HR and finance activities. When considering which processes to install in an SSC, the obvious first choices would be the high-volume, transaction-based processes, like purchase ledger. Such activities are generic and yield obvious synergies when centralized. Other support services fitting this category include:

- purchase order processing (purchase-to-pay)
- sales order processing (order-to-cash)
- management information process
- accounting to reporting
- planning to budgeting
- treasury to cash management.

However, further investigation will reveal that the SSC concept is also suited to the provision of specialist services, like legal. Quite often business units, depending on their size, cannot justify employing in-house expertise for these services and find that a centralized specialist unit, which has full corporate knowledge, is the ideal solution. Other specialist services that fit into this category include:

- human resources
- logistics
- property management
- taxation
- IT
- internal audit.

3.3 CHECKLIST OF TECHNICAL CONSIDERATIONS IN ESTABLISHING AN SSC[3]

How can accounting and legal differences be catered for?

Unfortunately, despite the progress towards the European Union's aim of a single market, considerable differences still exist in terms of accounting and legal requirements in the different member countries. There is no single set of European accounting standards (yet) and the method of regulation is peculiar to each country.

For example, in Germany and France the government regulates accounting standards, but both have recently passed laws permitting group accounts to be prepared according to International Accounting Standards Committee (IASC) rules. In Italy, accounts must be notarized and all pre-printed documents prepared by state-authorized printers; such problems with documents can be overcome by the use of document imaging. However, there is a commitment to standardize by 2005. Another issue that needs careful examination is the different legal requirements of each country, not least with regards to employment law.

Group taxation opportunities and problems created by the location of an SSC

The key driver for opportunities in terms of taxation is the methods chosen to charge business units for the services provided by the SSC. This is, of course, first and foremost a commercial decision, but the method needs to be agreeable to individual country tax authorities. Europe operates an arbitration convention to obtain corresponding adjustments to iron out any difficulties caused by differing tax treatments due to inter-country transfer pricing. The principle of arm's-length negotiation should be adopted and documented to avoid problems.

Some tax considerations to be taken into account when deciding in which country to locate the SSC are:

- variable corporation tax rates, which are over 40% in France and Germany;
- methods of calculating profits eligible for taxation, e.g. capital allowances, financing costs, intangible asset treatments;
- utilization of tax losses;
- transfer of goodwill;
- tax incentives offered by different countries, such as the Netherlands;
- commission structures, which could be beneficial, meaning that sales are made from the central unit, which pays commission to local sales offices as agents, providing the opportunity to earn more profit in a low-tax regime;
- VAT and other indirect taxes;
- document compliance.

How IT can facilitate an SSC

Recent developments in IT have provided the following essential capabilities in:

- Managing language requirements; these can be handled on-screen by ERP software and calls from different countries can be diverted via telecommunications, but generally staff with the necessary language skills will need to be employed.

- Improving accessibility of information via enterprise-wide networks and other technological advances – avoiding the need to duplicate information.
- Dealing with diverse processing requirements, such as multiple currencies – different VAT treatments are handled well by ERP solutions.
- Virtual transaction processing via web technology – this, combined with the shift to self-service for individual employees, managers, suppliers, customers and partners, will eventually result in an SSC eliminating data-entry tasks altogether.

3.4 PHASES IN THE IMPLEMENTATION OF AN SSC

Some organizations phase in the implementation of an SSC by first progressing through one or more of the following stages with the level of sophistication rising and costs falling at each stage (*see* Fig. 3.2):

- simplification
- standardization
- centres of excellence
- national SSC
- regional SSC (pan-European)
- global SSC (in a lower-cost economy like India)
- e-SSC ('lights out' processing).

Fig. 3.2 Possible phases in the implementation of an SSC

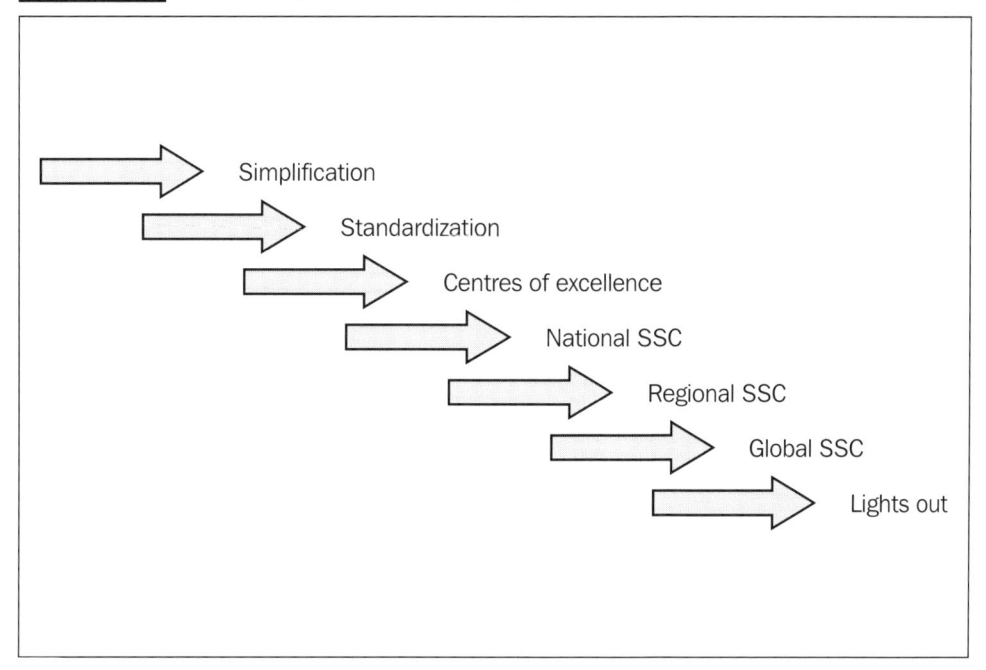

- Simplification
- Standardization
- Centres of excellence
- National SSC
- Regional SSC
- Global SSC
- Lights out

The lifecycle of an SSC project will include the following stages (*see* Fig. 3.3):

- Making the business case:
  - understand financial issues;
  - understand non-financial issues;
  - communicate the business case and get 'buy-in' from senior management and staff;
  - demonstrate added value to shareholders and stakeholders.

Fig. 3.3 Stages of an SSC project

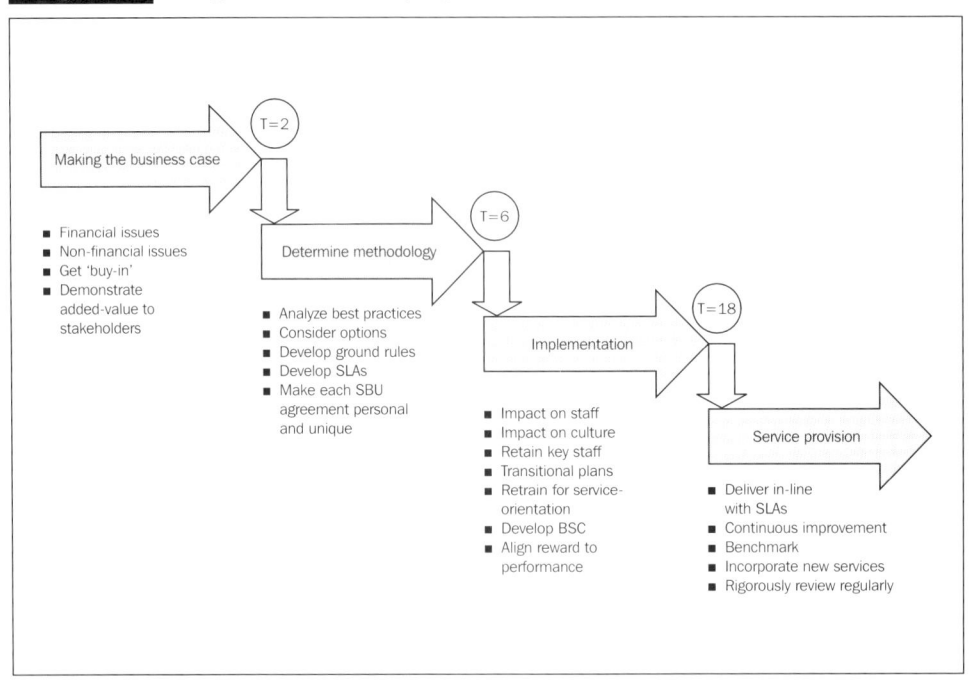

[Diagram showing stages: Making the business case (T=2) → Determine methodology (T=6) → Implementation (T=18) → Service provision

Making the business case:
- Financial issues
- Non-financial issues
- Get 'buy-in'
- Demonstrate added-value to stakeholders

Determine methodology:
- Analyze best practices
- Consider options
- Develop ground rules
- Develop SLAs
- Make each SBU agreement personal and unique

Implementation:
- Impact on staff
- Impact on culture
- Retain key staff
- Transitional plans
- Retrain for service-orientation
- Develop BSC
- Align reward to performance

Service provision:
- Deliver in-line with SLAs
- Continuous improvement
- Benchmark
- Incorporate new services
- Rigorously review regularly]

- Determine methodology:
  - analyze best practices;
  - consider options;
  - develop ground rules and service-level agreements;
  - make each business unit's agreement personal and unique.
- Implementation:
  - calculate the impact of changes on staff morale and corporate culture;
  - plan well in advance for the people issues, ensuring that key staff are retained;
  - develop and get 'buy-in' to transitional and implementation plans;
  - retrain as necessary to provide a service-oriented, standardized approach;
  - develop and agree a balanced scorecard of performance measures;
  - align reward to performance.

- Service provision:
  - deliver operational services to business units in line with SLAs;
  - continue to improve services and performance and reduce costs/prices over time;
  - benchmark performance externally;
  - identify new services that could be incorporated into the SSC;
  - rigorously review processes, customer satisfaction and progress regularly to ensure that benefits identified in the business plan are realized.

3.5 BENEFITS OF THE SSC APPROACH

- Provides better, more timely, more relevant information.
- Ability to utilize the latest web technological developments to reduce costs and provide faster processing and access to information.
- Enhances the efficiency and effectiveness of the services provided.
- Cost savings in the region of one-third claimed in Europe.
- Ability to standardize on one common and consistent data model across the whole organization.
- Facilitates the re-engineering of processes and management by process across the whole organization.
- Delivery of better quality of services as a centre of excellence.
- Focuses on core activity of SSC and provides customer focused and service oriented culture.
- Better and measured management of services provided, which can be benchmarked.
- Continual monitoring of service provision with flexibility to change quickly as required.
- Facilitates transparency of services and costs through SLAs.
- Adoption of best practice and company-wide standards.
- Move to eSSC removes need to centralize processing staff as web-enabled systems allowing for business-to-business (B2B) integration and self-service by decentralized staff (B2E), customers (B2C), suppliers, partners etc.

3.6 Case study
SSCs at Ciba Speciality Chemicals (CSC)[4]

CSC is an example of a company that has set up SSCs and run them in-house. It established a string of 12 SSCs around the world, all based on the same standardized systems – a scheme in which finance costs would be only some 1.5% of revenues. A working group of 12 systems staff (one to take charge of each SSC) decided how the SSC would operate and a set of common best practices and 700 harmonized data definitions were drawn up. The project was completed in one year and operational at the time the company was floated as an independent concern in March 1997.

4 Outsourcing

- 4.1 Introduction 51
- 4.2 IT outsourcing – risks, problems and lessons learnt 51
- 4.3 Outsourcing the finance function 53
- 4.4 Application service providers 58
- 4.5 Outsourcing partnerships 59
- 4.6 Case study – Outsourced shared services at the BBC 60

4.1 INTRODUCTION

Outsourcing is the transferring of internal business functions or processes, together with any associated assets, to an external supplier or service provider, who offers a defined service for a specified period of time, at an agreed set of rates. Organizations are recognizing that many of their non-core activities and processes can be operated more efficiently by an outside company that specializes in added-value outsourcing. It is not unusual for organizations to source part of a function or to selectively source a function, retaining significant parts in-house. The public sector, driven by compulsory competitive tendering legislation imposed by the Government during the 1990s, has been one of the main outsourcers.

Larger outsourcing companies have been consolidating and are now able to develop end-to-end systems combined with global reach. IBM Global Services is the world's, as well as the UK's, largest provider of outsourcing services, with worldwide income of $32 billion in 1999. It is its ability to offer software, hardware, services and training alongside outsourcing that helps give it the edge. In the twenty-first century outsourcing is continuing to evolve; with an already established and growing business-process outsourcing market the move is now towards application service providers (ASPs). ASPs meet the need of the business to establish market and brand position quickly. ASPs offer access to applications over the internet or a private network. The advantage for businesses is that they neither have to buy applications or licences, nor maintain and support them. The total UK outsourcing market is predicted to grow from £6 billion in 2000 to more than £20 billion in 2003, with the provision of outsourced e-services expected to represent 30% of that total.[1]

This fashion for outsourcing has benefited India, which has built an export business around solving other people's software and staffing problems. This was worth $2.65 billion in 1998–9 – 80% of the offshore outsourcing market and way ahead of its rivals, who include Ireland, Eastern Europe, China and the Philippines.

4.2 IT OUTSOURCING – RISKS, PROBLEMS AND LESSONS LEARNT

Historically, service functions such as security, cleaning, catering and payroll have been outsourced, but during the 1980s information technology became the main target for outsourcing. The rationale was that IT was not part of the core business and that it would be good business sense to transfer its running to an organization for which it was a core activity. Eastman Kodak is thought to be the first company to have outsourced its IT in this way. Research carried out by Andersen Consulting, commissioned by Harris Research, revealed that 90% of the organizations it interviewed had discussed outsourcing, 70% at board level.[2]

Main reasons for outsourcing

- Poor in-house computer systems, which were inefficient and ineffective.
- Reduction in costs, better value and improved quality of service.
- Greater flexibility.
- Access to expertise at a time of impending system changes.
- Focus on core activities at a time of major change and intense competition.
- The need for relocation or other space constraints.

Reasons for rejecting outsourcing

- Concern about loss of control.
- Lack of identifiable benefits.
- Decision that IT is strategic to the business.
- Effect of outsourcing on staff morale.
- What to do with existing IT personnel.
- Contract difficulties.
- Large-scale business change.
- Not the right time.

Risks in outsourcing

- Hidden costs of contract.
- Credibility of vendor claims.
- Irreversibility of contract.
- Lack of expertise in managing contracts.
- Loss of control over operations.
- New IT expertise from vendor fails to materialize.
- Loss of control over strategic use of IT.

Main problems experienced during outsourcing

- Defining service levels.
- Managing the contract and its details.
- Getting different contractors and vendors to work together.
- Vendor's lack of flexibility.
- Vendor's lack of responsiveness.

Lessons learnt from experience: what is needed for successful outsourcing

Preparation

- Detailed strategy and objectives for outsourcing.
- Clearly defined requirements specification and invitation to tender (ITT) process.
- Thorough vetting of vendors for claims and culture.
- More sensitive treatment of staff.
- Detailed financial and quantitative evaluation.

Contractual

- Tighter contract terms.
- More detailed, comprehensive service-level agreements.
- Anticipation of 'hidden' costs.
- Inclusion of penalty clauses.

Contract management

- Active management of supplier.
- Regular reviews of performance.
- Clear agreements on multi-vendor situations.
- Flexibility built into contract.
- Sufficient in-house staff dedicated to IT.
- Maintenance of staff vendor quality.

4.3 OUTSOURCING THE FINANCE FUNCTION

Outsourcing of the finance function is a more recent occurrence. According to J. Brian Heywood,[3] the first major private-sector clients to outsource a significant part of the finance function were BP Exploration (in 1991), Conoco and Sears, all three of which outsourced to Andersen Consulting. A survey carried out by Manchester Business School in 1997 among 400 small, medium and large organizations found that over 50% were outsourcing some aspects of the finance function.

Those finance function processes commonly outsourced are the low-value-adding, transaction-processing activities, such as:

- primary data capture and checks
- transaction processing

- information and reporting preparation
- control systems
- function management.

A survey of the top 1,000 companies carried out by Walker International[4] found that payroll was outsourced in 20% of those companies and accounted for 50% of all accounting services outsourced, followed by asset management, tax advice, internal audit and accounts payable.

Steps in an outsourcing project

Gather basic information

- Possible options for outsourcing, e.g. purchase ledger only or whole accounting function.
- Number of people who will need to be transferred, their roles and locations.
- Quantitative information on number of cost centres, number of transactions in ledgers, details of reporting process.
- Maps of existing processes and services being outsourced.
- Management and location of each part of the process.
- Details of related IT, telecommunications and other shared services.
- Information to be provided to potential outsourcers:
  - background details of the organization
  - reasons that outsourcing is being considered
  - objectives of outsourcing
  - other alternatives being considered
  - anticipated contract length
  - any joint-venture possibilities.

Begin dialogue with providers

- Hold discussions with potential outsourcers, utilizing basic information.
- Select a short list of three or four possible providers based on culture, reference sites and credibility.

Prepare the invitation to tender

- General company details.
- Levels of confidentiality required.
- Background to decision to outsource, including strategy, objectives, extent of outsourcing, current projects.

- The processes to be outsourced with details on each, including:
  - objective of process
  - transaction details, volumes per year
  - process maps, staffing details
  - current working practices
  - strengths and weaknesses of current process
  - features/changes required from any new outsourced system.
- Timing of ITT and contract.
- IT strategy as it affects outsourcing.
- Details of staff to be transferred.
- Transitional arrangements.
- Details and format required in outsourcer proposal.

Fig. 4.1 The stages in an outsourcing award

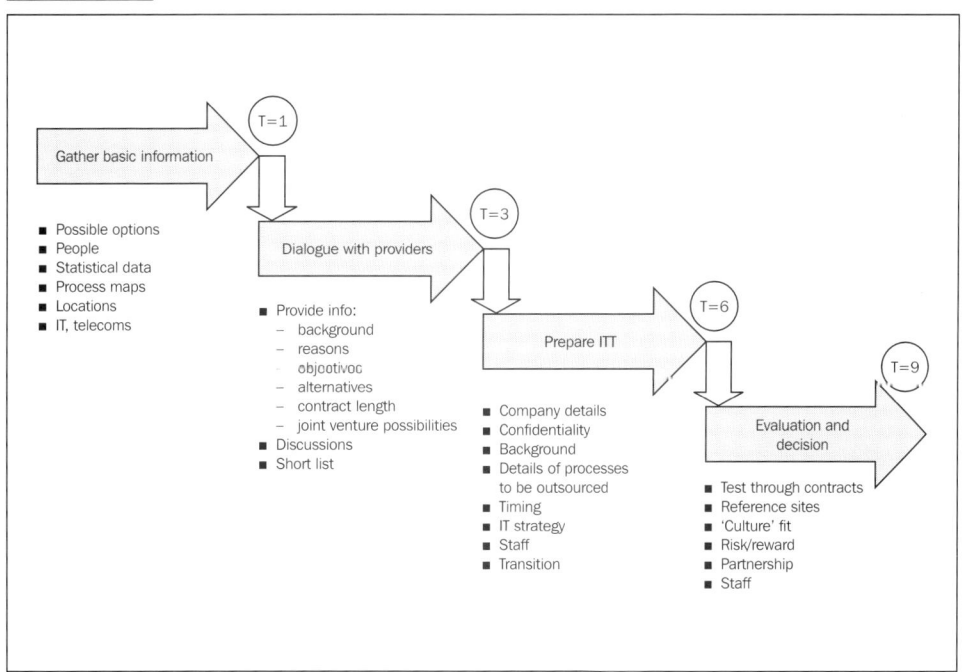

```
T=1: Gather basic information
  - Possible options
  - People
  - Statistical data
  - Process maps
  - Locations
  - IT, telecoms

T=3: Dialogue with providers
  - Provide info:
    - background
    - reasons
    - objectives
    - alternatives
    - contract length
    - joint venture possibilities
  - Discussions
  - Short list

T=6: Prepare ITT
  - Company details
  - Confidentiality
  - Background
  - Details of processes to be outsourced
  - Timing
  - IT strategy
  - Staff
  - Transition

T=9: Evaluation and decision
  - Test through contracts
  - Reference sites
  - 'Culture' fit
  - Risk/reward
  - Partnership
  - Staff
```

Provide assistance to outsourcers during bid process
- Increase the chances of a better match by providing as much assistance as possible.
- Ensure a level playing field for all bidders, providing the same support to all.

Evaluate bids
- Test suppliers through conventional contracts first, if possible.
- Always check out reference sites and take care to ensure that there is a 'culture fit'.

- Look for innovative risk/reward-sharing proposals that give both sides of the partnership incentives to make it work cost effectively.
- Are the staff to be transferred to be treated equitably? Will staff have enhanced career prospects with the outsourcer?

Decision

- Ensure that the contract allows for flexibility, change and development over the length of the contract.
- Set up a balanced scorecard to monitor performance.
- Build in regular meetings of senior management on both sides of the partnership.

These stages in an outsourcing award typically take around nine months to complete (*see* Fig. 4.1). It can take a further 18 months between the award and the full service delivery (*see* Fig. 4.2) which looks at the stages is an outsourcing implementation, following the decision on the preferred supplier.

Fig. 4.2 The stages in an outsourcing implementation

[Diagram showing stages: Board approval (T=3) → Contract (T=6) → Interim service delivery (T=12 plus) → Full service delivery (T=18)]

- Proposal
- Heads of agreement

Contract:
- Transitional plans
- Communication plans
- Agreement
- Draft SLAs
- Delivery plan
- TUPE letters

Interim service delivery:
- Final service delivery plans
- Final outsourcing agreement
- Quality plan
- Performance improvement plans

Full service delivery:
- Improvements in service
- Updated SLA
- Updated agreement
- Quality procedures

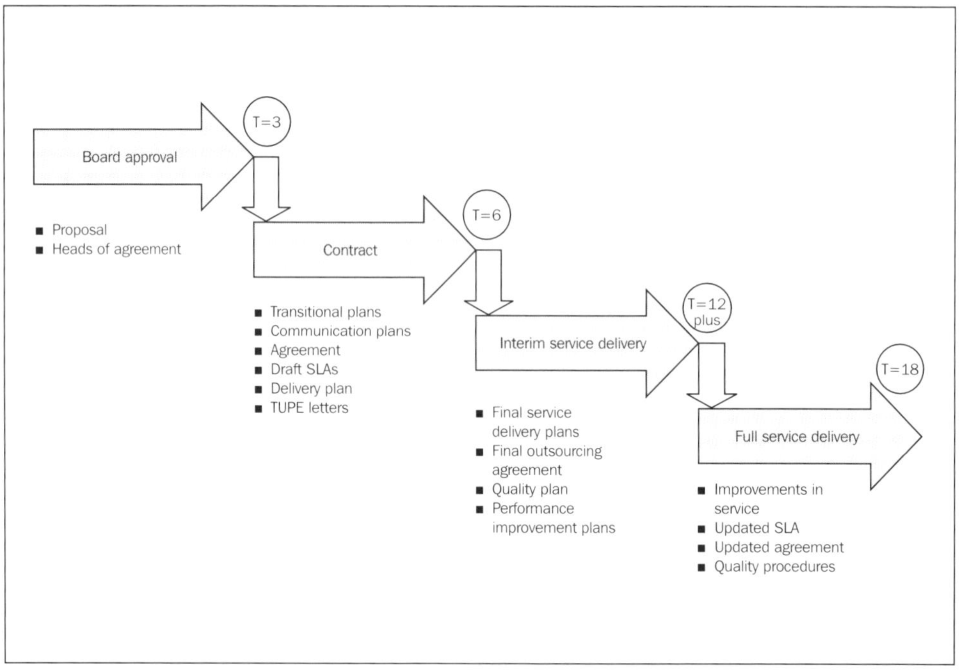

Potential benefits from outsourcing finance

- Reduced operating costs through re-engineering, introducing best practice and the economies of scale available to the provider.
- Avoidance of one-off costs associated with new equipment and systems.

- Greater control and predictability of expenditure.
- Significant improvement in service, resulting from enforceable service-level agreements.
- Increased flexibility arising from the provider's ability to reallocate staff between different contracts and service centres.
- The possibility of lower capital costs if the involvement in a shared service centre is acceptable.
- Resources freed up to focus on core financial value-adding services.
- The buying in of expertise to make the necessary transformation that may not exist in the current finance.
- A way of changing the culture of an old-established finance department to become customer focused, service oriented and commercial.

Potential risks of failure in outsourcing finance

James Creelman[4] claims that the potential risks of failure are:

- loss of control over the decision-making process;
- selection is made on lowest-cost basis alone;
- failure to consider the longer-term requirements;
- failure to incorporate continuous improvement into service-level agreements;
- difficulty in harmonizing the objectives of the two parties;
- lack of flexibility to allow for inevitable changes in assumptions made at start of contract;
- a tendency to try to 'get the better of' the other party, usually favouring the supplier;
- under-management of the contract, due to lack of appreciation of amount of work involved or loss of staff who were familiar with the contract negotiations (sometimes due to their transfer to the outsourcer!);
- inadequacy of communication channels;
- poor management of people issues.

The move to outsourcing

The outsourcing of the whole of finance, often linked to IT, started in earnest in the late 1990s and is becoming commonplace as we move into the twenty-first century. The need to move to new structures (such as shared service centres and process management) new technology (including web-enabled ERP); and new levels of customer service-oriented, are all encouraging finance directors to outsource. Many organizations, like the BBC case study at the end of this chapter, quote the need to 'buy-in' the necessary expertise. Others, like Lincolnshire County Council, quote the lack of necessary capital to install ERP being available from the Local Authority, as their prime motivator to outsourcing their finance and IT to Hyder. There is little evidence that outsourcing itself saves money – in fact, it often costs 10–15% more as a profit margin is made – but countered against that is the question as to whether the benefits could be realized without the assistance of the outsourcer. In the past it has been primarily the larger organizations that have been able to take advantage of outsourcing but, particularly with the advent of e-services and application service providers, smaller businesses are now beginning to benefit equally and move with speed to new technology.

4.4 APPLICATION SERVICE PROVIDERS (ASP)

Application service providers (ASPs) deliver computing resources via a one-to-many model: owning the resources being delivered; taking responsibility for delivery; and acting as a single point of contact. Users rent software applications through on-line links with a service provider, avoiding the initial costs of purchasing applications and the problems associated with implementing them. Potentially this is a very big market and it is SMEs (small to medium-sized enterprises) that can best take advantage of using ERP and other packages that would previously have been out of their reach. The industry expert Gartner estimates that companies can save 20–40% on application costs based on estimates of internal systems support charges. It obviously keeps costs low if the vanilla version is taken.

In practice it has been larger organizations that have tested this new concept. For example, BP Amoco went to ASP Asera to implement and manage a new web-based ordering system for its specialist chemicals customers and benefited from a time-to-market of just 90 days to roll out this new channel. Powergen are switching to the ASP version of QSP Financials used by 600 staff to provide a more predicable cost pattern.

There are four ASP payment methods:

- per transaction;
- fixed contract, variable applications – a flat fee per person for multiple applications;
- fixed contract, standard applications – e.g. ERP, with cost per user;
- pay-per-use – based on total time users spend on the system.

4.5 OUTSOURCING PARTNERSHIPS

In the second half of the 1990s, outsourcing deals moved into a second generation. Matthew May[5] explains that no longer is the emphasis on highly prescriptive contracts, but instead on risk sharing, partnerships and joint ventures. Michael Beebe, President of CSC's chemical, oil and gas group, is quoted as saying:

> *In the past, companies would ask how much of a contract would be value-added services, but never made any buying decisions on that. Now they are making decisions on the basis of what added value can be provided.*

Some examples of the sort of deals being struck include:

- In 1997 Thames Water formed a joint collaboration with Andersen Consulting (now Accenture) creating Connect 2020 to run Thames Water's supply chain. Wholly owned by Thames Water, the operation is run under contract by the consulting firm. The brief runs from negotiating the purchase of £300 million in goods and services a year to managing their fleet of lorries. A seven-year extendable contract includes Accenture getting a share of any improvements in working capital savings. Thirty payment and purchasing staff and 130 other employees transferred. Savings have been substantial, with £22 million shaved from the costs in the first two years. Quarterly reviews with a balanced scorecard are undertaken.
- In 1998 Elf Oil, the UK marketing arm of Elf Aquitaine, outsourced its financial accounting staff to PricewaterhouseCoopers (PwC), although it chose to keep the staff located on the company's premises. The contract provides that any savings and improvements in existing business processes will be split 50:50 between the parties.
- In 2000 Sainsbury's announced a seven-year outsourcing deal with Accenture, which involved the moving of 800 people, including the finance function, to the outsourcer.
- In 2001 BT announced its transfer of accounting and financial services to Xansa, the business consulting, information technology and outsourcing company. This is in line with BT's strategy of maximizing shareholder value by focusing on its core telecommunications. Some 500 BT employees will transfer to Xansa.

These arrangements recognize the shortcomings of earlier outsourcing contracts and, through various different innovative partnerships, have tried to overcome them. In particular, the inevitable conflict of interests and lack of incentive to save money and add value – inherent in the old-style deals – are being addressed.

4.6 Case study

Outsourced shared services at the BBC[6]

Background

The British Broadcasting Corporation (BBC) receives around £2.8 billion of licence fee funding annually (linked to RPI) and earns around £400 million from its commercial activities. It operates in a competitive environment, which has major cost implications, and a sophisticated internal market where programme makers have choice on source and supply. The challenges facing the BBC include:

- convergence of telecoms, media and computing
- flat licence fee income
- moves into new businesses
- introduction of digital terrestrial channels
- expansion of commercial activities
- non-strategic asset sales (e.g. transmission)
- re-organizations on a regular basis.

The changes faced and the diverse nature of its operations result in a number of specific financial management issues across the BBC including:

- separate requirements of the several businesses within the BBC;
- a range of different financial processes, supported by different (and incompatible) financial systems;
- the difficulty of obtaining timely and appropriate financial information;
- key finance functions devolved to organizational layers;
- financial processing activity occurring at many sites and involving a large number of staff;
- finance people perceived merely as 'score-keepers'.

The BBC's requirements

The BBC's business imperatives are to:

- reduce substantially the processing and administrative costs of the BBC;
- improve the quality (including accuracy, relevance and timeliness) of information delivered to programme makers and line managers;
- modernize the approach to information management, and the systems and services that support it.

The objectives of what the BBC calls the APOLLO Campaign are to streamline and standardize finance and business systems and processes across the corporation, based on SAP R/3 software, and to create and manage a shared service centre for all financial transaction processing and finance system support. The implementation of the integrated and common financial, administrative, purchasing, personnel and business information system throughout the BBC is based on standard SAP/R3 software for up to 30,000 users.

When the BBC decided to introduce SAP, it chose to outsource rather than go it alone. Finance Director John Smith explains:

> We thought it would be better value for licence payers to have a joint venture to achieve all this. We needed expertise to make the changes, and we recognized that we had only limited capability in-house.

In February 1997 the BBC awarded the contract to EDS and PricewaterhouseCoopers for a ten-year period and they formed Media Accounting Services Limited (MedAS) to deliver the contract, structured as shown in Fig. 4.3.

Fig. 4.3 BBC – Overview of the arrangements

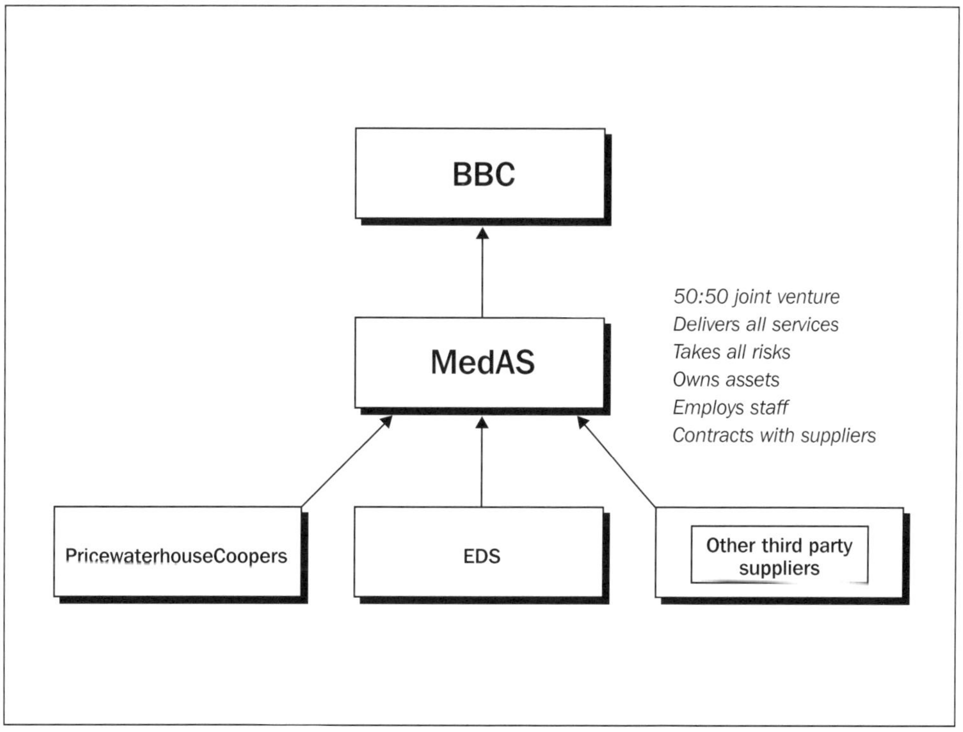

```
                    BBC
                     ↑
                     |
                   MedAS         50:50 joint venture
                     ↑           Delivers all services
                    ↑ ↑          Takes all risks
                                 Owns assets
                                 Employs staff
                                 Contracts with suppliers

PricewaterhouseCoopers    EDS    Other third party suppliers
```

During the contracting process the BBC applied the EU procurement process, which resulted in four bidders being short-listed. Contractual negotiations were undertaken with MedAS, who could deliver all components of finance and IT services (see Fig. 4.4), with the entire process from OJEC notice (purchasing contract) to signed agreement taking around 18 months. Other key features of the contract included:

- ten-year duration;
- fixed charges regime;
- significant consulting effort for transformation work;
- creation of an IT and finance shared services operation with contractual and enforceable SLAs;
- TUPE arrangements apply.

Fig. 4.4 BBC – MedAS delivers all components of finance and IT services

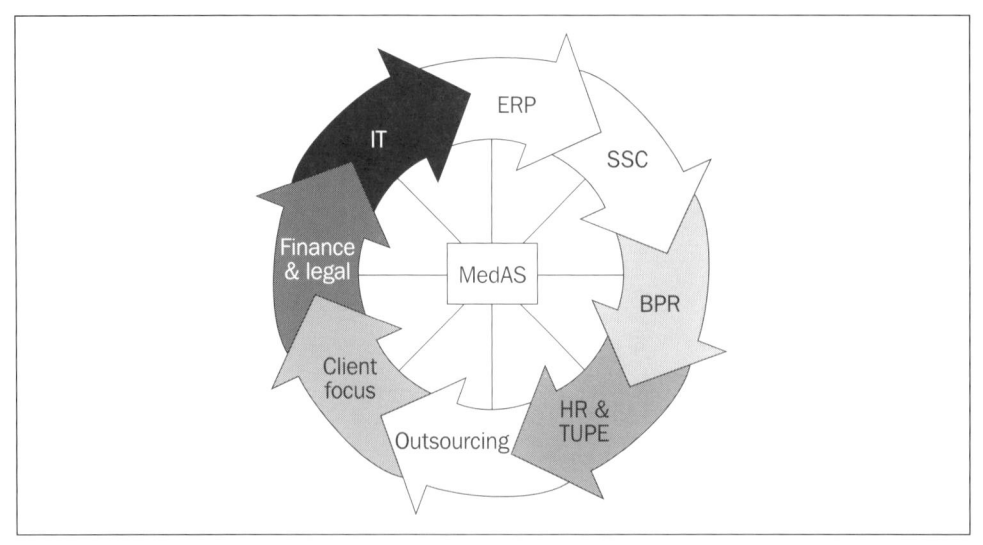

Finance IT staff and contractors and a range of legacy systems were transferred to the new company on 1 March 1997, with the priority of continuing to operate and maintain financial systems. MedAS then commenced re-engineering the BBC's 18 financial processes, followed by the transfer of a further 400 finance staff on 1 March 1998 together with a range of financial processing activities and provision of services to the BBC. The implementation of the re-engineered processes with SAP R/3 software started later in 1999.

Why outsource finance and IT services

Figure 4.5 shows a variety of service delivery models.

Fig. 4.5 BBC – Service delivery models

Client (More services outsourced →)				
All build and operational services delivered by internal resouces	Most build and operational services delivered by internal resources	All operational services provided by internal resouces	Some operational services provided by internal resources	Strategic services retained by BBC
No services	Some specialized IS/IT services (e.g. SAP) provided by contractor(s)	Turnkey facility is built by the contractor(s)	Turnkey facility is built and operated by contractor(s)	Turnkey facility is built and operated by contractor(s)
(← Less services outsourced)				Third party supplier

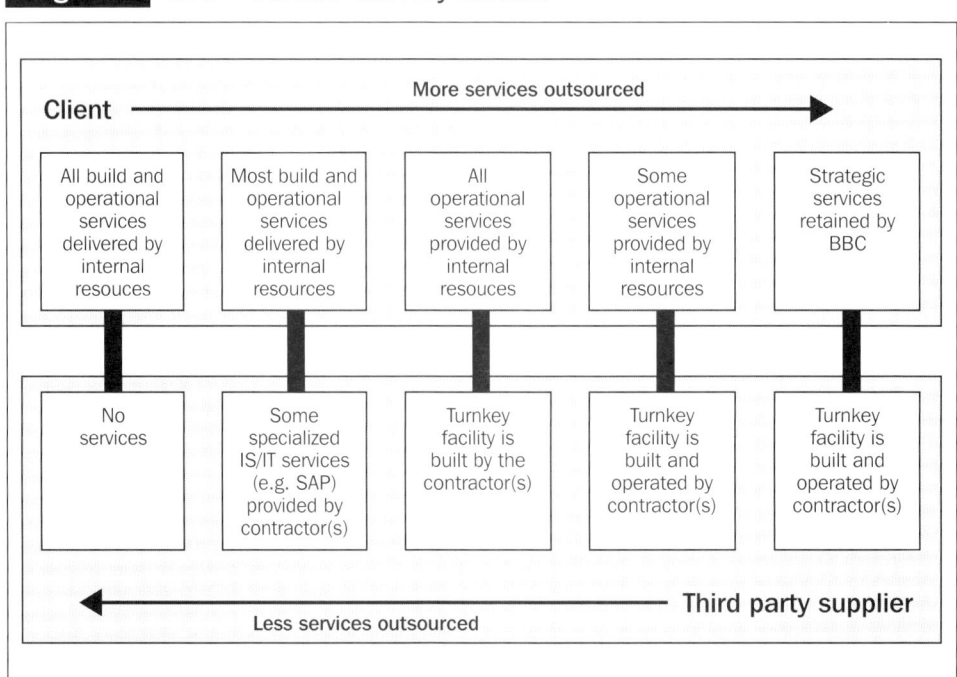

Issues to be addressed when considering outsourcing should include:

- pricing/funding arrangements (e.g. cost-benefit, fixed-charge profile, funding requirements);
- willingness to take risks (e.g. project and service delivery, financing, benefits realization);
- internal capabilities and past performance (e.g. demonstrated ability to deliver projects and services);
- diversity, complexity and vested interests (e.g. the diversity/power of the business units);
- partner(s) capabilities and experience (e.g. able to deliver the requirements);
- service flexibility (e.g. ability to change services to meet new requirements).

Figure 4.6 contrasts some of the main differences in the two methodologies, while Fig. 4.7 shows the three main contractor model alternatives.

Fig. 4.6 BBC – Examples of in-house v outsourced service delivery

In-house	Outsourced
self-funded	external funding
cost budgets	fixed charges regime
retain all risks	transferred risk
internal SLAs	enforceable SLAs
cost centre focus	profit focus
non-core activity	core competencies
single-customer focus	multiple customers
internal culture	refreshed culture

Some of the conditions where outsourcing could be appropriate are:

- sufficient scale of operation;
- significant service transformation requirements and organization concerned with the risks;
- service integration requirement (e.g. from merger and acquisition activity);
- business requirements for guaranteed and lower cost profile;
- changes to regulatory or statutory requirements.

Benefits accruing from outsourcing finance and IT services may include:

- fixed price regime with guaranteed price for the services outsourced, and inclusive of funding arrangements;

- services delivered by organizations whose core competencies and management are directly focused on these services (core v non-core);
- transfer of key risks (finance, service, project, benefits realization) to external organizations;
- external service providers can apply functional and industry best practice;
- there may be improved opportunities for staff (cost reduction focus v multi-client growth focus);
- removal or reduction of internal organization blockages, which affect existing services;
- external service providers are in a better position to provide flexible service arrangements (e.g. price arrangements, service components).

Fig. 4.7 BBC – Outsourcing service delivery models

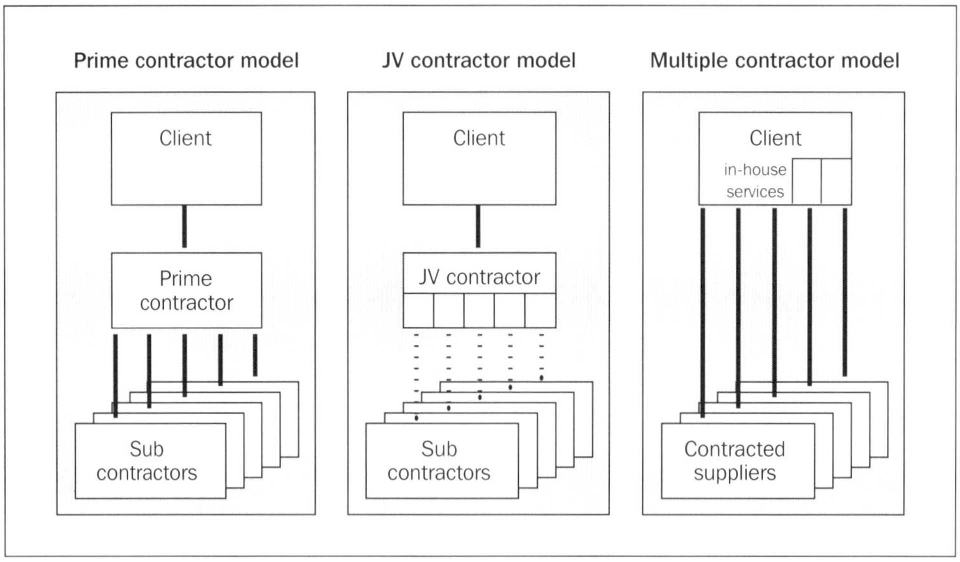

Considerations and conclusion

For outsourcing arrangements to be successful they require considerable commitment from both sides and are unlikely to happen without:

- client sponsorship throughout;
- changes in approach and procedures requiring training and change management support;
- leadership and input to transformation work (resources, decision making, prioritization);
- ongoing management of finance and IT across the client organization.

Figure 4.8 illustrates some of the areas that need to be dealt with in an outsourcing contract and why it takes a long time to negotiate – 18 months in the case of the BBC.

Different (and conflicting) agendas exist within an organization (see Fig. 4.9, for some indication of the differences that can occur), all of which needed to be carefully managed. In addition:

- Executive sponsorship is required for the outsourcing arrangements to be successful.

Outsourcing

- Although the contract is important, a partnership approach must be adopted with compromises being made from time to time.
- The customer–supplier interface needs to be clarified and implemented as a priority.
- Expectations need to be managed about the pace of service improvement following a TUPE transfer.

Fig. 4.8 BBC – Outsourcing contracts can be complex

Scope of services
Services performance obligations
Term of contract
Fee and payment arrangements
Roles and responsibilities
Assets and intellectual property
Liabilities
Staffing issues
Premises and location
Transition arrangements and timing

BBC responsibilities
Financial guarantees and deposits
Warranties and indemnities
Monitoring and control procedures
Dispute arrangements
Termination arrangements
Confidentiality and publicity
Contractual variation procedures
General contractual clauses
Arrangements for next contract

. . . and can take a considerable amount of time to finalize.

Fig. 4.9 BBC – Different (and conflicting) agendas within an organization

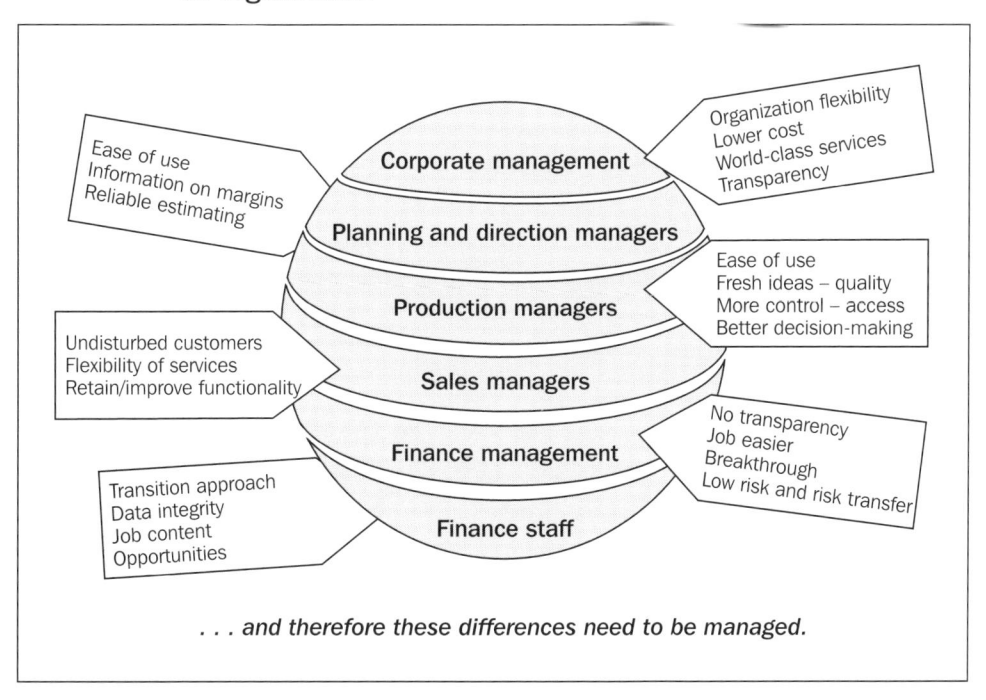

Corporate management
- Organization flexibility
- Lower cost
- World-class services
- Transparency

Planning and direction managers
- Ease of use
- Information on margins
- Reliable estimating

Production managers
- Ease of use
- Fresh ideas – quality
- More control – access
- Better decision-making

Sales managers
- Undisturbed customers
- Flexibility of services
- Retain/improve functionality

Finance management
- No transparency
- Job easier
- Breakthrough
- Low risk and risk transfer

Finance staff
- Transition approach
- Data integrity
- Job content
- Opportunities

. . . and therefore these differences need to be managed.

John Smith believes the BBC's outsourcing contract lays the foundation for the BBC's aim of greater business efficiency and improved financial information into the digital age:

> *The BBC is pleased to have reached this position and looks forward to a successful partnership with MedAS. There is a significant task still ahead of us, but the result will be the best possible finance systems for the BBC and its staff, and substantial savings will be ploughed back into programmes and services for licence payers.*

5

Information management delivering business intelligence

- 5.1 Introduction   69
- 5.2 Defining the business requirement   70
- 5.3 Technological developments   72
- 5.4 Formulating a company-wide information strategy   73
- 5.5 Knowledge management   75
- 5.6 Decision support and business intelligence tools   77
- 5.7 Case study – Data warehousing at Nationwide   82

5.1 INTRODUCTION

During the last part of the twentieth century, finance, aided in part by separate computer systems, managed to adopt an insular approach to its function within the business. Located at head office, concentrating on its financial, control and statutory obligations, it had far too frequently lost sight of the need to produce relevant, timely, meaningful information for the business. This had been, in part, a consequence of the drive in the 1970s to merge costing, management and financial accounting systems into one super-integrated system. Management information became the financial accounts, which were slightly modified, compared to budgets and then issued as the monthly management accounts pack. This information had little relevance to the operational managers of the business. This inevitably resulted in the growth of informal information systems throughout the organization, with each department having its own dedicated team producing the management information that it needed to run the business.

In the twenty-first century the role of the information manager is pivotal within the organization. The latest technological advances mean that it is now possible to have just one holistic, organization-wide information system, delivering business intelligence. The same information management system can now be used by everyone around the organization – with no conflicting data produced by different departments. Decision making can be based on one set of good, reliable information to reduce risk, facilitated by the new breed of finance professionals, who are now devoting large amounts of time to this crucial activity.

The role of chief information officer (CIO) in the modern organization must be held by a professional who understands how the whole organization operates and can facilitate the production of information that combines financial and non-financial, internal and external, qualitative and quantitative data. The CIO must be able to facilitate the design of an enterprise-wide integrated performance and information management system using the latest web-enabled technological developments – including ERP, CRM, SCM, business intelligence software such as data-mining, OLAP and enterprise portals. In addition, the CIO needs to be able to access the wealth of external information available through the web using online software.

Many organizations are now taking steps to identify all knowledge and information so that it can be recorded, managed, retained and used by everybody within the company. However, care must be taken to ensure that the end result is not 'information overload'. The key is to identify and filter the useful information and utilize such tools as alerts, exceptions, rules, traffic lights and trend analysis to present and highlight only those areas needing attention.

According to CIMA:[1]

Information management is the process of managing data so as to deliver information that adds insight, understanding and value for users by providing management information for:

- *organizational effectiveness – performance*
- *developmental activities – looking to the future*
- *operational efficiency and economy – improvement.*

> Information × (Knowledge + Understanding + Experience) = Decisions

The information manager needs to:

- *understand how organizations operate in order to identify information critical to success;*
- *appreciate that principles remain applicable over time although techniques and technologies may change;*
- *be able to use the range of techniques to provide information to meet users' specific needs;*
- *understand different contexts, needs, perceptions, attitudes and motives of users;*
- *be able to select and utilize the most appropriate tools and technology;*
- *be able to promote a broad and balanced perspective on how the organization is achieving its objectives.*

Typically, companies spent tens of millions on large-scale system changes driven in haste by the need to replace old equipment to beat the millennium bug, and often failed to take the necessary steps to ensure that they had properly thought through the massive investments. The all-too-frequent failure of IT to deliver on business goals means that in future the crucially important role of information management is more than ever likely to form part of the newly transformed finance operation.

5.2 DEFINING THE BUSINESS REQUIREMENT

Traditionally, companies have had scores of independent IT systems, often dependent on, and driven by, individual functions, built up over decades. They usually consist of a raft of different technologies, making integration very difficult and expensive or sometimes even impossible. The 1990s became the decade when companies came to realize the importance of breaking down their functional boundaries and viewing their organizations through streamlined processes. With this realization, there is not only an appreciation of the need for a process-oriented, enterprise-wide decision-support system, but also an urgent demand for its implementation, to enable companies to maintain their competitive advantage. In the modern organization, these processes will extend far beyond old company and geographic boundaries to link its IT systems with those of its suppliers, partners and customers worldwide.

The days are over when managers produced their own set of business information and time at meetings was wasted, arguing over whose figures were correct. No longer is it acceptable to take management decisions relying on 'gut feel', or to spend time 'fire-fighting' problems rather than eliminating the causes. Technology can now provide real-time access to decision-support information that combines quantitative and qualitative, financial and non-financial data, from internal and external sources.

Main areas of input to an information system will include:

- data from companies' ERP, CRM, SCM and other legacy systems;
- specific external data on such areas as competitors, customers, partners, suppliers and benchmarking;
- general relevant external information on the economy and the stock markets;
- the organizational objectives with links to other sources of information to show how these are being met, for example balanced scorecard and forecasts.

The primary role for a company's information system[2] is to provide an integrated understanding of the financial and operational position of the company in a dynamic business environment. It should have the following characteristics:

- be flexible enough to change as the business does;
- support the company's strategy;
- provide multiple views of the same data;
- provide a balanced scorecard of operational and financial performance measures;
- support a process/activity view of the business, in addition to a functional view;
- provide for the fast collection and dissemination of data;
- utilize exceptions, alerts, rules, trend analysis and other such tools to guard against information overload.

Figure 5.1 shows how a modern IT environment would cope with transaction processing and then pass this to a data warehouse. On top of this data warehouse would sit business intelligence tools, which in turn would analyze the data and disseminate the information electronically via such tools as EIS (enterprise information systems), portals, the internet and intranet. The process of designing such a system and descriptions of some of the technology available are outlined in the sections below.

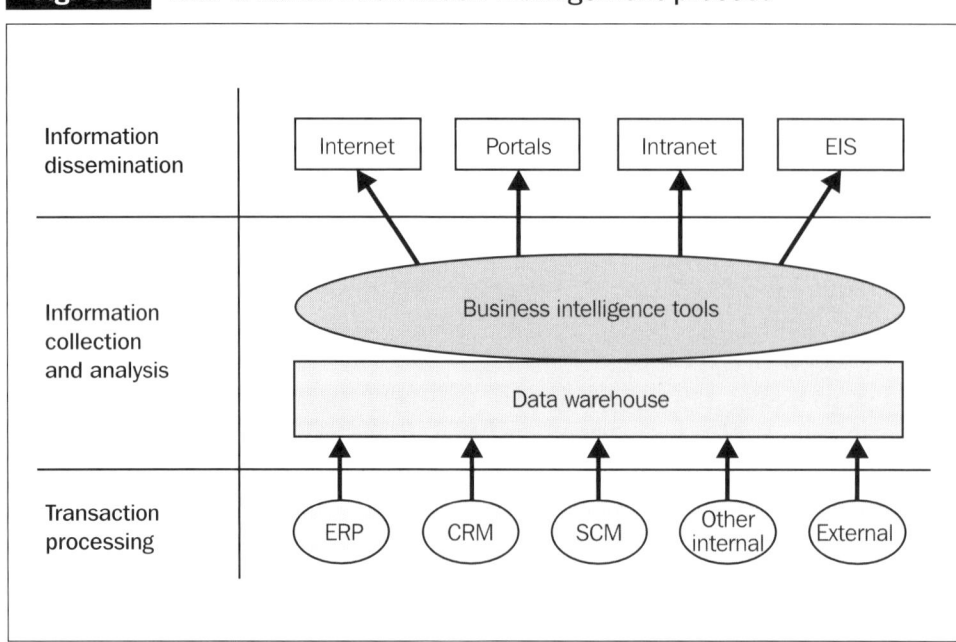

Fig. 5.1 Web-enabled information management process

```
Information           Internet    Portals    Intranet    EIS
dissemination           ↑           ↑           ↑         ↑
                    ┌─────────────────────────────────────────┐
                    │        Business intelligence tools       │
Information         └─────────────────────────────────────────┘
collection          ┌─────────────────────────────────────────┐
and analysis        │              Data warehouse              │
                    └─────────────────────────────────────────┘
                       ↑      ↑      ↑        ↑        ↑
Transaction          ERP    CRM    SCM    Other    External
processing                                internal
```

5.3 TECHNOLOGICAL DEVELOPMENTS

- Enterprise-wide systems – e.g. enterprise resource planning (ERP) and middleware.

- Company-wide desktop personal tools operating as self-service centres – e.g. Microsoft Office and Lotus SMARTSuite products, including such applications as word-processing, spreadsheets, databases, mapping tools, project management, shared diaries, organizers, internal mail, compression software, web browsers and presentational tools.

- Personalized portals – these enable employees to access selected data, information and services, from internal and external sources, both to help them with their jobs and to enable inputting of source data into the integrated company-wide systems. Examples include direct input of hours worked into a payroll system (manually or by reader) and interactive learning systems. Business-to-employee (B2E) systems are an important component of the web-enabled organization.

- The internet – this has revolutionised the way in which organizations can conduct their business through end-to-end, web-enabled systems linking directly to suppliers and partners (B2B) and customers (B2C). It facilitates business community integration and electronic application integration (EAI) middleware; supply chain management (SCM); customer relationship management (CRM); internet standards and security; web services; application service providers (ASPs); telecommunications services, technologies and mobile devices.

- Collaborative computing – through such tools as workflow, document management systems and groupware, making the need for manual intervention in processes redundant.
- Business intelligence tools – essential for organizations to turn the mass of data produced from its ERP and other systems into a form in which it can be accessed and turned into meaningful, relevant, timely information. For example, in the Manchester Housing case study in Chapter 9, on the balanced scorecard, Business Objects and the intranet were used to display its information to all staff (*see* section 5.6 below on page 77).

The other technological developments discussed above have been dealt with in detail in *Business Process Management*.[3]

5.4 FORMULATING A COMPANY-WIDE INFORMATION STRATEGY

Set up a project team

The information manager needs to start the process of formulating an information strategy by setting up and leading a project team of colleagues, representing all parts of the organization.

Analyze existing company, supplier and customer systems

An analysis of existing systems includes systems local to individual departments, some of which may be PC and some manually based. Look also outside the organization to possible links into the systems of suppliers and customers. These days the use of electronic commerce and business-to-business (B2B) integration through electronic data interchange (EDI) and extensible mark-up language (XML) standards, working in partnership with suppliers and customers, often removes the need for paper and duplicate keying of data, as well as speeding up such processes. Analyze the key features of these systems, including:

- inputs
- outputs
- frequency of use
- purposes
- interfaces with other systems
- technical requirements.

Analyze 'future' business needs

Although it is not the intention when setting out, often under pressure of time constraints, far too many IT implementation teams simply end up replacing legacy systems with new ones, which operate in exactly the same way as the old ones. It is essential to re-engineer processes and design in new high-level management techniques that allow the organization to add value continually. Examples explained in this book include:

- value-based management
- process-based management
- the balanced scorecard
- integrated performance management
- decision support
- business intelligence
- improved and standardized end-to-end community-wide processes
- benchmarking
- business process re-engineering
- priority-based budgeting
- forecasting and resource allocation.

Consult independent experts

Independent experts may be specialists and/or potential outsourcers/partners. Remember that an information strategy is one of the most important decisions that the organization will make, not just in terms of an IT investment strategy costing tens of millions but in making an essential contribution to the company's future ability to compete successfully.

Prepare the business case

Compile a detailed and compelling business case, evaluating all the benefits, costs and risks of all the elements of the proposed implementation project. Following the very large IT projects at the end of the 1990s driven by Y2K, many of which overran in terms of budget and time and often failed to deliver on promised objectives, organizations are now far more cautious in their approval of IT spending in the twenty-first century. Projects are often smaller and targeted to a specific improvement/development that is deliverable and certain to pay off in the short term. It is no longer acceptable for IT to be mismanaged and it is more likely than ever that it will be put under the overall control of the finance function.

Consult widely throughout the organization

While time is of the essence in moving towards new technological advantage, remember that the new transformed finance function no longer prescribes what information the business needs but facilitates the provision of relevant information for operational managers. It is they who will be using it and therefore they who can offer constructive thought on the design. It is, therefore, strongly advisable to win support from all parts of the enterprise before proceeding with implementation. This will lessen the pain later.

Continuous improvement

Once the system is installed, it is important that a culture of continuous review and improvement is adopted. It is recommended that, at a minimum, an annual audit should be undertaken.

5.5 KNOWLEDGE MANAGEMENT

Figure 5.2 shows how information is about understanding relationships, knowledge is about understanding patterns and trends and wisdom about understanding principles. However, a collection of data is not information, a collection of information is not knowledge, a collection of knowledge is not wisdom and a collection of wisdom is not truth.

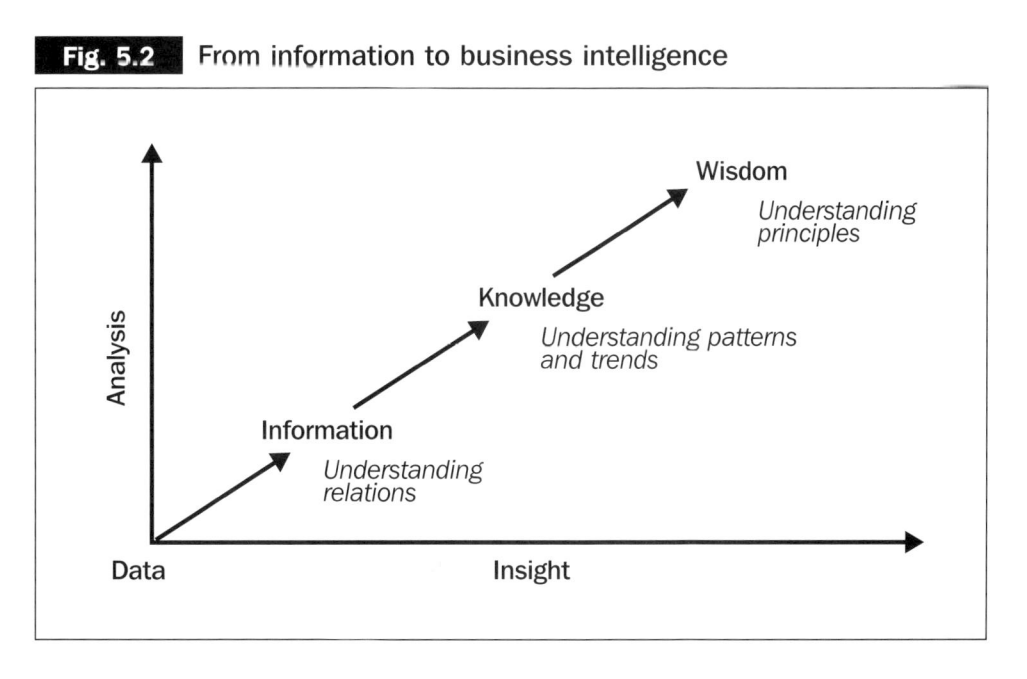

Fig. 5.2 From information to business intelligence

Research[4] reveals that chief knowledge officers have two principal design competencies:

- they are technologists, able to understand which technologies can contribute to capturing, storing, exploring and sharing knowledge;
- they are environmentalists, able to create social environments that stimulate and facilitate arranged and chance conversations, or to develop events and processes to encourage deliberate knowledge creation and exchange.

Characteristics of knowledge officers include breadth of career experience, familiarity with their organizations and infectious enthusiasm for their mission. Knowledge management (KM) initiatives need to address the basic cultural and organizational issues of how knowledge is shared, distributed and created and how these processes relate to key business goals. The success of an IT solution in KM is in how well it encourages the necessary interaction between people and the knowledge sharing culture within the organization.

Cap Gemini Ernst & Young (E&Y) has one of the largest knowledge infrastructures in the world,[5] and needs to use this knowledge daily to win work and improve its service to its clients. E&Y's intranet, called the KnowledgeWeb or KWeb, is used by its 85,000 professionals based all over the world. The KWeb, which was developed and maintained by its Centre for Business Knowledge, consists of a web-based front end, which is linked to an extensive back end that includes information retrieval technology from Verity, Lotus Notes/Domino databases, web pages and others. The challenge was to bring all the discrete repositories of knowledge content together in one architecture that could be searched by an engine similar to those available on the public internet – using key words or phrases. Since information is classified into information directories organized by familiar business categories, taxonomic searches are also possible, allowing users to navigate information directories easily and combining searching and browsing for more intuitive knowledge discovery.

Law firms are also reliant on large amounts of paperwork and by adopting document management systems can become more productive and competitive. Legal firm McGrigor Donald uses iManage, because it provided a solution with a minimum amount of tailoring and support at a price affordable to a smaller firm that has all transactions now wholly electronic and automated. The most valuable features are its sheer speed of searching for data across the database, the accuracy of that data and the overall resilience of the system.

5.6 DECISION SUPPORT AND BUSINESS INTELLIGENCE TOOLS

Business intelligence (BI) systems enable a business professional to access the information that describes the enterprise – to analyze it, gain insight into its workings and take action based on its findings. The aim is not just to gather large volumes of data from systems but to turn them into business intelligence to gain competitive advantage. The objective is to have one integrated company-wide information system to support the performance management and decision-making process and it can be achieved with modern IT and provide good business intelligence. Gartner predicts the market for BI software to grow to $7 billion by 2003 with over half the top companies having an e-intelligence capability. The growth is partly due to the internet, which allows companies to gather more information about customers and suppliers and share it with employees around the world, but equally driven by the demand of business to receive relevant timely information in place of volumes of data.

Modern BI is simpler to use for both query and drill-down and no longer needs specialists. Many have added charting features, like drill-down, web maps and dashboard representations, with a move to wireless technology enabling field workers to use a variety of devices. Intelligence is now in-built into the technology so that it can alert the user if a key performance indicator (KPI) is under-performing or the user can calculate the likelihood of cross-selling to a given customer. Tools vary from OLAP and data-mining, enabling companies to create their own BI systems, to packaged applications like Cognos, InterBiz, Brio and Business Objects.

Data warehousing

Data warehousing[6] allows companies to build, maintain and manage large amounts of data and query them at will. Data entering the warehouse from multiple sources are placed in a common format and then 'mined' for important information. The database software itself operates in a client/server architecture, usually needing very powerful servers. Features of data warehouses include:

- transactional-level database, usually a relational database;
- the data warehouse holds a copy of data from other systems;
- used in conjunction with ERP, SCM, CRM and other packaged software to avoid degradation through excessive querying on the live system;
- its purpose is to optimize enquiries rather than data entry;
- it is time variant, i.e. date-stamped historical data;
- non-volatile data (static);
- often consisting of one or more data marts – a subset of the data warehouse or standalone covering, say, one function;
- organized by subject or entity not application;
- can feed a multidimensional database, i.e. OLAP.

Figure 5.3 shows how data warehousing can improve quality whilst reducing costs.

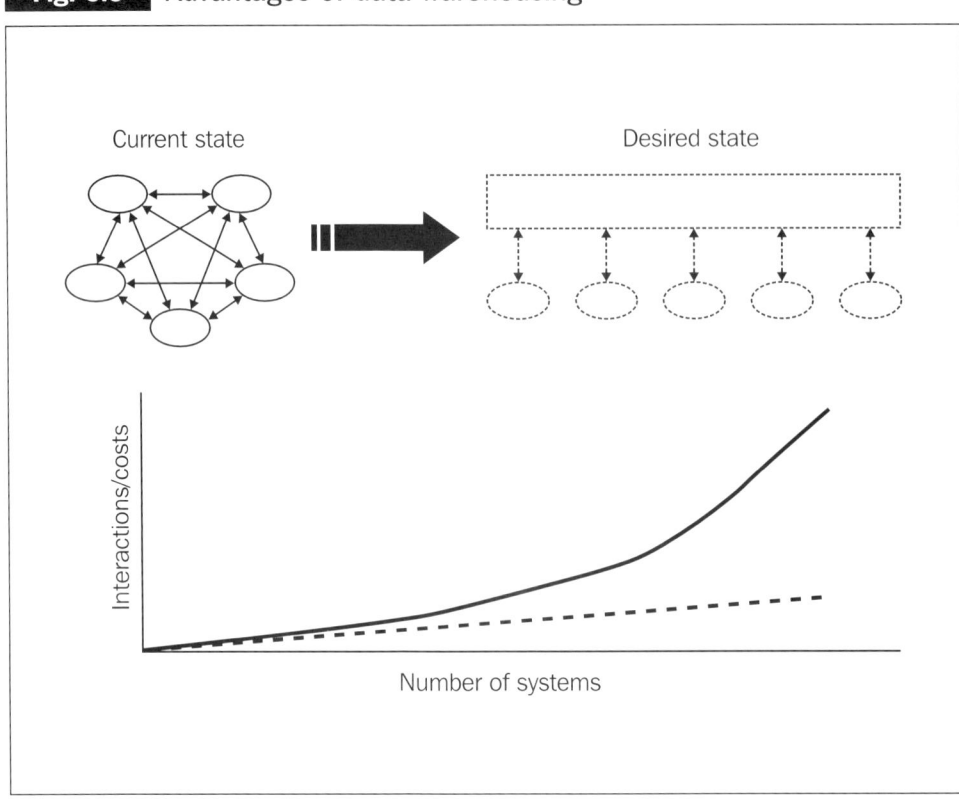

Fig. 5.3 Advantages of data warehousing

On-line analytical processing and decision-support systems

On-line analytical processing (OLAP) is a technology that enables users to gain insight into data through fast, consistent and interactive access to a wide variety of possible views of enterprise-wide information. OLAP products, such as iTM1, Essbase and Microsoft SQL, transfer the data to a separate multi-dimensional database for accounts using a spreadsheet link, like Visual Basic. OLAP occurs in many forms with greatly varying features and functionality, offering different advantages and disadvantages for both IT and end users. These include:

- cost
- level of detail
- data capacity
- speed of operation
- types, e.g. Desktop OLAP (DOLAP) and JOLAO (Java OLAP).

The terms decision-support systems (DSS), enterprise information systems (EIS) and management information systems (MIS) appear interchangeable and refer to end-user information-delivery systems that come in all shapes and sizes, offering simply managed queries or more complex drilling and simulation. These tools often incorporate OLAP. Most of the DSS tools could be used to access data directly from source applications, but the data warehouse provides the ideal foundation for integrating the data and taking it off-line, and as such is becoming increasingly popular as part of modern IT architecture.

Global Networking giant 3Com[7] has implemented an SAP and Peoplesoft ERP system, which feeds a massive data warehouse containing sales, service, manufacturing, distribution and financial information with daily snapshots. For analysis and reporting 3Com use Hyperion Essbase multi-dimensional OLAP. This allows drag and drop and moves things into Excel and Business Objects, which is a desktop reporting tool creating links to a cube of data, which it stores in memory and then pulls answers to queries from the main database.

Process/activity-based DSS

Organizations have recognized the need to link strategy to operational performance through identifying those drivers that create value. Figure 9.1 (page 147) illustrates the necessity of linking any value-based management initiative to strategy with a balanced scorecard, and underpinning it with detailed process/activity-based management information that drills down through the organization to ensure that all decision making is properly informed. Having established the need for process/activity-based information, this should be designed into the heart of the IT systems, not treated as a 'bolt-on extra'. Most ERP systems are process based.

Specialist vendors produce linked modules for process mapping, activity-based costing, customer profitability, process-based management,[3] priority-based budgeting, performance measurement and balanced scorecards, in addition to link engines to manipulate data between external systems and report-writing tools. These modules are linked to a common database, which holds the central process/activity analysis, integral to most ERP solutions, around which all the other techniques are based. Full integration of DSS tools with ERP or other packaged software must be the best solution and at the start of the new millennium most software vendors have developed these tools or formed alliances with specialist DSS vendors. A review of the functionality provided by the top 18 accounting software vendors[8] shows that all either have their own module or a recognized partnership to deliver ABC analysis. Figure 5.4 shows some of these links between products.

Fig. 5.4 DSS and ERP alliances

Software	– Vendor	ERP	/ Packaged software vendor
OROS	– ABC Technologies	SAP	/ Panoramic Business Views (BSC)
Profit Manager	– KPMG	Peoplesoft	/
Activa	– PwC	Oracle	/
Metify (Hyper)	– Armstrong Laing		/ CorVu (BSC)
NetScore/Prophet	– Sapling		/ Hyperion Solutions

DSS selection criteria

- User-friendly – providing ease of use and accessibility and graphical presentation.
- Integrated – providing the ability to access information that is financial, non-financial, internal, external, quantitative and qualitative from many different base systems and applications.
- Integrity – the data held must be consistent, robust and inspire confidence.
- Multi-user capabilities – providing information to all users across the organization.
- Multi-dimensional – providing the ability to view information across multiple dimensions, e.g. by department, by process, by channel, by SBU etc.
- Responsive – needs to be interactive and responsive to changing conditions.
- Size – must be able to cope with volumes of data, calculations and number of users.

Enterprise business planning tools

Many of the new planning and budgeting applications use complex databases designed to help organizations monitor, report, analyze and react to developments in their business in a timely manner. Latest developments in this area include support for activity-based budgeting, continual planning and web-based collaboration.[3] Packages include:

- SAS CFOVision – web-based financial consolidation, analysis and reporting together with budgeting and planning.
- Adaytum e Planning 2.2 – web-based solution for enterprise business planning, providing an online forecast into likely future operating performance. It contains

modules for financial analysts, line managers, executives and administrators and combines planning and modelling with budget, sales forecasting and workflow.

- Comshare MPC 4.0 – planning, budgeting, consolidation, management, reporting and analysis application that runs over the web.
- Hyperion Planning and Modelling 2.0 – the solutions align day-to-day operations with more strategic tasks to aid more informed decision making, providing organizations with the ability to move beyond traditional budgeting.

Enterprise information portal

Enterprise information portal (EIP) technology utilizes a web browser interface to give employees access to various data and information systems. The portals are modelled on internet portals like Yahoo and Ask Jeeves, which enable a search to be carried out to extract the relevant information. Most EIP products will allow search, retrieval, filtering, knowledge mapping, document management, workflow and personalization. Portals do not solve the incompatibility problems of proprietary software; they simply avoid them – they provide a gateway to look at things. By embedding application program interfaces (API) into the portals (often dubbed pagelets, portlets or gadgets), the need for complicated back-end integration between programs is eliminated – data gets integrated at the portal level. Vendors, like Peoplesoft's CFO Portal and Plumtree, have developed finance-specific packages, although many organizations have develped their own in-house via their employee portals. The use of portals by the largest organizations is expected to rise from 50% in 2001 to 85% in 2003.

Hewlett Packard (HP) spent $20 million constructing its employee portal (B2E) in 2000, providing a gateway called @HP to 90,000 employees in 150 countries. Among other things, this can update human resources records, change benefit electives and book business trips. HP claims that in its first year it has delivered a ROI of $50 million.

Ford Motor Company replaced about 1,000 intranets, each serving individual business units around the world, with a single portal for the whole organization, using Plumtree. This enables staff in any part of the organization to retrieve information from other parts, in addition to removing the need to maintain duplicate data on local intranets. One example of savings made by Ford is the use of its portal to display and access pay-slips, which are estimated at $18 million a year.

Website and CRM analytics

E-commerce has enabled the collection of vast amounts of customer data that can be analyzed. So-called web-mining enables companies to measure site usability, gain a better understanding of user behaviour and make significant improvements to their websites. Internet server logs provide data that, when combined with personal data obtained from customers, builds up highly detailed marketing intelligence. This in turn informs customer support and service strategy decisions to improve user experience and sales. Methods of data collection include:

- HTTP server log analysis – log entry for each HTTP request containing details of number of hits, number of visitors, visitor duration, visitor origin, visitor IP address, platform, browser type and version.
- Server monitors through Application Programmer Interface (API) – unique visitor IDs, referrer pages.
- Network monitors – client requests, server responses, cookies, stop requests, server response times, form data transmitted and HTML files.

This data then needs to be fed into a relational data warehouse to permit analysis through web mining and analytics tools like Hyperion's Web Site Analysis suite. This service is also available through ASPs, e.g. IBM's web traffic analysis service Surfaid, specializes in the collection and integration of very high volume data and was used during the Sydney Olympics. Xelector, a Dublin-based financial service operation, calls itself a B2B2C operator, sitting between product providers and portals like First-e, the internet bank. Its aim is to collect information in the financial services industry and analyze it to remove the need for 'gut feel' decisions. The company uses the SAS e-intelligence suite and Questor reporting tools.

Pharmaceutical outsourcing company Innovex[7] has 600 representatives collecting data electronically using an electronic territory management system (ETMS). BO WebIntelligence is used to disseminate the information to low-level users. A cube satisfies 95% of the need for standard reporting, which includes 40 key business measures pre-calculated across six dimensions – time, geography, product, etc. – on a weekly basis. For those that need more flexibility they can carry out ad hoc enquiries.

Whitbread Beer Company has installed a web-based Informix database management system which resides on an IBM RS/6000, with over 100 sales and marketing cubes created by Cognos Powerplay and Impromtu. Staff use laptop computers running Windows NT to access the data through the web.

5.7 Case study

Data warehousing at Nationwide[9]

Background

Nationwide Life and Nationwide Unit Trust Managers were formed as the regulated financial services subsidiaries of Nationwide Building Society. They began trading in January 1996, offering good-value products to customers introduced through the society's branch network.

Development of the systems and processes took over two years, from a greenfield site in Swindon. A substantial part of the operation was outsourced to third parties.

It was obvious that implementation of a management reporting function faced a number of challenges. The requirements specification took place while the full management team was still being recruited, requirements were changing and the systems architecture was still developing, so an adaptive approach was essential. With around a dozen production systems being developed, a client/server data-warehousing approach was chosen for the provision of management information. Although this was a high-risk approach relative to the traditional method of report production from production systems, the advantages far outweighed the downside. Those advantages were:

- ability to produce ad hoc reports
- local control of reporting
- low development costs
- flexibility of reporting
- ability to analyze data across diverse systems
- ability to produce operational reporting.

The specification

The system was developed around a high-specification central server, with distributed report access available from around 50 local client PCs using a graphical query tool. This allowed access to pre-defined reports where the user chose report parameters and provided the ability to produce ad hoc queries with 'super user' training – no reports were produced centrally for paper distribution to these users. Furthermore, the system allowed different data views to different categories of user.

The system was built from the bottom upwards – including tackling the issues of data integrity, quality, consistency and control across different platforms. This approach to data-warehouse development permits the system to be used as the basis of an executive information system. Data warehousing permits analysis of the complete lifecycle of a product sale, from initial customer contact to post-sale events.

The data warehouse approach represents an ideal solution in a multi-platform systems environment, allowing consolidation of atomic-level business data from diverse systems on to a central relational database. Such an implementation requires less analysis of data, but carries a greater overhead in future development of the system, which can largely be carried out locally by the system administrator.

Management reporting solution

Delivery of a system was a small (but key) part of the development of the management reporting solution. This involved addressing cultural and educational issues around implementation of a solution, addressing data and information ownership, development of critical success factors and key performance indicators and a monitoring basis for all business areas.

An integrated balanced business scorecard approach was adopted for management reporting, aligning the corporate vision with guiding principles and a balanced business plan.

The emphasis was not on just the traditional financial measures but also on non-financial business measures (see Fig. 5.5).

Fig. 5.5 Nationwide–balanced scorecard

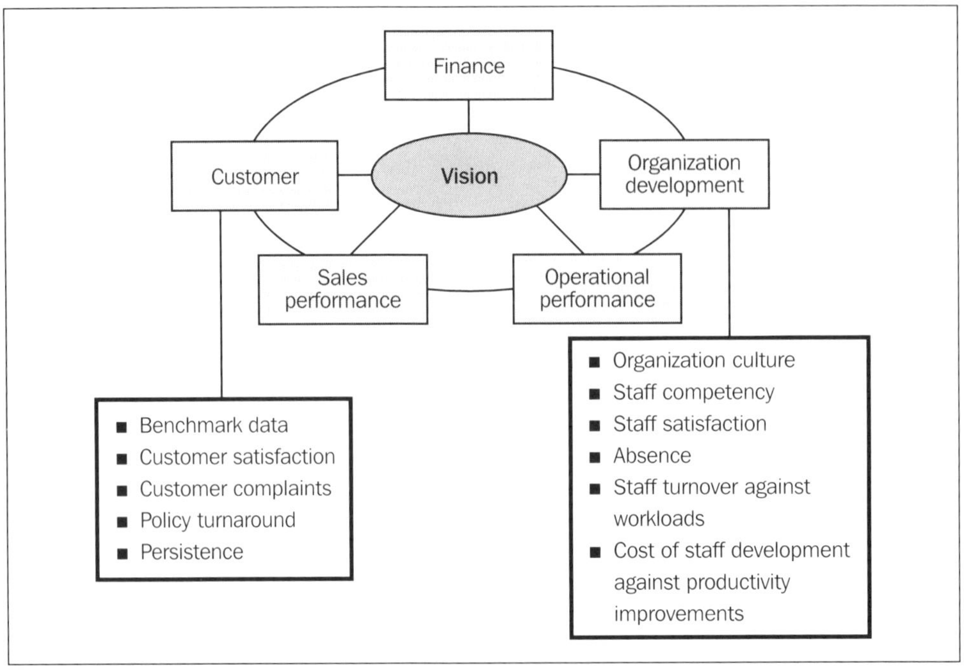

```
                    Finance
         Customer   Vision   Organization
                             development
              Sales      Operational
              performance  performance
```

- Benchmark data
- Customer satisfaction
- Customer complaints
- Policy turnaround
- Persistence

- Organization culture
- Staff competency
- Staff satisfaction
- Absence
- Staff turnover against workloads
- Cost of staff development against productivity improvements

The objective was to divide company reporting to monitor performance against the corporate vision and values (customer perspective, organization development, sales performance and operational performance). These are the business determinants that deliver financial performance – the ultimate consequence of corporate success. Although traditional monthly management accounts have tended to focus on financial measures alone, they have not monitored the 'levers' that drive corporate performance.

The board information pack was a largely graphical balanced scorecard of mainly non-financial measures, providing information and detailed analysis of results. This included a section on organizational development, measuring a number of human resources performance measures:

- organization culture
- staff competency
- staff satisfaction
- absence and staff turnover against workloads
- costs of staff development against productivity improvements.

Benchmark data is also used to measure performance against the industry.

The customer perspective covers the following areas:

- customer satisfaction
- customer complaints

- policy turnaround
- persistence.

Transformation of the finance function

With a high level of automation of reporting, the management accounting function can devote resource to providing value-added support to the business, as opposed to the traditional view of the finance function as a group of 'bean-counters' producing historical financial information. This transformation of management accounting needs to be implemented in a number of ways:

- development of a vision for the finance function
- establishment of guiding principles
- alignment of objectives with corporate goals
- measurement of team performance, including customer satisfaction
- benchmarking against best practice
- measurement of productivity
- application of quality processes and standards.

Traditionally, the management accounting function has measured performance of the operation, but has rarely had the confidence to measure its own performance. The result of such a focus has been to stifle continuous improvement and limit the influence of finance within the organization. The alternative is to establish metrics to monitor performance, measuring performance and implementing a development plan to improve the service provided by finance.

The measurement of finance performance exposes the function to the same disciplines that operational areas of the company have. Priorities of the finance function can be easily established through consultation with its customer areas: by asking what are the key corporate objectives and how finance can help the company achieve these.

Conclusion

Corporate priorities can be ranked in terms of both short- and long-term importance to establish a comprehensive strategic plan for the organization, resulting in an action plan for future development. A formal monitoring framework will allow progress reporting against the action plan.

It is important to manage resource to minimize the part of that resource dedicated to operational activities and increase the amount of time available to perform value-added tasks. This involves managing the balance between 'urgent' and 'important' – investment in the latter produces significantly greater returns.

In conclusion, management reporting has developed into a proactive commercial management function, committed to adding maximum value to the business through the implementation of leading-edge solutions to business problems. The emphasis has moved from reporting historical financial statistics to analyzing the full range of business determinants and influencing corporate strategy.

Part 3

Value-based management

- 6 Delivering shareholder value/best value   89
- 7 Valuing intangible assets/intellectual capital   111

Delivering shareholder value/best value

- 6.1 Introduction 91
- 6.2 Rappaport's theory 92
- 6.3 Shareholder value calculation models 93
- 6.4 EVA exercise 95
- 6.5 EVA example 96
- 6.6 SVA options matrix 97
- 6.7 Best Value 97
- 6.8 Embedded value-based management 99
- 6.9 Characteristics of VBM organizations 101
- 6.10 Inter-business unit charging and service level agreements 101
- 6.11 Case study – Creating corporate value at Wienerberger 102
- 6.12 Case study – Value-based management at British Aerospace 103

6.1 INTRODUCTION

In research carried out by Price Waterhouse in 1997,[1] maximizing shareholder value stood out as the number one priority of chief finance officers worldwide. The challenge is to link strategy successfully to operational goals and set measures and targets that ensure that added value is achieved. Performance-management frameworks must incorporate far more than measures; they need to incorporate processes that ensure that the necessary change occurs to execute the strategy.

The finance function must be transformed to take the lead role in building and running such a framework and facilitating the necessary changes, as it is the only part of the organization that holds the key pivotal role linking shareholder demands with business strategy and operational performance. There is no time to waste in replacing those traditional information systems consisting of individual operational data – the management accounts pack of financial data and performance-management systems of individually set targets with no clear link to corporate strategy, added value or achievement-measurement systems.

In today's world, keeping shareholders happy is more complex than was previously the case. Institutional investors control larger stakes in companies and have correspondingly greater powers to influence events in the boardroom. This means that companies need to start valuing their businesses in the same way as their shareholders do and ensure that decisions taken at whatever level are consistent with adding shareholder value. Not doing so can lead to many unwanted consequences, including:

- the inability to raise the necessary capital funds;
- falls in share price as investors switch to higher-yielding opportunities;
- the requirement for directors to justify their remuneration packages;
- the risk of hostile take-over.

Traditionally, companies have measured their success using such indicators as profit margin, return on assets and return on equity, judging the viability of investments using discounted cashflow measures such as net present value (NPV) or internal rate of return (IRR). Meanwhile the shareholder measured the company's performance using such indicators as earnings per share (EPS) and the price/earnings ratio (P/E). It is generally agreed that today many accounting entries are made on the basis of management judgement, for example pension funding, goodwill, depreciation, deferred tax and acquisitions policies, and profit as a measure has, therefore, become complex and a gulf has opened up between it and cash generation.

This recognition of the need to understand the drivers of shareholder value has resulted in many organizations becoming above-industry-average in growth, margins and capital efficiency (including intangible assets) over the last five years.

With the advent of e-business, where a high proportion of assets are in the form of intellectual capital, it is more important than ever that the finance function finds ways of measuring, managing and monitoring these intangibles as they are the key to enhancing shareholder value. Maintaining corporate reputation necessitates the implementation of an enterprise risk-management system, which also must take account of ethical, environmental and social issues.

6.2 RAPPAPORT'S THEORY

In 1986 Alfred Rappaport published *Creating Shareholder Value*,[2] which finally brought together shareholders and managers with one common approach to measuring company performance that could replace all previous methods. This was cash generation, because that represents fact rather than opinion. Rappaport based his theory on five drivers of cash and two other value drivers:

- Those that influence '*cash in*':
  - turnover growth rate
  - operating profit margins.
- Those that influence '*cash out*':
  - the percentage tax rate actually paid
  - the percentage of incremental revenue spent on fixed capital net of depreciation
  - the percentage of incremental revenue spent on working capital.
- The value growth potential period – the future timeframe over which the cash drivers need to be measured for evaluation, which represents the company's perceived 'competitive advantage period'.
- The weighted average cost of capital (WACC) – which takes the cost of debt and equity and weights them according to the book or projected book gearing. This is considered more representative than the 'interest' shown in the profit and loss account.

Using these seven value drivers, Rappaport's formula for evaluating shareholder value is:

> *Shareholder value = Corporate value – Debt*

where:

corporate value = the future free cashflow (cash in – cash out) that the company is expected to generate over time, discounted by the weighted average cost of capital.

6.3 SHAREHOLDER VALUE CALCULATION MODELS

Since Rappaport's book a number of different models have been developed, all building on Rappaport's proposition and value drivers. These can be grouped into three main categories.

Economic value added (EVA™)[3]

Economic value added (EVA) is the trademark of Stern Stewart & Co., US consultants, and is a methodology that is growing in popularity, particularly in the USA, with many companies quoting EVA measures in their annual reports. This model starts with profit and then makes up to 160 different adjustments to cater for the distortions caused by accounting methodologies and management judgements. These adjustments are based on two guiding principles:

- Investment decisions taken by the company should result in assets regardless of how they are treated in the accounts, for example training and marketing expense will be capitalized.
- Assets once created cannot be eliminated by accounting treatments, for example goodwill written down in the books will be reinstated under EVA.

The model is calculated as follows:

$$EVA = Profit - (Net\ capital \times Cost\ of\ capital)$$

It is supplemented by market value added (MVA), which reflects the spread between the capital invested in the company and the market value of the business, which includes future growth value (FGV):

$$MVA = Discounted\ value\ of\ future\ EVA\ including\ FGV$$

where:

- returns are expressed as the percentage of net operating profits, after cash taxes, to the economic book value of the assets employed in the operations of the business.
- equity capital is calculated in accordance with the capital asset pricing model in order to take account of risk in the weighted average cost of debt and equity capital.

Companies using this methodology include Lucas Varity and Burton in the UK and Coca Cola in the USA. Roberto Giozueta, former Coca Cola CEO, is quoted as saying:

I get paid to make the owners of the company increasingly wealthy with each passing day. Everything else is just fluff.[4]

In an article in *Financial Director* magazine in April 2000, Stern Stewart used their trademarked techniques and applied them to 152 UK mid-market companies (between £200 million and £1 billion) based on data at the 30 December 1999.[5] This analysis showed how top performer Ryanair can have a current EVA of just £36 million and an FGV of £504 million, giving it an MVA of £540 million, with most of its worth generated in future growth expectations. In contrast, Express Dairies, number 8 in the ranking, has an MVA of £279 million. This is made up of an FGV of –£2 million and an EVA of £281 million, earning an EVA of £27 million in its current year and a WACC of 9.7%, with nothing built into the share price for future expectations except continued returns at current levels.

Cashflow return on investment

Promoted originally by the Boston Consulting Group and HOLT Value Associates, cashflow return on investment (CFROI) is popular in the UK as it values performance using similar methods to those traditionally used in evaluating individual items of investment. It compares future cashflows to the weighted average cost of capital, either as a sum of money or as an internal rate of return. Calculations vary, but they all strive to compare inflation-adjusted cashflows to inflation-adjusted gross investments to find CFROI. Generally, a distinction is made between replacement capital, which is regarded as negative cashflow like normal expenses, and growth capital, which is seen as genuine investment. A computer program, VALUAD.com, utilizes the CFROI theory.

Cash value added (CVA™)[6]

Developed and trademarked by Swedish consultants FWC AB, cash value added (CVA) has similarities to CFROI as it also starts with cashflow and makes a distinction between strategic and book investments. The premise is:

> *If the average discounted CVA index over five years = or > 1, then value is being created*

where:

- operating cashflow demand (OCFD) = annual cashflow amounts, growing by the assumed rate of inflation to yield an internal rate of return (IRR) equal to WACC on the original investment;
- the CVA index equals the present value (PV) of the operating cashflow divided by the PV of the OCFD.

6.4 EVA EXERCISE

Traditional statements

(i) Profit and Loss Account	Company A £m	Company B £m
Turnover	635	266
Operating expenditure including depreciation	(399)	(117)
Interest	(32)	(10)
Tax	(22)	(23)
Dividends	(76)	(53)
Retained profit	106	63

(ii) Balance sheet	Company A £m	Company B £m
Fixed assets	2453	1169
Current assets	274	56
Current liabilities	(381)	(278)
Long-term liabilities	(692)	(101)
Long-term creditors and provisions	(236)	(33)
	1418	813
Shareholders' funds	1418	813

(iii) Notes

- Current assets include cash of £146 million (Company A) and £1 million (Company B).
- Current liabilities include short-term loans of £27 million (Company A) and £72 million (Company B).

Economic value added statements (assuming 8% cost of capital)

$$EVA = Profit - (Net\ capital \times Cost\ of\ capital)$$

(i) Net capital × Cost of capital	Company A £m	Company B £m
Shareholders' Funds	1418	813
Cash	(146)	(1)
Short-term loans	27	72
Long-term liabilities	692	101
Net capital	1991	985
× Cost of capital (8%)	159	79

(ii) EVA statements	Company A £m	Company B £m
Turnover	635	266
Operating expenditure includes deprecation	(399)	(117)
Profit before interest	236	149
Net capital × Cost of capital (8%)	(159)	(79)
Tax	(22)	(23)
Economic value added (EVA)	55	47
Compared to retained profit	106	63

6.5 EVA EXAMPLE

Figure 6.1 shows how a company followed traditional ROCE criteria for decisions on investments and found the share price fell because SVA calculations revealed the switch to be a poor investment.

Fig. 6.1 EVA published example

Sector	Current return on assets	Required ROCE to return cost of capital
Specialty chemicals	13%	16%
Plastics	10%	7%
Chemicals Europe	21%	32%
Chemicals USA	7%	10%

Historic target ROCE of 14% – Group switched investment to Chemicals Europe from plastics and share price fell

6.6 SVA OPTIONS MATRIX

Figure 6.2 shows what strategic decisions need to be made based on the SVA information.

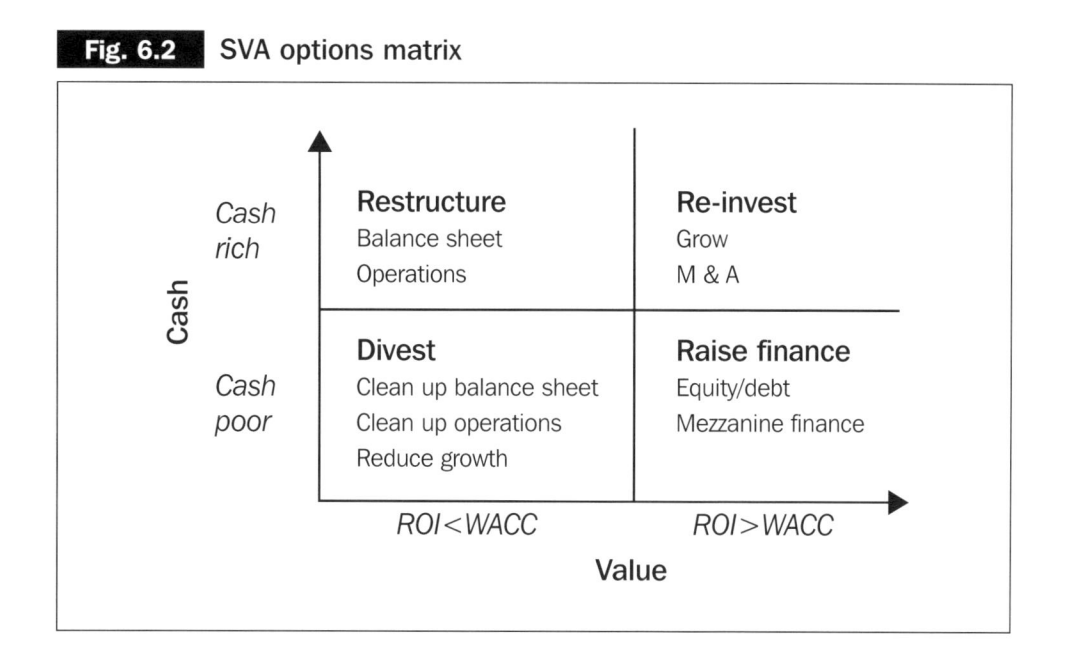

Fig. 6.2 SVA options matrix

	ROI<WACC	ROI>WACC
Cash rich	**Restructure** Balance sheet Operations	**Re-invest** Grow M & A
Cash poor	**Divest** Clean up balance sheet Clean up operations Reduce growth	**Raise finance** Equity/debt Mezzanine finance

(Axes: Cash (vertical), Value (horizontal))

6.7 BEST VALUE

At the end of 1998 the Government issued the Local Government (Best Value and Capping) Bill.[7] Through this bill, the Government aims to modernize local government in England and Wales, by placing principles of best value on a statutory footing and introducing reserve powers to limit excessive council tax increases. Best Value requires local authorities to deliver services to clear standards by the most effective, economic and efficient means available. It aims to strengthen accountability both to local people and taxpayers generally. And it should lead to healthier partnerships between local government and the private and voluntary sectors. The bill abolished compulsory competitive tendering on 2 January 2000.

The Local Government Bill states:

> *A best value authority must make arrangements to secure continuous improvement in the way in which its functions are exercised, having regard to a combination of economy, efficiency and effectiveness.*

Specifically, the new Best Value powers:

- require local authorities to review their services over a five-year period;

- require local authorities to set new and demanding targets for each service and publish these in local performance plans;
- introduce new external audit and inspection arrangements to ensure that local people have confidence in their authority's performance;
- give ministers wide powers to intervene where local authorities are failing to provide Best Value services;
- allow ministers to remove any obstacles to local authorities working with others, including other public bodies and the private sector, to provide Best Value.

Best Value has four components:

- Fundamental performance reviews (FPRs) or service reviews – reviews of all the local authority's services over a five-year period, which must:
    - challenge
    - compare
    - consult
    - demonstrate the test of competitiveness

    with the purpose being to ensure that service delivery satisfies the citizens who pay for services and to ensure that continuous improvements are made.

- Local performance plans (LPPs) – published annual plans to provide a clear, practical expression of an authority's performance in delivering local services and its proposals to improve. These are the principal means by which authorities are held accountable to local people.

- National performance indicators (NPIs) – these include:
    - council-wide 'general health' indicators
    - key indicators reflecting cost effectiveness and quality of each main service, focused on what services have been delivered (outcomes) rather than what resources have been devoted to them (inputs).

- Audit and inspection arrangements – new arrangements to give a clear view of whether Best Value is being obtained, including rigorous external checks on the information provided by authorities in LPPs and the management systems that underpin them. Regular external inspection of performance has been established in the form of an inspectorate similar to the existing inspectorates, e.g. OFSTED.

Best Value is essentially about demonstrating to the community and the stakeholders that service provision provides value for money. To demonstrate Best Value through FPRs, LPPs and NPIs, local authorities need to present and use information based on a consistent set of principles. In short, the financial and performance information used to assess Best Value is worthless unless it is prepared in accordance with a robust and consistently applied framework of accounting. This framework utilizes all the value-adding tools and techniques that are used in the private sector and included in this book.

Tony Redmond, Chief Executive and Director of Finance at the London Borough of Harrow, is quoted as saying:

> *Best Value is already proving very important. Take the Government's new public service agreements, which have been piloted in 20 local authorities during 2001, as an example. They seek to focus on particular areas of activity and actually identify targets for achieving improvement and service delivery. The idea is that an authority undertakes to improve delivery in a particular service in return for extra funding. This creates a contract that has measurable objectives. These could be general – such as ancillary services in education – or specific, such as boosting performance at a named school.*[8]

The rest of the public sector, although not subject to the Best Value legislation, is undergoing similar initiatives, which are forcing a reappraisal of the role of the finance function. For example, the Highways Agency Corporate Business Controller, Tony Dart, says his finance function has been at the heart of a new management plan and performance system, which has been introduced during 2001. It covers external service delivery and internal performance. It is supported by a board-level, performance management action group, which meets monthly. He believes that the new system is already showing through in 'delivery outcomes' and attributes some of the success to the involvement of front-line managers in setting the performance indicators, thus gaining their commitment. The improved focus on delivery has seen half of the 70 management accountants devolved to local operations.[6]

6.8 EMBEDDED VALUE-BASED MANAGEMENT

Value-based management (VBM) is a comprehensive approach to managing a company to maximize total shareholder/stakeholder returns over time. It involves focusing all levels of the organization on creating value in the commercial marketplace through identifying appropriate drivers and incorporating them into a clear strategy, thereby realizing value in the capital marketplace. It is based on the following logic:

- Publicly traded companies are in business to create wealth for shareholders.
- Creating wealth for shareholders is the key to protecting the interests of all stakeholders, e.g. employees, consumers, community, government, regulators.
- Market value is determined by investors' expectations of future cashflows.

- The ability to generate positive cashflows over time depends on profitability and growth.

While most companies are now responding to this pressure by using shareholder value analysis to drive strategic decision making and using the shareholder value calculations to determine the overall value creation of their strategic business units, few are linking this into the operational levels of the business. It is necessary to change the mindset of employees to understand what long-term value creation means for them in the language they speak within their business units. Value is created at the point where decisions are made, and in the 'bottom-up empowered' organization that is discussed in section 8.2 (page 129), that is at middle-management level or below.

Embedding VBM principles into the business, so that all decision making is based on it, is the goal. This requires detailed activity/process-based information/models on the operations of the business, in addition to the need to integrate all the corporate management processes, as shown in Fig. 6.3. This figure demonstrates the importance of aligning corporate governance, organizational structure, strategy, planning and budgeting, performance management and employee compensation. Linking employee compensation to value creation, rather than to accounting results or budget negotiations, is crucial for the success of the embedding process. An embedded VBM system driven by the transformed finance function will make the shift from scorekeeping to true business partner. The value created by each part of the business will become transparent, with project evaluation using value-based techniques rather than discounted cashflow (DCF). Each business unit then becomes a value-generating centre with targets for each value driver.

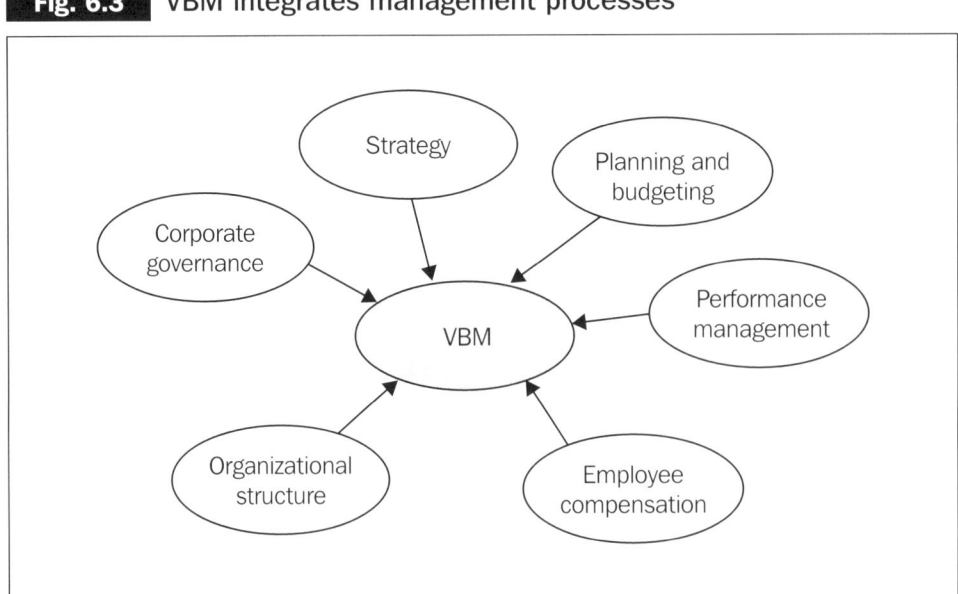

Fig. 6.3 VBM integrates management processes

6.9 CHARACTERISTICS OF VBM ORGANIZATIONS

According to Marakon Associates, specialists in VBM, whose clients include Coca Cola, BP, Disney and Lloyds TSB, organizations that adopt VBM share a number of common characteristics:

- Have only one objective – to 'maximize shareholder value'.
- Manage risk to focus on strengths, e.g. Coca Cola concentrated on its US markets.
- Do not accept investment that does not provide growth.
- Manage costs through strategy (not brute force) – no across-the-board cuts.
- Insist on choice of strategies (encouraging innovation).
- Use shareholder value analysis (SVA) to motivate employees and delegate accountability.
- Fundamentally change their organization structures every 30 months.
- Define world class as best in value-creation, not among obvious competitors.

In a 1999 survey of 453 big European firms by KPMG, two-thirds of respondents (more than 80% in Germany) claimed they were implementing VBM.

6.10 INTER-BUSINESS UNIT CHARGING AND SERVICE LEVEL AGREEMENTS

In organizations that have recognized the need to be service oriented and customer facing, the creation of business units that operate as autonomous profit centres is becoming the norm, particularly where value-based management principles have been adopted. This necessitates trading between all organizational business units, both operational and support. The setting of inter-business unit charges from support business units, such as IT and finance, requires the drawing up of service-level agreements (SLAs) between the supplier business support unit and the customer business units.

Service-level agreements

The concept of SLAs has been used by many IT departments for several years, particularly if the services have been outsourced. Similarly, the public sector has been accustomed to market testing and compulsory competitive tendering over the last decade. The preferred methodology behind setting SLAs is to use activity-based techniques, discussed in *Business Process Management*,[9] to analyze the current level of service being provided and alternative levels that could be provided, in addition to the current cost of the provision. Negotiations with customers will determine an appropriate level of service at an agreed selling price, in the same way as dealing with an external supplier. It would be reasonable within such a process for customers to obtain outside competitive quotes, if a similar service were available, to benchmark the competitiveness of the internal business unit service.

Setting 'ground rules'

A note of caution in setting these inter-business unit trading situations: it is essential that 'ground rules' be set by the organization before negotiations commence. For example:

- It may not be feasible to allow business units to buy from an outside supplier in preference to the internal supplier, particularly in the short term.

- There will need to be rules that ensure that each business unit is not allowed to optimize its own results or profitability at the expense of other business units and/or the organization as a whole.

If remuneration for business unit staff is linked to performance, which would be the norm under VBM, then great care must be taken with the setting of those incentives, because performance measures drive behaviour.

6.11 Case study
Creating corporate value at Wienerberger[10]

Wienerberger revealed how it grew from a tiny Austrian brickmaker in 1986 to the biggest brick manufacturer in the world by 1996, growing revenues sevenfold, net profits tenfold and increasing dividends by an average 22%. However, its shares underperformed, falling by 30% in the five years to 1995. The finance executive in charge of investor relations explained that: 'We had to grow by acquisition because the market was stagnant in Western Europe. But our problem was to grow while optimizing our capital.'

So in 1997 the company introduced VBM, assessing every business decision it made on the basis of ROCE and EVA. In the following two years, while the pace of acquisitions has not slackened, the firm's shares have beaten the market by 10%. More importantly, analysts say that Wienerberger now has focus and transparency and that VBM is really driving its value. Interestingly, Wienerberger is one of several companies who preferred to talk about the creation of corporate value, by advertising the creation of stakeholder value, which ties shareholder value with devotion to employees and customers – suggesting a virtuous circle of riches for everyone.

6.12 Case study
Value-based management at British Aerospace[11]

Background

British Aerospace (BAe) is Europe's largest aerospace and defence company, with some 48,000 employees at the end of 1998. Turnover in 1998 was £8.6 billion, with 89% of sales generated overseas, making BAe the UK's leading exporter. The order book at the end of 1998 was over £28 billion. BAe has two key fields of operations: the global defence market and the commercial aerospace market.

Following a difficult period in the early 1990s that saw the share price fall to below £1, BAe has undergone significant change through the disposal of non-core businesses and its role in the consolidation of aerospace and defence companies, both in Europe and internationally. The share price increased over 20-fold and the company has been working on a corporate change programme, reshaping the business through concentration on five values.

VBM at BAe

This programme includes the implementation of value-based management, a methodology that helps identify and set priorities for the company and ensures that the actions taken to address these priorities are those that will bring the greatest benefit. The objectives for VBM at BAe include:

- aligning internal objectives to value creation;
- understanding where and how value is created;
- driving improvements in operating performance at all levels in the business;
- measuring the important and stop measuring the unimportant.

VBM can be defined as a way of linking business goals and managerial decisions to their impact on shareholder value. This process of managing the business for value is beneficial because it:

- sets the agenda for management action through identification of a handful of key performance indicators;
- creates a common language and objective across the group;
- can be cascaded throughout the organization;
- focuses all staff on valuable tasks and highlights unproductive activities;
- acts as an umbrella framework for other initiatives;
- assigns priorities to the allocation of capital and resources;
- motivates employees through incentives driven by value creation.

In the words of the Chief Executive of British Aerospace:

> *VBM methodology is fundamental to the setting of priorities in our business and ensuring that our actions are driven by value creation.*

Implementation at Regional Aircraft

VBM was trialled in the Regional Aircraft business unit at Woodford, part of BAe Commercial Aerospace, which produces the Avro RJ range of regional jet aircraft. Other Regional Aircraft activities comprise Jetstream engineering support and customer-training operations at Prestwick in Scotland; and marketing of the Avro RJ and customer support for the Avro RJ, BAe 146 and Jetstream range of aircraft, both centred at Toulouse in France. The main spares distribution centre is at Weybridge, and there are marketing, customer support and spares centres in Washington, USA, and Sydney, Australia. Other activities include a complete range of support capabilities, including Jetspares, aircraft maintenance and refurbishment, aircraft flight testing, engineering test facilities, customer training, specialized design services, paint finishing, information services operation, aircraft cabin crew emergency training and airport firefighter training.

An initial VBM pilot scheme was in Avrotec, the aircraft maintenance and refurbishment business. This project ran from February to May 1997 and proved very successful, turning around a £0.5 million loss into a £2 million profit. Application of the VBM process involved an understanding of the relationship between cashflow and the Avrotec operations and the setting of key performance indicators (KPIs) to ensure focus on those drivers. Through a four-month rigorous process, the KPIs were identified from a combination of value driver chains and sensitivity analysis using a VBM spreadsheet model, simulating cash generation at an operational level. Attention was focused on those drivers yielding the greatest efficiency in the labour and parts process.

Following this success, attention was turned to the Regional Jet assembly process and this second VBM project ran from September to December 1997. This resulted in fewer than ten KPIs being identified and prioritized, replacing the previous 250 performance measures, which were reduced to monitor status or dropped completely. This was another success story, realizing efficiencies in such indirect areas as engineering change and logistics, which resulted in attention being turned to a third Regional Aircraft business, Jetspares.

The Jetspares business

Jetspares is a £20 million business, which provides a service for airlines flying the Regional Jet and 146 aircraft used, for example, in the Queen's Flight. This service provides spares and repairs as and when needed and is charged for on a 'rate per hour flown' basis. The process, which can be seen in Fig. 6.4, involves Jetspares holding stocks of parts in a large warehouse and a smaller number of parts at customer sites. When a part needs to be replaced, it is returned to the warehouse and a new part is immediately despatched; the worn part is refurbished and returned into store.

The key steps followed within the VBM process were as follows:

- team interviews conducted;
- financial analysis carried out;
- value drivers mapped, heavily linked to cash (*see* Fig. 6.5);
- the VBM economic model constructed;
- five KPIs identified and respective targets set by the management team.

Fig. 6.4 BAe – Jetspares

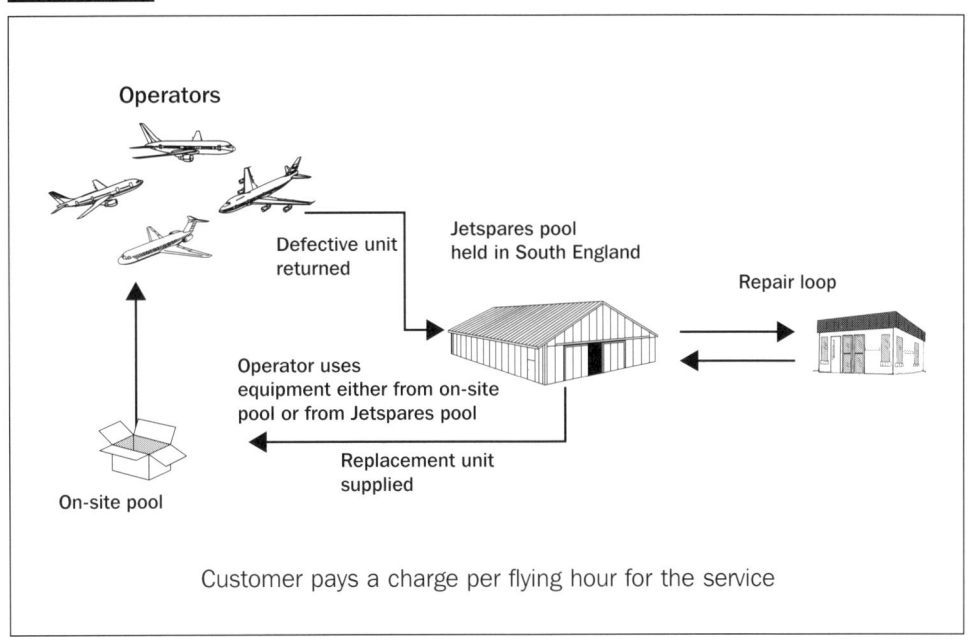

Operators

Defective unit returned → Jetspares pool held in South England ↔ Repair loop

Operator uses equipment either from on-site pool or from Jetspares pool

Replacement unit supplied

On-site pool

Customer pays a charge per flying hour for the service

Fig. 6.5 BAe – Value driver map yielding performance indicators

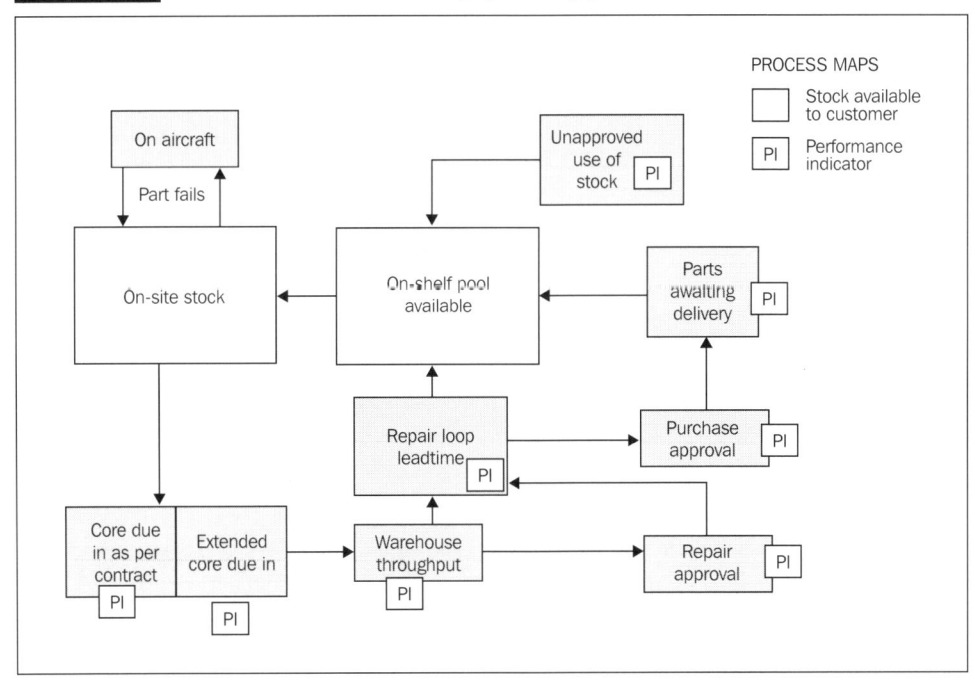

PROCESS MAPS
- Stock available to customer
- PI Performance indicator

On aircraft → Part fails → On-site stock ← On-shelf pool available ← Unapproved use of stock [PI]

On-shelf pool available ← Parts awaiting delivery [PI]

Repair loop leadtime [PI] → Purchase approval [PI]

Core due in as per contract [PI] — Extended core due in [PI] → Warehouse throughput [PI] → Repair approval [PI]

The top five KPIs were selected from ten performance indicators, as seen in Fig. 6.6. These were:

- Jetspares sales rates
- reliability in terms of average time duration between failure of parts

- average repair cost per transaction
- purchase price reduction index
- repair turnaround time for defective parts.

Fig. 6.6 BAe – Value impact of a 1% movement in top 10 KPIs

£ millions cash (NPV)

Performance indicators:
- Jetspares rate — KPI
- Reliability — KPI
- Average cost per repair — KPI
- Purchase price reduction — KPI
- Repair turnaround time (TRT) — KPI
- Scrap cost per aircraft (efficiency)
- Repair agent share
- Value of overstock
- Variable indirect labour per aircraft
- Debtors fixed payment debt days

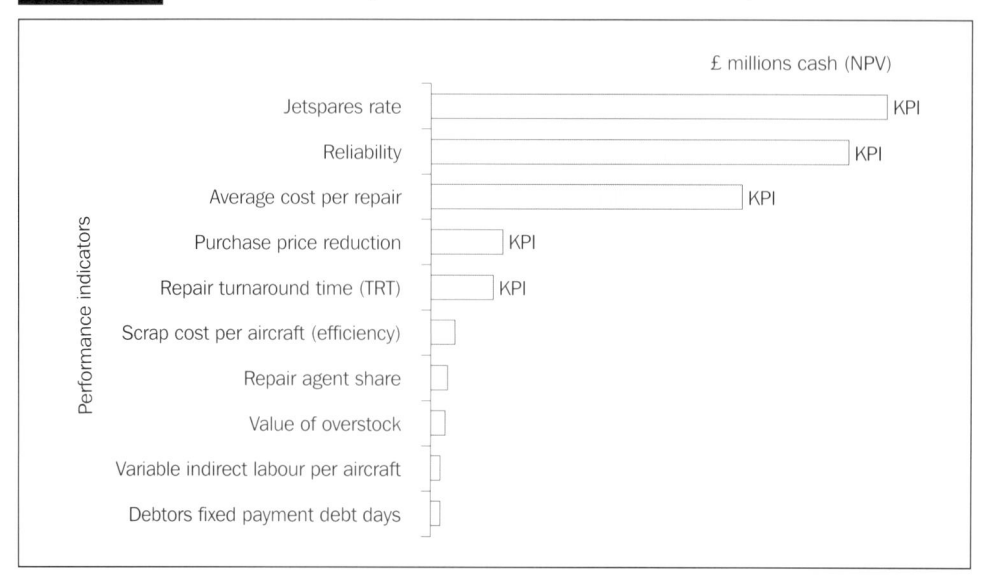

Figure 6.7 clearly shows the characteristics that are sought in VBM KPIs:

- large impact
- controllable
- measurable
- linked to cash.

Fig. 6.7 BAe – Characteristics of KPIs

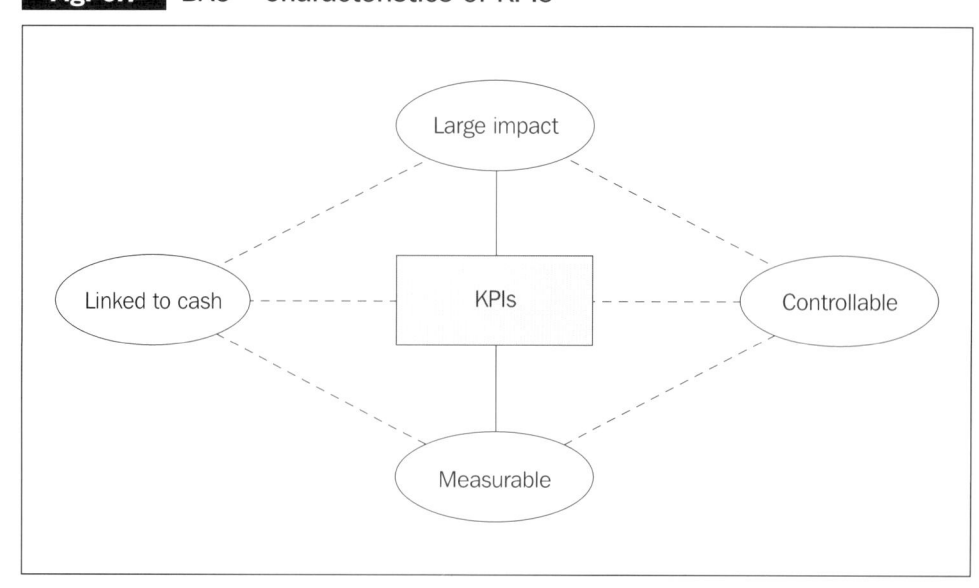

KPIs:
- Large impact
- Linked to cash
- Controllable
- Measurable

Figure 6.8 illustrates how KPIs must be assigned priorities so that management can identify the main KPIs on which to concentrate. Figure 6.9 shows that over a seven-year period the VBM study identified significant additional value for Jetspares, shown in Fig. 6.10. Improving a KPI such as reliability of aircraft parts by just 1% will mean a cash saving in repair bills alone of almost £2 million over the life of the product.

Fig. 6.8 BAe – Identification of KPIs

- Monitor
- Manage actively
- Key performance indicators
- Low priority
- Hedge or change strategy

Management influence: Low → High
Value impact: Low → High

Fig. 6.9 BAe – The initial management view of movability on KPIs

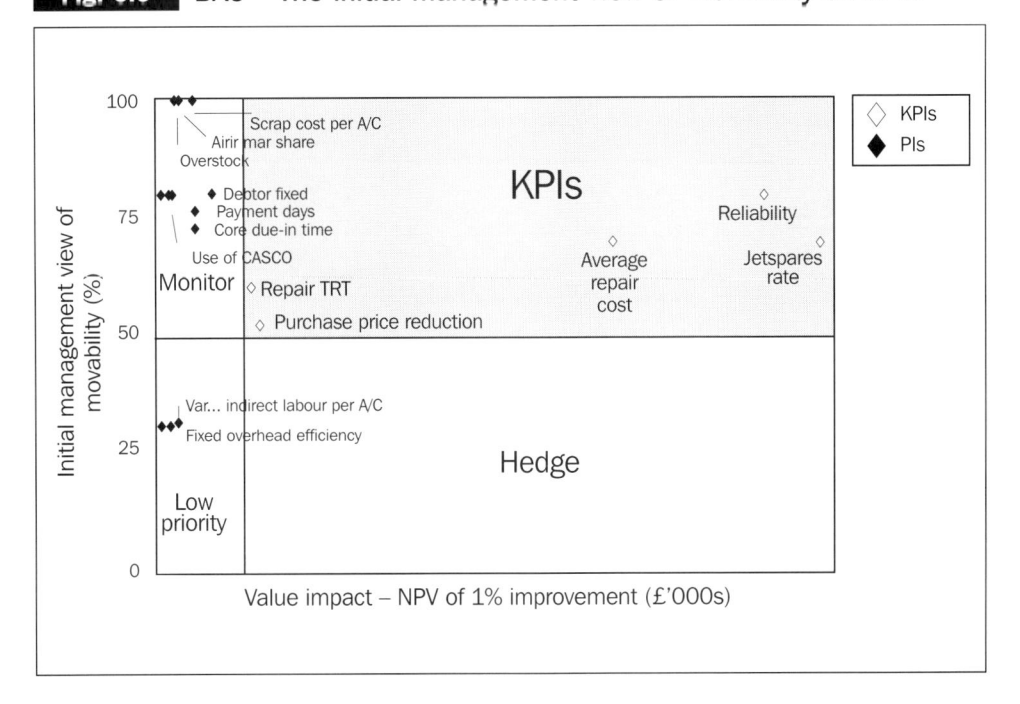

◇ KPIs
◆ PIs

KPIs quadrant:
- Scrap cost per A/C
- Airframar share
- Overstock
- Debtor fixed
- Payment days
- Core due-in time
- Use of CASCO
- Repair TRT
- Purchase price reduction
- Reliability
- Average repair cost
- Jetspares rate

Monitor

Low priority:
- Var... indirect labour per A/C
- Fixed overhead efficiency

Hedge

Y-axis: Initial management view of movability (%) – 0, 25, 50, 75, 100
X-axis: Value impact – NPV of 1% improvement (£'000s)

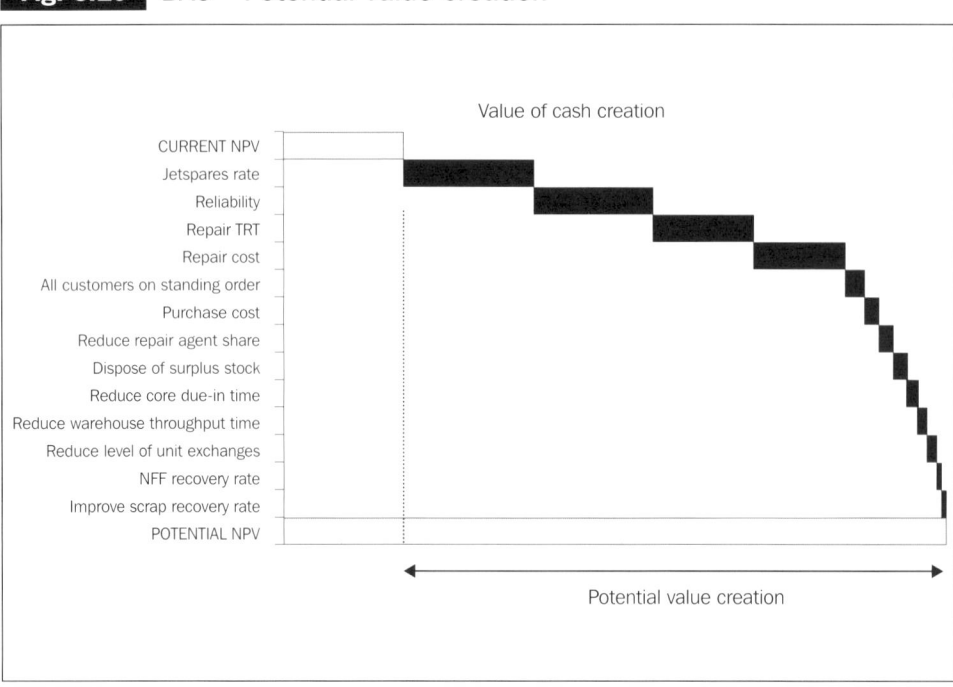

Fig. 6.10 BAe – Potential value creation

```
Value of cash creation

CURRENT NPV
Jetspares rate
Reliability
Repair TRT
Repair cost
All customers on standing order
Purchase cost
Reduce repair agent share
Dispose of surplus stock
Reduce core due-in time
Reduce warehouse throughput time
Reduce level of unit exchanges
NFF recovery rate
Improve scrap recovery rate
POTENTIAL NPV

            ←— Potential value creation —→
```

It was realized that prior to the VBM project, increases in sales were in fact destroying value; the business was operating at an economic loss. Improvements were made immediately to several processes, including working capital, reduction of stock levels per aircraft as volumes increased, and realignment of sales incentives towards cash and away from the traditional volume measures.

The future

This success story proved a milestone for Regional Aircraft and encourages three further projects to be started in 1999 covering:

- sales and marketing
- purchasing and bill of materials process
- spares.

These are all being managed internally by Tony Bryan, VBM Executive for Regional Aircraft, with teams of three to four people on each project. At the same time, a series of six training modules has been developed aimed at a range of people, from team leaders participating in the project to specialist trainer training for the implementors. These training modules cover the two phases of the VBM programme:

- Phase I – identifying KPIs in the businesses (taking from four to six months).
- Phase II – aligning all core management processes to KPIs, for example the reporting, budgeting and planning processes. This phase is expected to take between 12 and 36 months to complete, and is effectively a change-management programme requiring a change in behaviours and the way in which decisions are made.

The success in Regional Aircraft is mirrored across BAe, with VBM implementation progressing in all its key businesses. VBM is providing valuable insights into all aspects of the business, including contract negotiations, bidding and estimating for new business, project tracking and management, manufacturing efficiency and working capital management.

VBM is a priority action for BAe, helping to deliver long-term sustainable growth in value for its customers, employees and shareholders.

7

Valuing intangible assets/intellectual capital

- 7.1 Introduction   113
- 7.2 Customer (relational) capital   113
- 7.3 Organizational (structural) capital   115
- 7.4 Human capital   116
- 7.5 Corporate reputation   117
- 7.6 Enterprise risk management (ERM)   118
- 7.7 Ethical, environmental and social reporting   122
- 7.8 Case studies – Managing intangibles   123

7.1 INTRODUCTION

In 1978 the book value of financial and physical assets on average equalled some 95% of market value. In 2001 it was nearer 20%. The other 80% derived from intangible assets/intellectual capital (IC), such as knowledge, brands, research and development, intellectual property, reputation, and relationships with employees, customers, suppliers and business partners. In organizations like Microsoft, Amazon, and Dell, physical assets now account for a tiny proportion of market value.

Tangible assets like property can be leased and manufacturing outsourced. Companies like Nike, Benetton and Cisco can be argued to have more value as virtual companies than if they owned their own production facilities. According to Mike Tierney, Cisco Systems UK Finance Director,[1] Cisco receives 90% of its orders from its network of a few hundred partners electronically – these are filtered through a European Revenue Shared Service Centre in Amsterdam. Scheduling for manufacture is then done electronically in the master scheduler in San Jose with the manufacturing outsourced to third parties in places like Scotland, from where it is shipped directly to the customer. This makes Cisco as near as you can get to a virtual corporation.

Despite this, only a few companies manage, measure and monitor intangibles; some, like brands, are assigned value if they are acquired but not internally generated. Techniques for valuing intangibles are still developing, but they are currently underreported and undervalued and lack of transparency and consistency adds to share-price volatility. Identifying and communicating the value of intangibles will impact shareholder views on the company performance and potential, and internally its understanding is essential to aid resource-allocation decisions.

The role of the finance function is to apply its skills in encouraging the creation and the integration of knowledge in their organizations; to direct and control the intellectual capital formation process; and to evaluate, report and audit the results of these processes on an ongoing basis. This will depend on the ability to classify knowledge-based assets, to identify how they form intellectual capital and how they are linked to overall strategic goals of the organization and to evaluate how they contribute to intellectual capital in the business and benchmark to other comparable organizations.

Intellectual capital can be categorized into three main types – customer, organizational and human – which are all interrelated and link with the financial capital to form the market value of the organisation and its corporate reputation.

7.2 CUSTOMER (RELATIONAL) CAPITAL

Customer value

For all businesses, the main purpose is to create a customer. For e-businesses, the customer is often the biggest asset and their success is determined by their ability to leverage it. To value the worth of a customer it is necessary to determine the costs of acquiring, serving and retaining it throughout its life and deduct this from the revenues that can be generated from delivery of products and services. According to findings in *eCFO*,[2] understanding, managing and improving the value of the customer base raises important questions:

- Does your company have customer relationships that provide profitable long-term growth?
- Do you really understand who your customers are, where they come from and how much they contribute?
- How do you deploy resources to acquire and retain the right customers?
- Does your investment in customer relationship management systems properly address customer value?

To find the answers it is necessary to:

- measure customer breakeven;
- build a weighted customer value index – scoring things like product usage, loyalty, payment method etc.;
- profile the customer;
- manage customer value – by using the analysis to target market, and reshape how products and services are priced and offered and relationships managed.

Brand value

Understanding the value of your brands has always been important in a traditional organization but is crucial in an e-business. As Sir Richard Branson has said: 'If you look at the values of companies on the internet with strong brands, they tend to be ten times higher than companies that have no brand'.[2] Brand valuation provides information both internally and externally. Internally, such information will provide the basis for such decisions as acquisitions and disposals and advertising and marketing spend.

Brand valuation approaches fall into four types:

- cost invested
- market value
- estimates of future income streams
- an economic assessment of all factors that could influence brand value.

Brand valuation methodologies have been developed by specialist consultancy firms. They go through a number of steps; for example, for Brand Finance:

- calculate economic value added (EVA™);
- identify the brand value added – identify the portion of EVA™ attributable to the brand by understanding and modelling the drivers of demand;
- calculate the discount rate;
- calculate the brand value – by applying the risk-adjusted discount rate to the brand-value-added cashflows;
- manage brand value – performance management, brand portfolio and strategy.

7.3 ORGANIZATIONAL (STRUCTURAL) CAPITAL

Research and development

Traditionally the finance function has allocated resource to research and development (R&D) based on a percentage of predicted revenue streams rather than basing it on the shareholder value it will generate. Stern Stewart' analysis[3] of the FT500 companies, based on 1998 figures, showed that four out of the top ten in MVA ranking are drugs and healthcare companies with Glaxo Wellcome as number one. This strong performance was attributed to a strong portfolio of new products in development and means that Glaxo had been able to show investors that it had reduced its exposure to the performance of just a few blockbusters. Guidance from Cedric Read[2] suggests:

- linking R&D investment to market value – by understanding how R&D variables affect shareholder returns so that alternative strategies can be evaluated;
- improving operational R&D decision making – by utilizing real options valuation (ROV)[4] to recognize the uncertainty of both development and marketing uncertainty;
- measuring the performance of R&D investments – by linking them to bottom-line, meaningful comparisons between different categories of R&D, highlighting the cost of failure, monitoring R&D's contribution to post-launch success/failure, and showing the level of R&D's responsibility for portfolio management.

Intellectual property

In the search to understand where the corporate value lies organizations have been finding that much of it relates to intellectual property (IP) – all those intangible assets that can be legally protected to some degree in the form of copyrights, patents, proprietary software and trademarks. Established firms are moving to exploit their IP; for example, BT recently discovered that it owned a patent relating to hyperlink. Patents account for 20% of Texas Instrument's profits and $1 billion a year in revenues to IBM. The advent of e-business has resulted in the breaking down of businesses, and a high degree of interconnection has been created between previously separate entities through joint ventures, alliances and partnerships. Often this requires a degree of sharing of assets, particularly trademarks or patented technology. However, it is possible to separate design from manufacture from distribution and retail. Companies who operate globally are being forced to check the validity of their IP protection across countries.

KPMG's IP Services have devised the following ten questions that organizations need to ask themselves:[5]

- Do we know what we have?
- Is our IP managed by multiple departments internally?
- Is our business direction threatened by another company's IP dominance?
- Has existing IP been evaluated for core and non-core usefulness?
- Is IP managed in a manner that enhances shareholder value?
- Are R&D efforts tied in to strategic direction and existing IP assets?
- Are systems in place to monitor and develop IP management?
- Should we dispose of IP that we no longer use?
- What internal focus and policies do we have to evaluate the effective use of IP?
- Is our use of IP protectionism, proactive or strategic?

Online IP of products that can be digitized – newspapers, books, music – is a very complex area with some issues still being decided. The questions hinge around who controls it, how best to distribute it and how to charge for it.

Infrastructure assets

Companies like Amazon are attempting to patent their unique business methods – this is one example of infrastructure assets. Similarly, IT company Dell has patented its order-processing system. Other infrastructure assets include management philosophy, corporate culture, information systems, networking systems, management processes and financial relations.

7.4 HUMAN CAPITAL

Investors have always emphasized the importance of management when deciding where to put their funds and today the value of human capital has become the key to a successful business. Retaining talented employees is proving one of the biggest challenges for twenty-first-century global organizations. Companies are having to grapple with the decisions on how best to motivate and remunerate their staff. Organizations adopting a value-based approach link remuneration to the achievement of objectives that deliver increased shareholder value.

Human capital refers to the know-how, education, qualifications, work-related knowledge, occupational assessments and competencies, and other capabilities, skills and expertise of the human members of the organization, not least entrepreneurial ability, the ability to innovative and flexibility. The emergence of knowledge and creativity as the principal determinants of competitiveness is forcing organizations to place a value on their human capital.

7.5 CORPORATE REPUTATION

These three categories of intellectual capital – customer, organizational and human – combine with financial assets to build corporate valuation and reputation, which must be managed with care (*see* Fig. 7.1).

Fig. 7.1 Corporate valuation

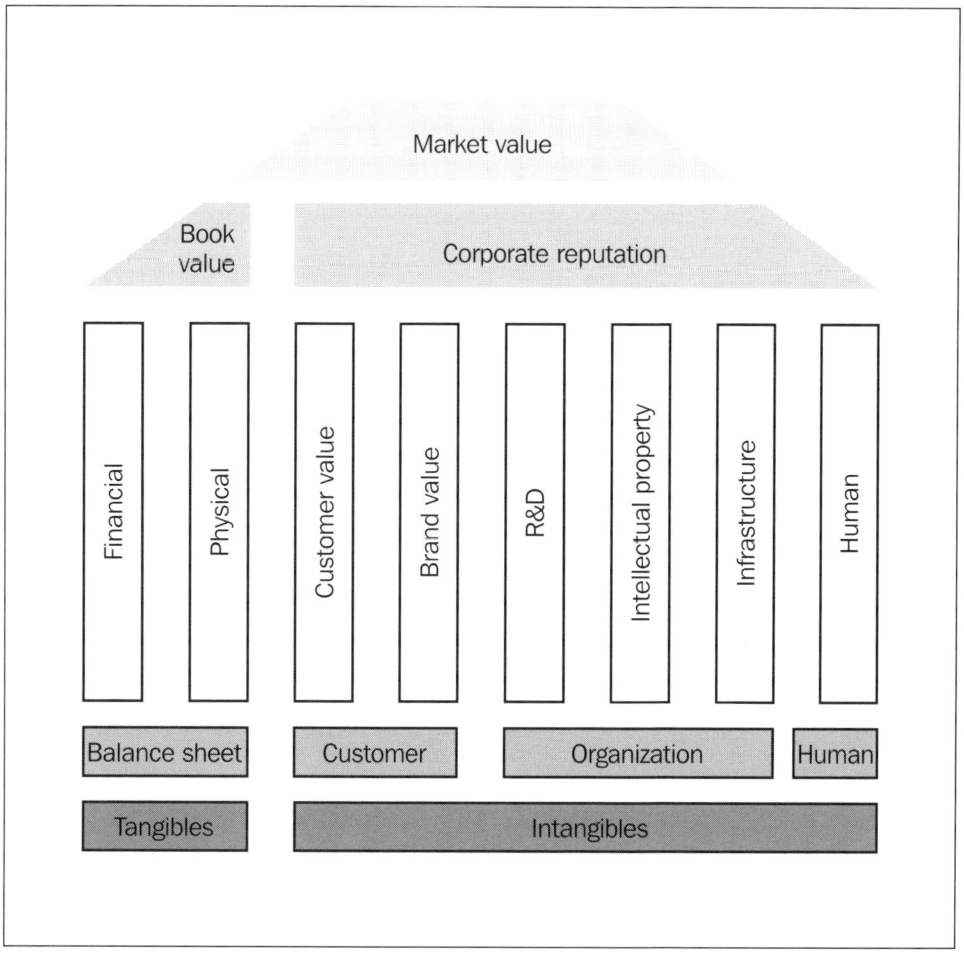

Every operational or strategic decision has the potential to impact on share price and reputation. This is why more and more finance departments are working ever closer with their public and/or investor relations (IR) departments. Investor relations is no longer a support service buried within communications departments – it is now more likely to have a prominent place in finance. An example of this is at Adidas-Salomon,[6] who found its share price tumbling when it announced that it was to take a stake in Bayern Munich Football Club on 18 September 2001. So the CFO and head of IR devised a joint plan for damage limitation involving a roadshow for key investors. By 1 October 2001 the share price rose back to pre-announcement levels. At Ericcson a close working relationship has developed between finance and IR, which includes interchange of staff between the two. In fact their current head of IR is a finance-trained professional

These close ties stress the importance of delivering consistent messages both internally and externally. Similarly, the importance of a clear and well-communicated enterprise risk management strategy cannot be over-emphasized.

7.6 ENTERPRISE RISK MANAGEMENT

If the transformed finance function is to be the driver of shareholder value throughout the business, then it must re-evaluate the way in which the organization manages its risk. Addressing financial risk alone is no longer sufficient; a comprehensive approach to managing technical, commercial, operational, strategic and financial risk needs to be adopted by the company and facilitated by the finance function.

High-profile examples of failure to evaluate risk fully are available, such as Barings Bank, where an employee was sent to prison, and Hoover's infamous 'Free flights to the USA' promotion, available to anyone who bought a new Hoover vacuum cleaner. The risks involved in offering a promotion worth at least four times the value of the goods sold were not picked up and dealt with effectively by the company's risk-management strategy. Instead the promotion had dire consequences for the company, its executives and staff, despite the organization's leading brand position. In hindsight, it is easy to see the errors – but how many organizations can confidently reassure their shareholders that their risk-management strategy effectively manages the risk inherent in all their business processes?

In addition to controlling risk within the organization, risk factors outside the control of the company need to be evaluated and incorporated into the decision-making process. Such external influences will include environmental and political issues outside the control of the company but significantly affecting it. Recent examples affecting most companies include the introduction of the euro and the terrorist attack on the World Trade Center. An example of a specific company being hit by an environmental issue outside its control was Greenpeace's reaction and subsequent campaign regarding Shell's decision on how to dispose of the Brent Spar platform. The key to maintaining shareholder confidence is how well such situations are handled when they do occur or, even better, to have anticipated and mitigated the possibility of the event occurring and to have communicated that to investors.

The requirement is to develop comprehensive company-wide processes and policies for identifying, understanding, assessing and mitigating risk. Taking risks is a part of every organization's normal activities. The greater the risk, the greater the reward – a fact that is recognized by shareholders in their investment portfolios. The risk-management system needs to offer assurances that controls are in place to assess significant risk and highlight strategic opportunities. When risk has been identified as an asset it must be managed to seize opportunities, create value, push to the limits, beat the competition and attract investors. When it is recognized as a liability it must be managed to reduce the possibility of loss, protect value, stay in control, avoid falling behind and reassure investors.

Research undertaken in 2001 covering 130 organizations worldwide reports that over 55% of finance directors surveyed believe that enterprise risk management (ERM) can help address their most urgent business issues.[7] More than 60% believe that ERM can assist with earnings' consistency and expense control, as well as address some of the underlying challenges of capital management and contingency planning. Organizations like Endisa, Alcatel SEL and Infineon are examples of companies that have gained competitive advantage from adopting ERM.

The case for enterprise risk management

Traditionally, each area of risk has been dealt with independently within its own department, for example:

- risks concerning exchange rates and investments – treasury;
- credit risks – sales ledger;
- supplier risks – procurement;
- internet risks – IT;
- insurable risks, e.g. property, employee liability product risks – marketing or product managers;
- customer risks – sales and account managers;
- employment practices such as succession planning – HR;
- contractual risks – legal;
- risks involved in mergers, acquisitions and other strategic decisions – strategic planning;
- technical and health and safety risks – operations;

- disaster-recovery contingencies and controlling system security – IT;
- change programmes – project by project.

This approach is susceptible to large areas of risks not being monitored at all, either because they fall between two departments or because a misunderstanding of responsibility has occurred. Instead they need to be viewed from the perspective of the whole organization, categorized as:

- strategic – risks of plan failing, e.g. poor marketing strategy;
- financial – risks of financial controls failing, e.g. fraud;
- commercial – risks of business interruption, e.g. loss of key executive;
- operational – risks of human error or omission, e.g. design mistakes;
- technical – risks of physical assets failing or being damaged, e.g. equipment breakdown.

Equally, there may be a knock-on effect from one risk to another. In the Hoover example quoted above a problem arose originally in offering an unsustainable promotion, but this was compounded many times over in the multitude of errors made in the handling of the problems created. This illustrates the links between risks and is further evidence of the need to adopt a holistic approach. The global, fast-moving environment of today's larger organizations, with their commercially aware shareholders, demands a different approach to risk management. In consequence, this issue has moved up the corporate agenda and become a key measure within corporate balanced scorecards.

With the drive to ever greater cost savings and increased profits year on year, the question of balance between product quality and costs of production raises questions about the risks involved in cutting corners, which ultimately must be tackled in the boardroom.

Building integrated risk management

- Assimilate information regarding the existing recognition of risk, noting which department takes responsibility for it and how it is assessed and mitigated.
- Collect information on historical risk problems that the company has suffered and categorize these in terms of their business impact. Include soft risks, like culture change and poor IT strategy, as well as hard risks, like interest rates and customer complaints.
- Reinforce the message throughout the company of the importance of the risk profile and the need to integrate and monitor it more closely, stressing its links to creating shareholder value.

- Set up a risk-management group, comprising the main departmental risk managers around the business.
- Evaluate existing departmental risk management and categorize materiality (*see* Fig. 7.2), identify gaps, shortcomings, interrelationships, management strategies and improvements from a holistic viewpoint.

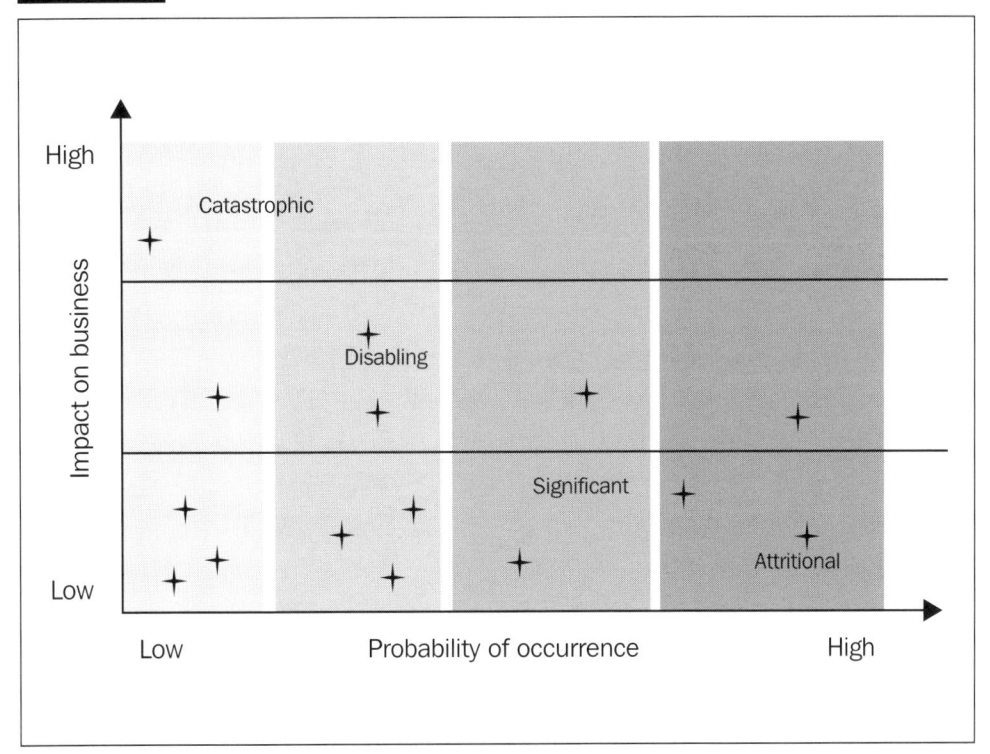

Fig. 7.2 Materiality of risk

[Chart: Materiality of risk matrix with "Impact on business" (Low to High) on the y-axis and "Probability of occurrence" (Low to High) on the x-axis, showing four categories: Catastrophic, Disabling, Significant, and Attritional]

- Build new models and scenarios, linking these where possible to shareholder value calculations.
- Determine and clearly set out your corporate risk strategy in a way that everyone in the organization can understand. Document policies and procedures and train employees to 'evaluate risk' in everything they do.
- Build risk performance measurement systems and controls to underpin the balanced scorecard's key performance indicators.
- Monitor and evaluate on a regular basis, using benchmarks, wherever practicable.

It is now a recommendation of good practice (since the beginning of 2000, following the Turnbull Report) to incorporate measures at board level that demonstrate the presence of an integrated ERM policy that is embedded in the organization. This internal control system must monitor important threats, including environmental, ethical and social risks.

7.7 ETHICAL, ENVIRONMENTAL AND SOCIAL REPORTING

Businesses are considering the ways in which environmental issues can secure competitive advantage. They need to look at how to link expenditure on good environmental management to improved performance and reputation. Fund managers now expect organizations to anticipate possible future legislation by investing wisely in environmental issues. In response to the interest of investors, the quality of environmental reporting is rising. For example, a 2000 survey of 'Britain's most admired companies' conducted by *Management Today* included a direct correlation between disclosure and reputation.[8]

Interestingly, the findings of CIMA-sponsored research[8] suggest that environmental auditing and kite-mark accreditation have little effect on reputation, regardless of annual report disclosure strategy. The importance of the annual report and the influence of disclosure style means that accountants can have a major impact on how the company is perceived by external stakeholders. The researchers found that higher reputation companies enjoyed superior profit-margin ratios, which in turn translated into a lower equity capital of approximately 1.35%. The research shows that, to be effective, annual report disclosures must describe the monitoring and implementation of environmental strategies. They will also add impact if they reflect the preferences of investment professionals and use quantifiable targets and performance against targets – companies less committed will show less convincing and more generalized disclosures.

Standards and frameworks

At the beginning of 2001 the Advisory Committee on Business and the Environment (ACBE) published advice for companies with more than 250 employees to help them review levels of sustainability. Similarly, AA1000 is the new standard for social and ethical accounting, launched by the Institute of Social and Ethical AccountAbility, which sets out a process and framework for taking decisions about a whole range of social and ethical issues. The Copenhagen Charter, produced by four firms of management consultants in Sweden, offers a management guide to stakeholder dialogue and reporting. It is split into three parts describing:

- how social and ethical reporting can be used to create both internal and external value;
- the principles of stakeholder reporting;
- how to make stakeholder reporting credible.

The Charter says: 'Companies that commit to stakeholder reporting do so with the aim of securing balanced and sustainable value creation for all key stakeholders'.

Core principles for social reporting

- Completeness.
- Comparability.
- Inclusivity.
- Regularity and evolution.
- Embeddedness.
- Disclosure.
- External verification.
- Continuous improvement.

Index of Corporate Environmental Engagement

Shell Transport & Trading tops a league table in the UK 2001 annual Business in the Environment Index of Corporate Environmental Engagement. The index revealed that one-third of companies do not measure their global warming emissions. Just 15% of companies set emission reduction targets of 10% or more, while 64% set no targets at all. Second to fifth in the index were Scottish Power, British Energy, Severn Trent and J. Sainsbury.

7.8 Case studies

Managing intangibles

Monsanto – risk management failure

An example of the effect that ethical and environmental issues can have on a company is Monsanto. Their development of GM crops as the answer to the world's food shortages suddenly became seen as 'Frankenstein foods'. The financial impact has been catastrophic: US analysts in 2000 rated the profitable $5-billion-a-year agricultural-business arm as effectively worthless.

Nike – risk management failure

It is no longer sufficient for a company to check that its own activities and systems are ethically sound, it must also check on its suppliers and business partners. An example of this is Nike, who suffered through the media discovery that children were being used to make its products in the developing countries.

Railtrack – corporate social responsibility

A good example of an organization that has been forced to adopt corporate social responsibility is Railtrack, who clearly demonstrated that good profits and returns for shareholders cannot be earned at the expense of other stakeholders and safety.

Body Shop – Ethical accounting

Bodyshop has a regular external verified process to understand, measure, report on and improve the organization's social, environmental and animal testing performance through stakeholder dialogue. The resulting report incorporates three separate (social, environmental and animal testing) reports.

Diageo and BP – corporate community involvement reports

Diageo and BP provide a description, illustration and measurement of community involvement policies and activities through occasional reports. This approach may also include benchmarking against other company performances.

Shell International – statement of principles and values.

Shell issues a statement that develops, evolves and describes the organization's principles in meeting its financial, social and environmental responsibilities.

Scandia – intellectual capital valuation

Scandia has a regularly disclosed process to understand, measure, report upon and manage various forms of capital, which includes intellectual, human, social environmental, organizational, structural and financial capital.

Interface – sustainability reporting

Interface is evolving a report process that identifies ways forward and reports upon progress against sustainability principles.

Black Country HA – social auditing

Black Country HA has a regular, externally verified process to understand, measure, report on and improve on the organization's social performance through stakeholder dialogue.

UNIPOL – social balance

UNIPOL issues a regular reconstruction and aggregation of financial data across stakeholder groups which specifies financial costs associated with 'social activities'.

Part 4

Beyond traditional budgeting

- 8 Scenario planning, forecasting and resource allocation 127
- 9 The balanced scorecard 145
- 10 Benchmarking 167

Scenario planning, forecasting and resource allocation

- 8.1 Resource allocation 129
- 8.2 Empowered organizational culture 129
- 8.3 Beyond traditional budgeting 132
- 8.4 Scenario planning 136
- 8.5 Forecasting 138
- 8.6 Case studies – Beyond traditional budgeting 140

8.1 RESOURCE ALLOCATION

Chapter 6 described how VBM organizations are focused on delivering value to investors, because they will invest their funds where the best opportunities for maximizing shareholder value occur. Allocation of funds within the organization must therefore be approached in a similar way, by viewing strategy as a series of options offering different opportunities, with different costs, values and outcomes. At least at a strategic level, the modern finance function needs to view its role as managing a portfolio of investments. It includes finding, evaluating and nurturing new opportunities that will attract resources, as well as its traditional role of trying to generate more value out of existing business models by the allocation of resources. The finance function today must:

- investigate any opportunities that exceed cost of capital;
- remember that availability of capital is rarely a constraint;
- value and have regard for intangible assets and other constraints in managing resources;
- manage the allocation or attraction of resource as a portfolio;
- supplement or replace discounted cashflow (DCF) and return on investment (ROI) with shreholder value analysis (SVA) like economic value added (EVA);
- disregard the annual budget cycle in resource management.

Traditionally, the planning and budgeting process was primarily concerned with how to manage the limited capital available for investments, often making allocations at operating company level based on history. The modern organization finds no shortage of capital available for the right investments, but other – often intangible – resources are becoming more scarce. These include skills, know-how, technology and experience, which are necessary to deliver a desired strategic scenario. In this new innovative, dynamic, empowered, web-enabled environment it is essential that the backward-looking, conventional budgeting and planning process is replaced with more appropriate forward-looking tools and techniques that support a culture that encourages innovation and thinking 'out of the box'.

8.2 EMPOWERED ORGANIZATIONAL CULTURE

Until the early 1990s most publicly owned organizations were focused on short-term results, often driven by the stock market demanding improvements in share price and dividends year on year, without interest or regard for long-term strategies, growth or value generation. This resulted in senior managers running the business based on financial and accounting information, which they used to plan the next cycle of required results and then to instruct the workforce accordingly, requiring them to manipulate processes and cajole customers to achieve them (*see* Fig. 8.1).¹

Fig. 8.1 The 'top-down' control cycle

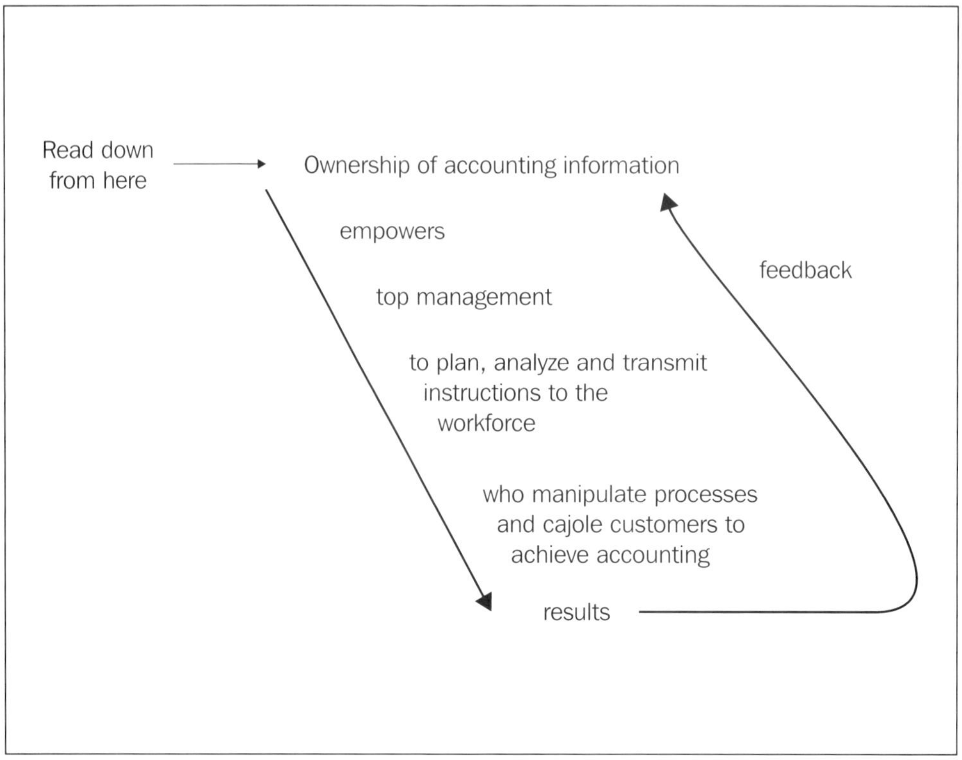

```
Read down
from here  ──→  Ownership of accounting information
                      ↓
                   empowers                            ↑
                                                   feedback
                 top management
                      ↓
              to plan, analyze and transmit
                  instructions to the
                      workforce
                      ↓
                who manipulate processes
                and cajole customers to
                   achieve accounting
                        ↓
                      results ─────────────────┘
```

Source: *Relevance Regained* (Johnson, 1992)

Typical characteristics exhibited by a top-down control cycle organization can be seen in Fig. 8.2.

Most organisations during the 1990s have made a conscious effort to switch their culture to that depicted in Fig. 8.3. This illustrates that in the new global age customers have so much choice that they are forced to be responsive and flexible and must empower their workforces to learn and make changes that continuously improve processes capable of better satisfying their customers. Moving to an empowerment culture takes time, requires determination and considerable change by organizations, and it can be seen that those who persevere are the ones who are the most successful. In the process of these changes, far too often the finance function lags behind the rest of the organization in making the necessary adjustments. Instead it ought to be leading the change by transforming the way it operates as a function and the way the business operates as a whole.

Fig. 8.2 Stifling innovation memorandum

TOP DOWN CULTURE ORGANIZATION

MEMORANDUM

To: All senior executives

Subject: **10 RULES FOR STIFLING INNOVATION**

1. Regard any new idea from below with suspicion – because it's new.
2. Insist that people, who need your approval to act, first go through several other levels of management to get their signatures.
3. Express your criticisms freely and withhold your praise. Let them know that they can be fired at any time. (That keeps people on their toes.)
4. Treat identification of problems as a sign of failure in order to discourage people from letting you know when something in their area is not working.
5. Control everything carefully. Make sure that people count anything that can be counted frequently.
6. Make decisions to reorganize or change policies in secret without any consultation and spring them on people unexpectedly. (That also keeps people on their toes.)
7. Make sure that requests for information are fully justified and that it is not given out to managers freely.
8. Assign to lower-level managers, in the name of delegation and participation, responsibility for figuring out how to cut back, lay off, move people around or otherwise implement threatening decisions that you have made. And get them to do it quickly.
9. Do not forget to launch a *new* cost-cutting initiative at least twice a year. This will score you points with the directors and leave the staff wondering what is going to happen next.
10. And above all, do not forget that you, the higher-ups, already know everything important about the business.

Fig. 8.3 The 'bottom-up' empowerment cycle

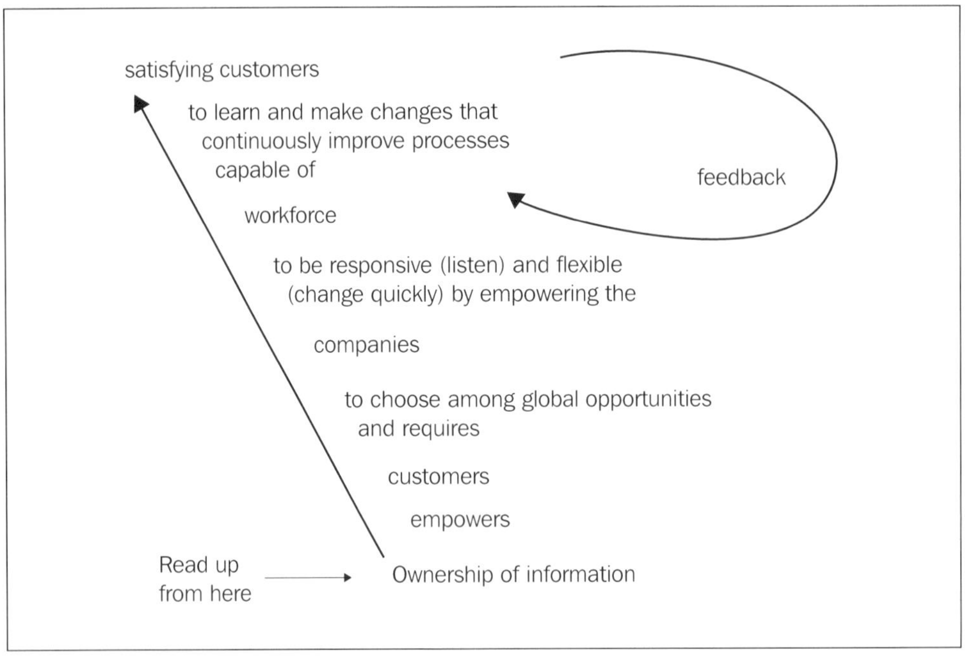

```
satisfying customers
    ↑
    to learn and make changes that
    continuously improve processes
    capable of                              feedback
                                               ↺
        workforce
            to be responsive (listen) and flexible
            (change quickly) by empowering the
                companies
                    to choose among global opportunities
                    and requires
                        customers
                            empowers
Read up  →   Ownership of information
from here
```

Source: *Relevance Regained* (Johnson, 1992)

A McKinsey Consultant's survey revealed the top three reasons that talented managers join an organization:

- values and culture – 58%
- freedom and autonomy – 56%
- exciting challenge – 51%.

Yet research by CAM-I[2] points out that budgets are well known for:

- reinforcing the command and control culture
- constraining freedom and autonomy
- stifling the challenges that excite prospective managers.

To change the culture it is necessary to deal with the budget.

8.3 BEYOND TRADITIONAL BUDGETING

The traditional finance function is focused on running the organization by means of traditional budgetary control techniques, which were designed in the first half of the twentieth century to control a producer-led business. The definition of budgeting is an annual process that sets the performance agenda for the year ahead. It has wide behavioural implications because it is a performance contract. The purpose is to commit people to achieving a certain result. Terms are likely to include a fixed target, time period, resources, limits of authority, reporting intervals and rewards. Once set, this process demands adherence to the plan. Over 90% of large and medium companies use the budget model but there is considerable evidence that most are dissatisfied with the results.

- Hackett Benchmarking Solutions, who studied over 1,400 global firms, found that the average company invests more than 25,000 person days per $1 billion of revenue in the budgeting and planning process and the average time taken for developing the plan is 4.5 months.
- A KPMG study showed that inefficient budgeting is eating up 20–30% of the time of senior executives and financial managers.[3]
- Despite this time invested there is no evidence that the budget adds any value to the business.
- *CFO* magazine reported in 1999 that 75% of managers make decisions with out-of-date, incomplete information.

These budgets are set without linking resource allocation to output volumes, priorities or value-added – at least not in service and support areas. Generally, resources are allocated based on such factors as who had what last year and which directors are most powerful within the organization. Under these traditional budget-led regimes, rigid adherence to whether cost centres are within the pre-set budget limits is maintained on a monthly basis, irrespective of changes in demand for products or services within individual cost centres or the business as a whole. If costs need to be reduced within this traditional budgetary framework, then all departments are instructed to reduce their costs by the required percentage. These arbitrary 'across-the-board' cuts are made irrespective of which departments are carrying out high-priority or customer-facing services and which are already being run in a very efficient, cost-effective manner. After several years of such arbitrary cost reductions, many organizations are finding that the long-term health of their businesses is being endangered.

Figure 8.4 summarizes these shortcomings. The corporate vision is not fully understood by all staff; there is a failure to link the corporate vision and strategy to departmental and individual goals; and a failure to link strategy to resource allocation – this is traditionally done based on history, not on what outputs are required. Finally, the traditional budgetary control feedback is usually a comparison of actual cost-centre expenditure against budget, with no direct link to outputs achieved. These are typical symptoms of the barriers, which can be traced back to this short-term, financial framework.

There is now a sense of urgency about the need to reinvent/supplement or replace traditional budgeting techniques that reinforce the old command and control structure and serve to stifle innovation. New methods of planning, control and allocating resources are being introduced before permanent, long-term damage is done to the health of many businesses.

Fig. 8.4 Barriers to strategic implementation

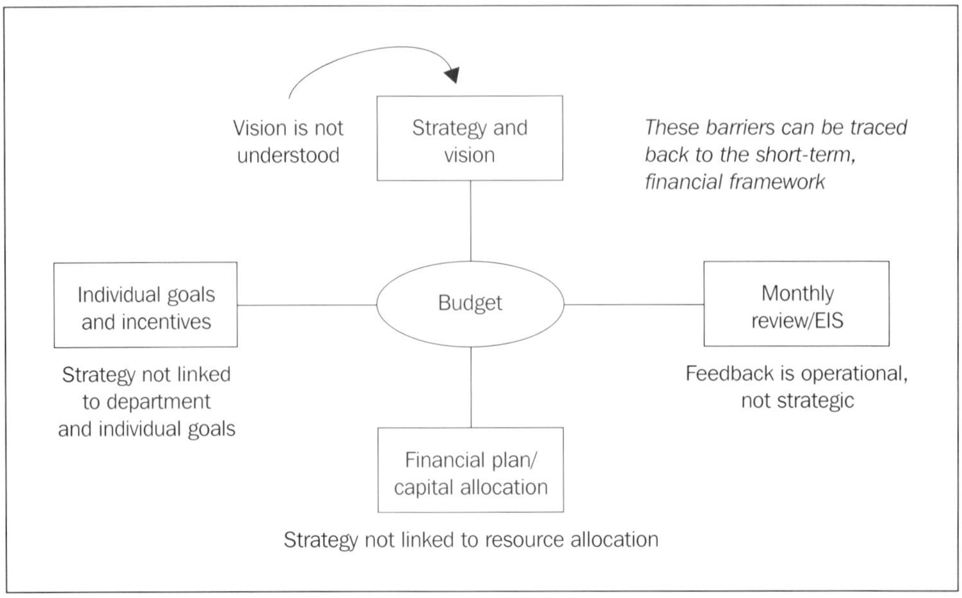

```
                    Strategy and
  Vision is not  ←  vision              These barriers can be traced
  understood                            back to the short-term,
                        │               financial framework
                        │
  ┌──────────────┐      │      ┌──────────────┐
  │ Individual   │──── Budget ─│  Monthly     │
  │ goals and    │             │  review/EIS  │
  │ incentives   │             └──────────────┘
  └──────────────┘      │
  Strategy not linked   │       Feedback is operational,
  to department         │       not strategic
  and individual goals  │
                   ┌─────────────┐
                   │ Financial   │
                   │ plan/       │
                   │ capital     │
                   │ allocation  │
                   └─────────────┘
           Strategy not linked to resource allocation
```

Tools and techniques that are being successfully used to replace traditional budgeting include:

- Enterprise-wide business intelligence (*see* Chapter 5, page 67) – providing one set of good reliable information (both non-financial and financial, external and internal, and qualitative and quantitative) to all levels within the organization.

- Value-based management (*see* Chapter 6, page 89) – helping organizations to focus on delivering value to their stakeholders and allocate resources accordingly.

- Rolling forecasts (*see* section 8.5, page 138) – helping to break away from the annual cycle and allow decisions to be based on the latest and best information.

- Balanced scorecards (*see* Chapter 9, page 145) – enabling the value-added strategy to be linked to operations and monitor its success, which is essential if the strategy is to be realized.

- Benchmarking (*see* Chapter 10, page 167) – internal and external, collaborative and competitive: encouraging performance improvement and innovation.

- Process-based management (*see Business Process Management*[4]) – enabling the effective analysis, costing and performance management of internal processes. Tools and techniques include activity based costing (ABC), business process re-engineering (BPR), business process analysis and model building, performance measurement, alternate service levels and priority-based budgeting (PBB), which facilitates the prioritization of resource allocation, particularly in support services. (BPR of the finance function is examined in Chapter 2, page 19.)

These tools allow resource allocation to be made based on value-added, efficiency, priority and output volumes, with internal process budgets based on unit costs and outputs, and performance benchmarked to best in class targets. Strategic plans and forecasts need to be based on matching competitors' KPIs, not beating last year's budget. These value-adding tools and techniques are the way in which a transformed finance function facilitates management of the organization in the empowered, twenty-first-century organization.

The *CAM-I Beyond Budgeting Round Table White Paper*[3] sets out 12 principles that will provide managers with a robust framework for implementing the new model, as shown in Fig. 8.5. The principles are split into two categories:

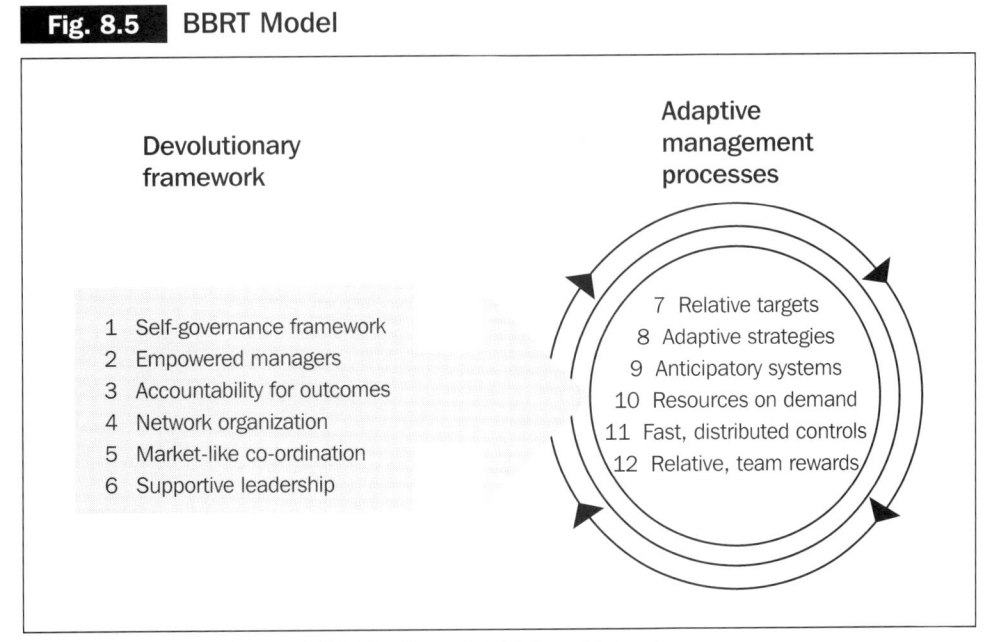

Fig. 8.5 BBRT Model

Devolutionary framework

1. Self-governance framework
2. Empowered managers
3. Accountability for outcomes
4. Network organization
5. Market-like co-ordination
6. Supportive leadership

Adaptive management processes

7. Relative targets
8. Adaptive strategies
9. Anticipatory systems
10. Resources on demand
11. Fast, distributed controls
12. Relative, team rewards

Source: Adapted from *CAM-1 BBRT White Paper* (2000) (www.bbrt.org)

Creating a devolutionary framework

- Governance – establish a framework for devolution by clarifying purpose, principles and values; *don't enforce central control through rules and procedures.*

- Empowerment – give people the freedom and capability to act; *don't control and constrain them.*

- Accountability – make people accountable for achieving competitive outcomes, *not for meeting functional targets.*

- Organisation – organize around a network of independent customer-oriented units, *not a hierarchy of functions and departments.*

- Co-ordination – co-ordinate cross-company interactions through 'market-like' forces, *not through central planning, budgeting and control.*

- Leadership – challenge and coach people; *don't command and control them.*

Adaptive management processes

- Goal setting – beat the competition, *not the budget.*

- Strategy process – make strategy a continuous and inclusive process, *not a top-down annual event.*

- Anticipatory systems – use anticipatory systems to inform strategy; *don't make short-term corrections to 'keep-on-track'.*

- Resource utilization – make resources available when required; *don't allocate them on the basis of annual budgets.*

- Measurement and control – provide fast, open information for multi-level control, *not detail for micro-management.*

- Motivation and rewards – base rewards on company and unit-level competitive performance, *not pre-determined negotiated targets.*

Members of the BBRT who have adopted these techniques include Borealis A/S, Carnaud Metalbox, Ahlsell, Bulmers, The AES Corporation, SKF, Boots, Volvo, Ciba Vision, Sight Savers International, UDV-Guinness, General Electric and BP-Amoco. Dr Jan Wallander of Svenska Handelsbanken was the pioneer who first dared to abandon the sacred budgeting model in the 1970s. Svenska Handelsbanken has since outperformed its Nordic rivals on just about every measure consistently for the last 30 years. It is the most cost-efficient bank in Europe and has recently been voted one of Europe's best internet banks.

8.4 SCENARIO PLANNING

It is now widely accepted that strategic planning is no longer the province of a few senior executives but should be driven to lower levels in the organization. Line managers know their market and the competition better than anyone else in the company. In addition, involving them in the process also has the advantage of gaining their consensus for and awareness of the strategy. Traditionally, companies used accounting tools like the profit and loss and balance sheet to plan the company's future, resulting in an internally focused illusion of numerical precision. Planners would discuss and agree what the most likely future would be and then develop strategies accordingly. Organizations are now recognizing that they need to examine all possible and relevant futures, not just one – hence the move to scenario planning.

Experienced scenario planners advocate that the technique works best when it is used to answer specific questions about the future that have commercial significance to the organization. Many argue that continual reassessments of plans, giving short-, medium- and long-term perspectives, are essential to an organization's success. Unlike budgeting, which is regarded as non-value-adding, scenario planning engages people in debate, opens minds to other possibilities and improves strategic outcomes.

According to Gill Ringland:

> *In a time of uncertainty, scenario planning unfreezes intellect, allowing intelligent people a framework within which it's not only OK, but even mandatory to admit that they don't know what the future will bring, but nevertheless to plan.*[5]

Some of the factors that need to be considered in such scenarios will include:

- *Europe* – will the UK enter the euro and what would be the impact?
- *Customers* – will your customers or their needs change in the future?
- *Environment* – how will environmental issues impact on your company?
- *Demographics* – what will be the impact of more elderly people in the West and more teenagers in Asia and South America?
- *Technology* – how will technology change your products and the ways you interact with customers etc?
- *Government* – with regulation on the increase, what demands is government likely to make on your business?
- *Competition* – where will competition be coming from in the future and what will the competitive drivers be?
- *Products* – what products will your customers want in the future?
- *Organization* – how will the company be organized in future and what skills will be needed?
- *Wild cards* – what unexpected events could blow the company off-course?

By imagining, as early as the 1980s, a future in which a new leader would emerge in the USSR and Communism would disappear, Shell was in an advantageous position when the scenario did eventually play out. Similarly, United Distillers built scenarios about the future of India as a market for whisky.

Another company that has used the technique is Amerada Hess,[6] the oil and gas firm. In 1997 executives had to decide whether its UK operation should expand beyond its traditional strengths of exploration and production and move into domestic distribution – half the company thought it should and half thought it should not. Using consultants, Amerada Hess assembled a 20-member team of junior and senior staff, together with external market experts, at a two-day retreat. They constructed a range of scenarios based on two key questions:

- Would the government tighten or loosen regulations?
- Would the market for gas and oil grow?

Six weeks were spent researching the scenarios before they met again to make their final decision. Based on the evidence that indicated that increasing deregulation would open up new opportunities and that the market for gas showed signs of growth, they decided with consensus to move into distribution – and they are delighted with their resultant market share.

8.5 FORECASTING

With the latest technological developments, forecasting can be more sophisticated and more frequent, and – unlike the annual budgeting process – much more accurate. Robert Fildes, President of the International Institute of Forecasting, has said:

> *So many disasters can be attributed to a failure of forecasting – the market analysis is not being done to illuminate strategic policy. Companies simply don't want to put in the work. Senior managers frequently cut corners when it comes to forecasting. Many of them contend that forecasting is nothing more than glorified fortune telling. And because businesses these days are changing so quickly and the future is so uncertain, they believe that there is little benefit in poring over old data to understand the trends that are likely to affect their companies' business plans in the months and years ahead.*[7]

More attention to forecasting makes sense: research shows that companies issuing profits warnings suffer an average 21.5% fall in their share price. For example, Invensys revealed that 2001 first-half profits fell by 30% when it issued its third profits warning in 10 months – the CEO and chairman have both since been replaced.

Forecasting in practice

At Aventis, the pharmaceuticals and agricultural company, 700 managers in 60 countries participate in four forecasting exercises, which take place five weeks before the end of each quarter. The last forecast of the year in November is used to prepare a rolling three-year plan. In addition, the SBUs have the opportunity to inform about marginal adjustments on a monthly basis, e.g. a change in exchange rate. Monitoring the quality of the information are small cross-functional teams which are set-up around product lines and based at head office. CFO Patrick Langlois explains that the accuracy of forecasting is part of the variable compensation packages of managers involved in forecasting. The accuracy of Aventis's forecasting illustrates the importance of both measuring the accuracy of forecasting and rewarding it accordingly.

Researchers John Mentzer, Carol Bienstock and Kenneth Kahn of the University of Tennessee, have spent five years examining the auditing and forecasting processes of 16 large US companies.[8] They have produced the following guide to world-class forecasting processes:

Who does the forecasting?

- There is collaboration, communication and co-ordination between finance, marketing, sales, production, logistics and forecasting.
- Forecasting is a separate function that provides forecasts in all necessary levels and time horizons.
- Each function receives its own forecast based on a single reconciled set of data. For example, finance gets its annual forecast while sales gets a quarterly report broken down by different territories.
- All personnel involved in the process have performance rewards based on the impact of forecasting accuracy.

What is forecast and how?

- There is top-down and bottom-up, with reconciliation.
- Vendor-managed inventory is a separate part of the process.
- Products are segmented into categories (such as low value versus high value, short shelf life versus long shelf life, customer sensitive).
- The motivation for sales to underforecast and distributors to overforecast is understood.
- Forecasts and business plan are developed simultaneously, with periodic reconciliation.
- There is regular training in quantitative analysis/statistics and in business environment, and senior management support of the entire process.

Which IT tools are used?

- Open-system architecture means all parts of a company involved in forecasting can provide electronic input easily.
- EDI/web-based links with major customers and suppliers improve key-customer and supply-chain staging of forecasting.

How accurate is the forecast?

- Forecasting error indicates a need to search for the problem; for example, demand might be forecast accurately, but plant capacity has prevented the production of the forecast amount.
- Performance evaluation is linked to the impact of accuracy on achieving a range of corporate goals, such as profitability, margin growth or supply-chain costs.

Figure 8.6 shows the cycle of forecasting. First is formulation – scenario planning, options review, resource attraction to value-adding investment and resource allocation to support services, forecasting and target setting. This is followed by execution – action planning and implementation, measuring, reporting and rewarding performance and taking corrective actions before starting the continuous cycle again.

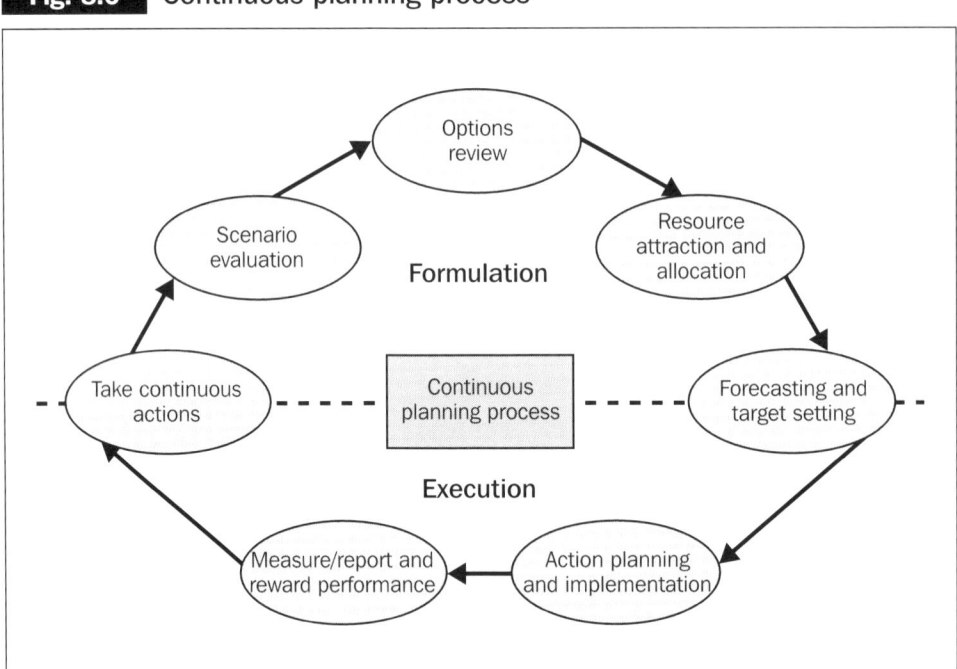

Fig. 8.6 Continuous planning process

8.6 Case studies

Beyond traditional budgeting

Volvo

Following losses in 1990–2 and a small profit in 1993, Volvo decided to tackle the problem of budgeting and planning because the existing system encouraged the old mindset of command and control and absorbed 20% of management time. Volvo decided instead to focus on strategy, action planning and beating the competition in a continuous process using:

- flash forecasts each month, covering a quarter;
- two-year rolling forecasts, updated each quarter;
- revised four- and ten-year strategic plans, updated annually;
- broad-brush targets including KPIs, with time spent on developing and implementing action plans.

Volvo's key performance indicators (KPIs) include market share, order intake, warranty costs, fault frequency, total ownership costs, product costs, dealer profitability and customer satisfaction, which are then benchmarked against the competition.

Borealis

Borealis is a privately owned Danish petrochemicals company, which scrapped the budget in 1995. Its four-pronged replacement for the budget (see Fig. 8.7) includes:

- quarterly rolling financial forecasts that always look five quarters ahead;
- a balanced scorecard that assesses financial and non-financial KPIs for target setting;
- trend reporting, cost targets and ABC methods to control costs;
- three categories for investments to help streamline the assessment process.

Fig. 8.7 Borealis – Performance measurement and reporting

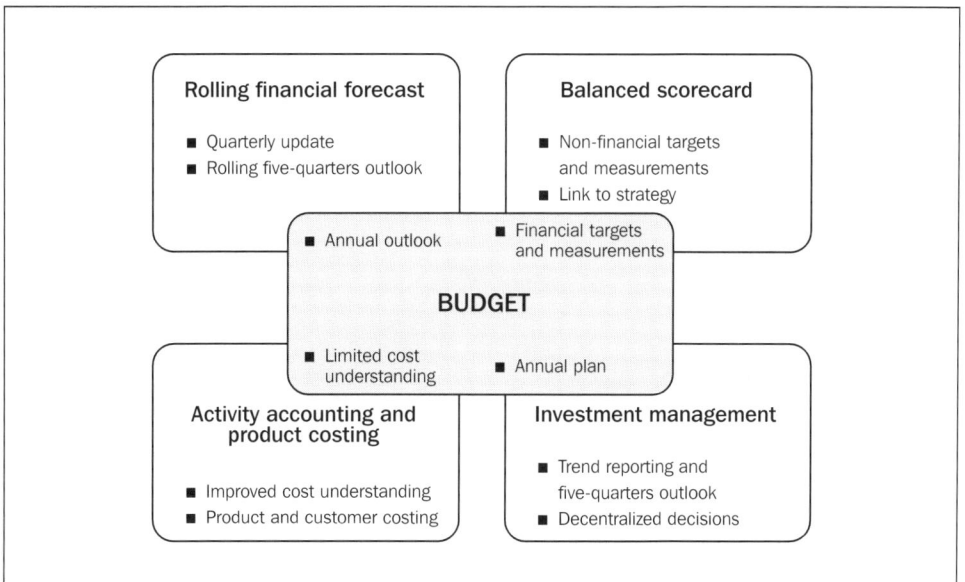

- Rolling financial forecast
  - Quarterly update
  - Rolling five-quarters outlook
- Balanced scorecard
  - Non-financial targets and measurements
  - Link to strategy

BUDGET
- Annual outlook
- Financial targets and measurements
- Limited cost understanding
- Annual plan

- Activity accounting and product costing
  - Improved cost understanding
  - Product and customer costing
- Investment management
  - Trend reporting and five-quarters outlook
  - Decentralized decisions

Diageo

According to Janet Kersnar,[9] Diageo, the £14-billion consumer giant whose brands include Guinness and Burger King, decided in October 1999 to scrap the firm's annual budget and replace it with a totally different approach. As a result, it joined a growing band of multinationals that have abandoned what Jack Welch, the boss of General Electric, once famously described as:

> The bane of corporate America. The annual budget is time consuming, labour intensive and seemingly never ending, and is, at best, an excuse for senior managers to gather numbers that they should have at their fingertips anyway; and, at worst, one of a company's biggest competitive handicaps.

Rather than using a budgeting process and a strategic planning process with annual targets, Diageo's CFO Phillip Yea says:

> We should try to have one single planning process of which year one was important but not so important that it stops you talking about years two, three, four and five.

Since that decision, managers across the company's four lines of business have identified KPIs that they need to use to track, predict and report improvements in their operations. They use leading market indicators and brand equity, reinforced by EVA™, and have implemented a balanced scorecard linking strategy to operations so that everyone had relevant metrics. The overall aim at Diageo is to benchmark itself against a peer group of 20 international consumer and branded-goods companies in terms of total shareholder return. By June 2003 it aims to be among the top five companies out of the 20 in the benchmarking process. It still uses budgeting in certain parts of the organization for expenditure control and cash management, but has eliminated much of the wasteful interaction between head office and strategic business units.

HP Bulmers[10]

HP Bulmer, which has a turnover of £225 million, realized that it needed to grow if it was to survive as an independent on the stock market, even though it held 68% of the British cider market. Finance Director Lesley Jackson believed that culturally the company was stuck in the 1950s; to drag it into the twenty-first century she advocated that conventional budgeting should be replaced. Instead the planning and control process should include:

- rolling quarterly financial forecasts
- monthly customer planning
- 12-weekly manufacturing planning
- KPIs, like cost per hectolitre.

The new financial management process encourages the sort of management behaviour that will help Bulmer to meet its ambitious growth targets. As Lesley Jackson has said:

> *The important thing is to make people connect to the drivers of growth. Now we are completely aligned in how we manage the City and our stakeholders and how we manage the business.*

Jabil Circuit[11]

Jabil Circuit is a US electronics manufacturing services firm which outsources its circuit board manufacturing and systems assembly to customers, who include Cisco and Dell. The Florida-based firm now serves 40 key clients and has 22 factories in nine countries on four continents with revenues of over $4 billion in 2001. It is a decentralized, customer-oriented organization, rather than one built around products or sites – each customer is served by an independent business unit. Chris Lewis, CFO, is credited with providing the tools and disciplines that permit managers to draw on resources throughout the company at a moment's notice and to keep everyone focused on working capital metrics. Because its growth has been organic, Jabil has been able to roll out one overall IT platform, enabling everyone to capture and access data in the same way. Managers are able to assign 94% of costs directly to business units, including those related to scrap, shop supplies and the amount of paste on a circuit board, plus investments in long-term assets and working capital. As Lewis says: 'This resolution gives them a ton of accountability'.

Planning at the company starts with a six-monthly rolling forecast that is updated every three months. A weekly snapshot of sequential trends in margins, inventory levels, asset returns and sales cycles by plant, customer and vendor helps detect variations and allows for more efficient use of production resources and available inventory. In addition, a monthly analysis of actual operating performance compares each business unit on the basis of return on net assets, forecast accuracy and asset utilization. This is managed through collaboration among operations, business development and finance. Even with the recent downturn, Jabil remains among the top players for working-capital metrics in the industry.

9

The balanced scorecard

- 9.1 Introduction 147
- 9.2 Measures that drive performance 148
- 9.3 The strategy-focused organization 149
- 9.4 Weighting the balanced scorecard 153
- 9.5 The ten commandments of implementation 155
- 9.6 Links to quality frameworks 156
- 9.7 Case studies – e-BSC 158
- 9.8 Case study – Manchester Housing's information strategy 160

9.1 INTRODUCTION

Performance-management systems controlled by the traditional finance function exhibit many of the following characteristics:

- too inward focusing
- too historical, lacking predictive power
- reflect the business functions and structure, not processes
- reinforce wrong behaviour
- focus on inputs not outputs
- too summary in nature or mistake data for information
- based on the way the company worked before change
- too financially oriented.

The balanced scorecard (BSC) is a tool designed by Kaplan and Norton[1] in 1992, which is now widely used across all industry sectors. It highlights the need to look at critical success factors (CSFs) or outcomes required to achieve the organization's strategy and set key performance indicators (KPIs) for all the company perspectives – including the customer, learning and innovation, and internal business, as well as the traditional financial perspective – when monitoring the organization's performance. These KPIs make up a high level monitor of performance for senior managers and they need to be linked to the more detailed operational measures so that any failure to perform to a target KPI can be pinpointed and corrected within the organization.

Figure 9.1 shows how this one holistic system links the value-adding strategy via the BSC to a detailed common data model containing activity/process-based information, which incorporates quality frameworks and HR measures as well as operational data.

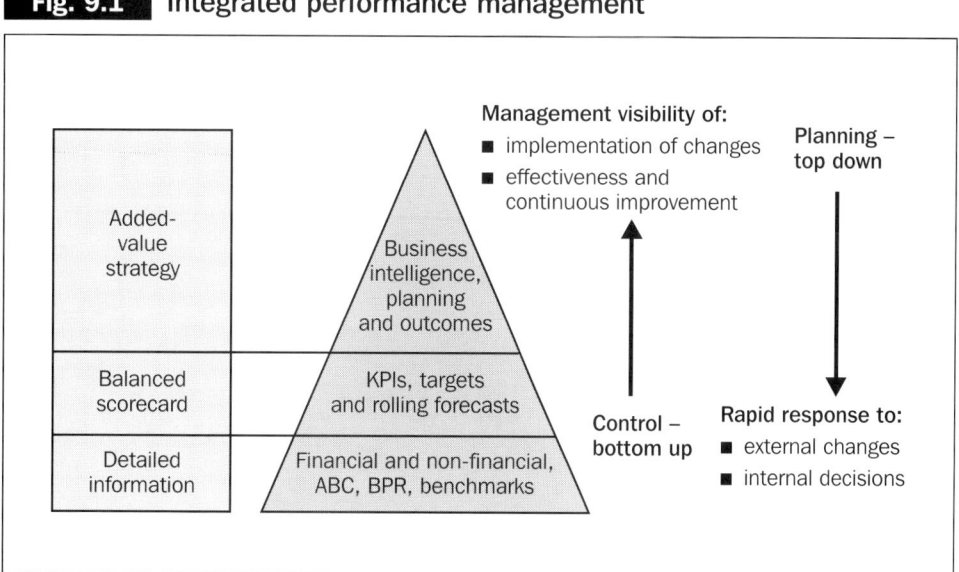

Fig. 9.1 Integrated performance management

9.2 MEASURES THAT DRIVE PERFORMANCE

During a 12-month research project with 12 companies at the leading edge of performance management, Kaplan and Norton[1] designed a set of measures that gave top managers a fast but comprehensive view of the business. They likened it to the dials and indicators of an aeroplane cockpit – the task of navigating and flying an aeroplane requires detailed information about fuel, air speed, altitude, bearings, destination and much more, and to fly without this information would be dangerous to everyone aboard. Similarly, a business that attempts to manage its complex operations with just a few measures, traditionally financial, cannot hope to be in total control or be sure of making the right decisions to meet its objectives.

The balanced scorecard encourages managers to look at their business from at least four different perspectives:

- The financial perspective – how do we look to stakeholders?
- The customer perspective – how do customers see us?
- The internal business perspective – what must we excel at?
- The innovation and learning perspective – can we continue to improve and create value?

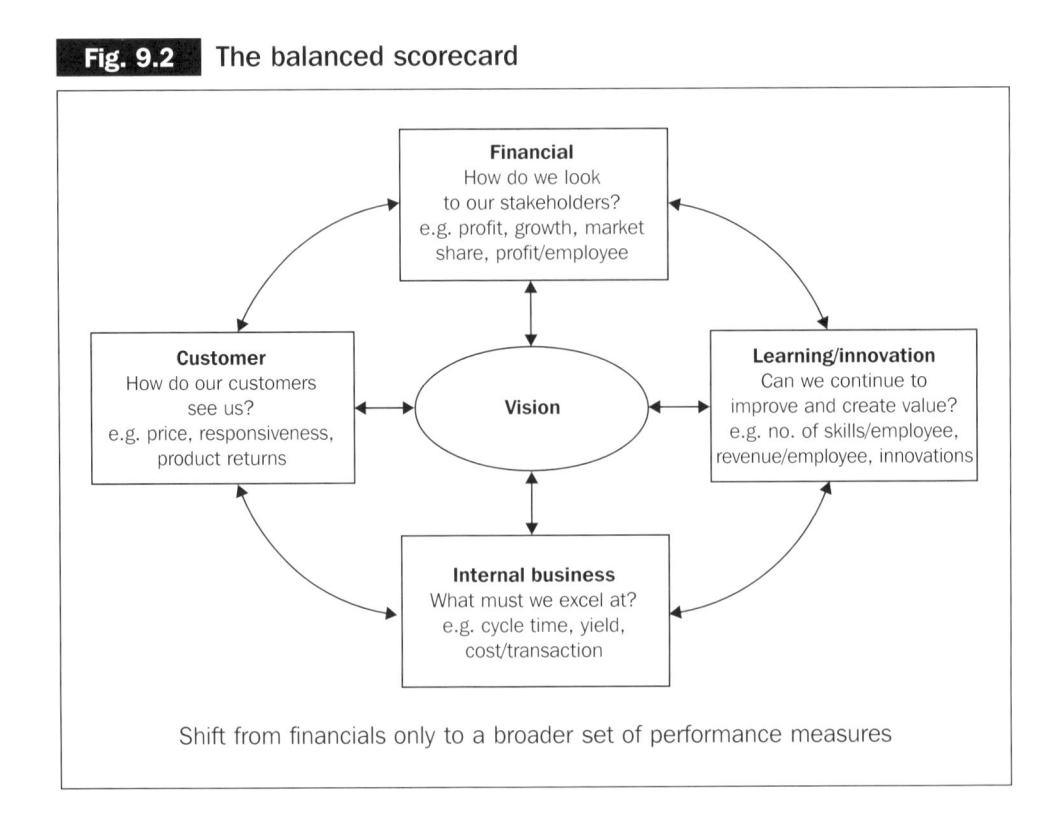

Fig. 9.2 The balanced scorecard

Financial
How do we look to our stakeholders?
e.g. profit, growth, market share, profit/employee

Customer
How do our customers see us?
e.g. price, responsiveness, product returns

Vision

Learning/innovation
Can we continue to improve and create value?
e.g. no. of skills/employee, revenue/employee, innovations

Internal business
What must we excel at?
e.g. cycle time, yield, cost/transaction

Shift from financials only to a broader set of performance measures

Figure 9.2 shows how to link the corporate vision to outcomes representing all perspectives of the business. Most companies have large amounts of information or data, usually in a form that is too detailed for senior managers to have time to digest. The idea at this level is to limit the number of measures to a minimum to ensure that the senior management team (SMT) concentrates on the achievement of the strategic goals. The 'balance' refers to balancing tension between the traditional financial and non-financial, operational, leading and lagging, and action-oriented and monitoring measures. It has the advantages of:

- bringing together in one report many of the seemingly disparate elements of the company's agenda;
- guarding against sub-optimization, by forcing senior management to consider all the measures together and ensuring that one objective is not achieved at the expense of another.

This can help to overcome the 'silo mentality' tendencies of some senior managers, who have traditionally pursued the objectives of their department irrespective of the effects and often to the detriment of the rest of the company. The SMT is forced to operate as a team, balancing the competing objectives to achieve the optimum result for the company as a whole.

The balanced scorecard fits in well with the 'bottom-up empowered' organization, putting strategy and organization, not control, at the centre. It establishes goals but assumes that people will adopt whatever behaviours and take whatever actions are necessary to arrive at those goals. The measures are designed to pull people towards the overall vision. Care must be taken in setting those measures, because performance measures drive behaviour.

When setting KPIs it important to appreciate that there are cause and effect relationships between measures and perspectives (*see* Fig. 9.3). Thus it recognises that it is improvements in learning and innovation that will help improve business processes, which in turn will benefit customers and have the desired impact in the financial results and contribute to the achievement of the strategy. When setting measures, it is important to be aware that some are lead indicators, e.g. the level of company orders, and others are lag indicators, e.g. profit. Careful monitoring of lead KPIs permits a business to take corrective action before it is too late.

Fig. 9.3 Defining the cause-and-effect relationships between perspectives

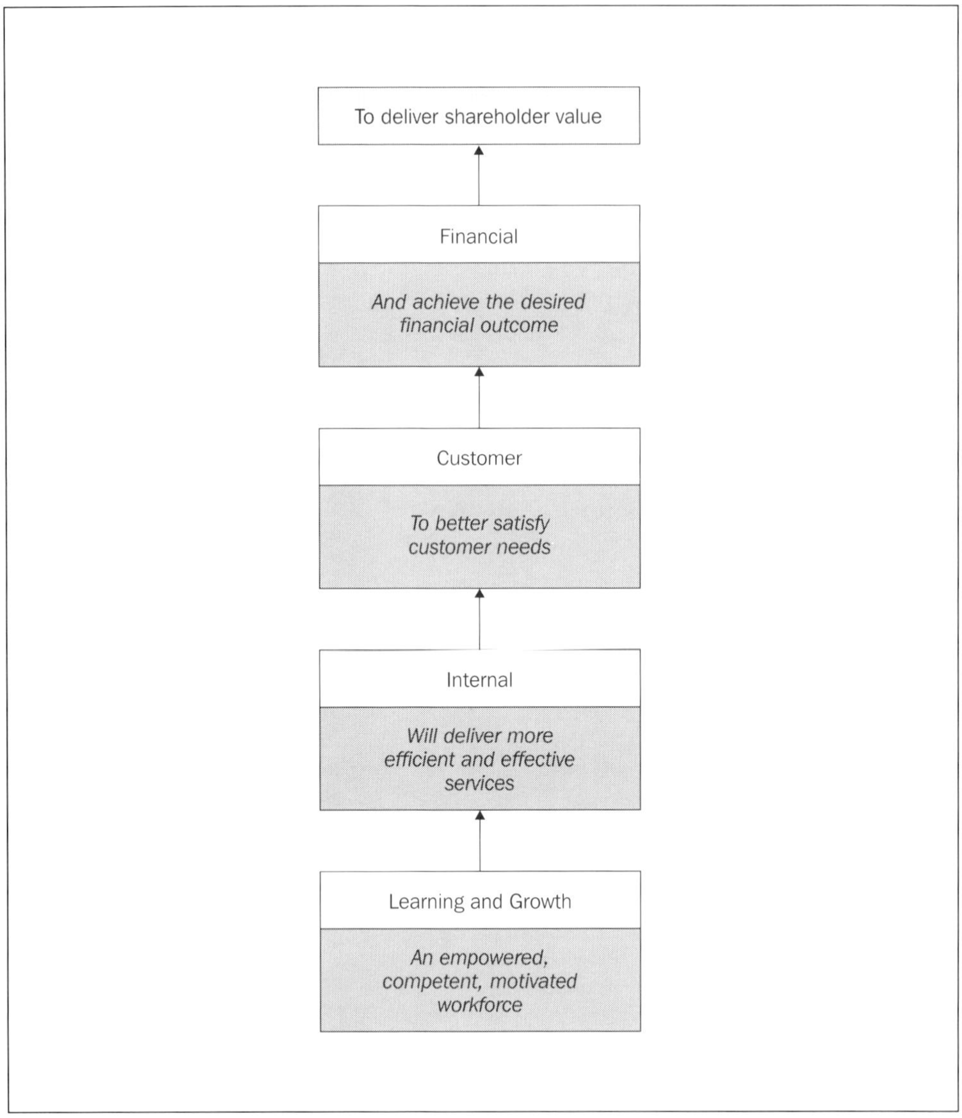

```
                To deliver shareholder value
                            ↑
                      ┌───────────┐
                      │ Financial │
                      ├───────────┤
                      │ And achieve the desired
                      │ financial outcome
                      └───────────┘
                            ↑
                      ┌───────────┐
                      │ Customer  │
                      ├───────────┤
                      │ To better satisfy
                      │ customer needs
                      └───────────┘
                            ↑
                      ┌───────────┐
                      │ Internal  │
                      ├───────────┤
                      │ Will deliver more
                      │ efficient and effective
                      │ services
                      └───────────┘
                            ↑
                      ┌───────────────────┐
                      │ Learning and Growth│
                      ├───────────────────┤
                      │ An empowered,
                      │ competent, motivated
                      │ workforce
                      └───────────────────┘
```

9.3 THE STRATEGY-FOCUSED ORGANIZATION

Kaplan and Norton[2] describe the evolution of the balanced scorecard from a measurement system to a system for managing change. They examine the impact of the BSC at some of the 200 companies that have implemented it, including Mobil Oil, Sigma Insurance and Charlotte City Council, and are able to demonstrate its success in operation. Bain & Company research shows that the BSC is now used by about half of North America's Fortune 1,000 companies; in Europe the estimate is between 40 and 45% and in Australia about 35%.

Kaplan and Norton show how closely the BSC in practice aligns itself with the concept of creating economic value. They emphasize again how the traditional budget makes it difficult to implement radical new strategies designed for the knowledge-based competition of the twenty-first century. Their research reveals that although most organizations are able to define a strategy, between 70% and 90% fail to execute it successfully. This is not surprising when research further reveals that 85% of management teams spend less than an hour a month discussing strategy. Kaplan and Norton found that although every organization had its own way of working, there were five principles that ran through the strategy-focused organizations:

- Mobilize change through strong executive leadership from the top.

- Translate strategy into operational terms using the BSC and strategy maps.

- Align the organization to the strategy by cascading it down through the organization to SBUs and SSCs etc.

- Make strategy everyone's everyday job and reinforce that by setting up personal goals and objectives and then link variable compensation to their achievement.

- Make strategy a continual process by linking strategies to the planning and budgeting process, the information systems and management meetings.

So in contrast to Fig. 8.4 (page 134), Kaplan and Norton are advocating a strategic management system designed around a longer-term view, where the BSC becomes the focal point in a continuous process that translates the vision, communicates and links to business planning and feeds back the learning to the vision.

Kaplan and Norton also describe strategy mapping.[2] A strategy map for a BSC becomes embedded in a chain of cause-and-effect logic that connects the desired outcomes from the strategy with the drivers that will lead to their achievement. The strategy map describes the process for transforming intangible assets into tangible customer and financial outcomes. It provides executives with a framework for describing and managing strategy in a knowledge economy. This generic architecture has four strategic themes:

- *Build the franchise* – create value and develop new products, services, markets and customer segments.

- *Increase customer value* – redefine, deepen and expand relationships with existing customers.

- *Achieve operational excellence* – create value through internal productivity and supply-chain management and efficiency.

- *Be a good corporate citizen* – manage relationships with external stakeholders and the environment etc.

For each of these strategic themes a cause and effect diagram of the four BSC perspectives needs to be drawn to explain the strategy and then linked to the BSC KPIs – *see* Figs 9.4 and 9.5 which both relate to the operating excellence theme of a retailer.

Fig. 9.4 Strategy map of a retailer

```
Strategic theme: operating excellence

Financial  ───────  Shareholder value
                    Grow revenues    Economies of scale

Customer   ───────  Prompt and courteous service
                    Attract and retain more customers
                    Good value prices

Internal   ───────  Quality shopping experience
                    Sourcing quality

Learning   ───────  Trained motivated staff
```

Fig. 9.5 Balanced scorecard of a retailer

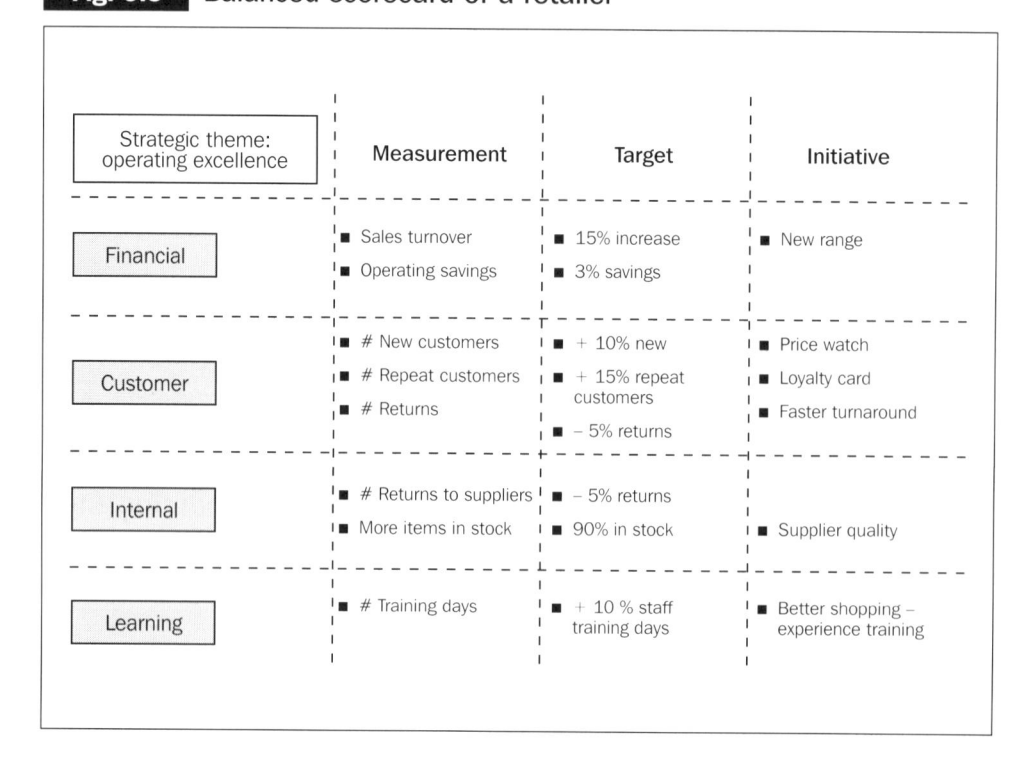

Strategic theme: operating excellence	Measurement	Target	Initiative
Financial	■ Sales turnover ■ Operating savings	■ 15% increase ■ 3% savings	■ New range
Customer	■ # New customers ■ # Repeat customers ■ # Returns	■ + 10% new ■ + 15% repeat customers ■ – 5% returns	■ Price watch ■ Loyalty card ■ Faster turnaround
Internal	■ # Returns to suppliers ■ More items in stock	■ – 5% returns ■ 90% in stock	■ Supplier quality
Learning	■ # Training days	■ + 10 % staff training days	■ Better shopping – experience training

Evidence is provided of the success of the BSC approach to strategy from many case studies, including Mobil Oil Division North America Marketing and Refining. It had consistently been the worst performer within its peer group in the four years (1990–4) leading up to its adoption of these new techniques. However, following the introduction of its new strategy and the BSC in 1994, it became the leading performer amongst its peer group/industry sector for the next four years (1995–8). This success was so quick that it could not have been through the introduction of major new launches or capital investments but instead must be a result of capitalizing on assets that already existed through focus on the BSC to disseminate strategy. The BSC created a performance mindset used by the new management team to cascade its strategy down the 18 SBUs and 14 SSCs.

Many of the principles that are prominent in value-based management are also now emphasized as crucial to the success of BSC implementation. These include the need to set up SBUs and SSCs, which operate autonomously and need to be linked via a cascade of BSCs back to the corporate, top-level BSC.

Equally important is the need to link incentives to the achievement of targets. An example given by Kaplan and Norton[2] emphasizes the importance of driving the desired behaviours by:

- linking 10% of the bonus to the corporate result;
- making up to a further 20% available, based on
    - the results of the division (6%)
    - the SBU itself (14%);
- setting the base pay at 90%;
- enabling up to 120% of previous pay for maximum achievement of targets.

9.4 WEIGHTING THE BALANCED SCORECARD

The scores applied to different parts of the balanced scorecard will vary according to the importance of that measure to the overall vision. The importance placed on different measures can often vary year on year, as the emphasis changes in the achievement of goals. Weightings are commonly applied on the BSCs used in managing outsourcing contracts.

Example of a weighted balanced scorecard for outsourcing the finance function

The scorecard criteria
- The provide company runs the finance company on behalf of the source company for an annual fee of costs plus a margin.

- The annual budgeted amount for 1996/7 of £750,000 fee is subject to a 'risk/reward margin' based on a BSC score comprised as follows:
  - financial perspective: overall costs of running the service 30%
  - customer perspective: satisfaction of functional user groups 25%
  - business perspective: satisfaction of internal management 25%
  - innovation: number of process/system improvements 20%.

% Margin	% Score
25	100
20	80
15	60
10	40
5	20
1	0

Score ratings are agreed as follows:

Points rating	Costs incurred (£k)	Number of innovations	User/management
5	650	3	10
4	700	2	8
3	750	1.5	6
2	800	1	4
1	850	0.5	2
0	900	0	0

Annual results and scores

Measure	Value (£k)	Points	Weighting (%)	Result
Costs incurred	800	2	30	0.6
Number of innovations	1	2	20	0.4
User satisfaction rating	8	4	25	1.0
Management satisfaction	6	3	25	0.75
				2.75

Margin calculation

- 2.75 as a percentage of maximum 5 = 55%.
- 55% score equates to 13.75% margin (maximum 25%) of £750,000 planned costs, giving £103,125 risk/reward margin earned on the contract.

NB: Actual costs of £800,000 are not used, as that would encourage higher costs!

9.5 THE TEN COMMANDMENTS OF IMPLEMENTATION

Research carried out in Europe in 1996 using seven European companies as case studies resulted in findings known as the 'ten commandments of balanced scorecard implementation'.[3] The objective was to try to understand the mixed success of the application of this simple, commonsense concept of using a balanced set of performance indicators to run an organization. The ten commandments to be followed for successful implementation were concluded to be:

The dos

1. Use the scorecard as an implementation pad for strategic goals.
2. Ensure that strategic goals are in place before the scorecard is implemented.
3. Ensure that a top-level (non-financial) sponsor backs the scorecard and that line managers are committed to the project.
4. Implement a pilot before introducing the new scorecard.
5. Carry out an 'entry review' for each business unit before implementing the scorecard.

The do nots

6. Use the scorecard to obtain extra top-down control.
7. Attempt to standardize the project. The scorecard must be tailormade.
8. Underestimate the need for training and communication in using the scorecard.
9. Seek complexity, nor strive for perfection.
10. Underestimate the extra administrative workload and costs of periodic scorecard reporting.

To these may be added an eleventh commandment:

11. Do not start implementing a balanced scorecard unless you know what you hope to achieve.

Together, these commandments provide good, sound advice that could be applied to almost any project undertaken by an organization.

9.6 LINKS TO QUALITY FRAMEWORKS

The Malcolm Baldrige measurement and management framework was developed in the USA in 1987, to recognize companies that are leaders in providing increased quality and value to their customers in an internationally competitive era. Funded by the European Commission, the European Foundation for Quality Management's (EFQM) Business Excellence model was launched in 1992, to raise the level of competitiveness throughout Europe by identifying role-model companies and disseminating best practice. Although not designed to assist implementation of strategy, these quality award frameworks are a way for companies to identify key processes. The EFQM Business Excellence model (*see* Fig. 9.6) uses nine elements to assess an organization's success against award criteria, specifically with reference to quality. In 2000 the EFQM drafted changes to its Business Excellence model to incorporate knowledge as well as people and to recognize the importance of partnerships in enabling customer-focused processes. The draft revision also amends business results to organizational performance. The Malcolm Baldrige National Quality Award similarly has seven award criteria (*see* Fig. 9.7).

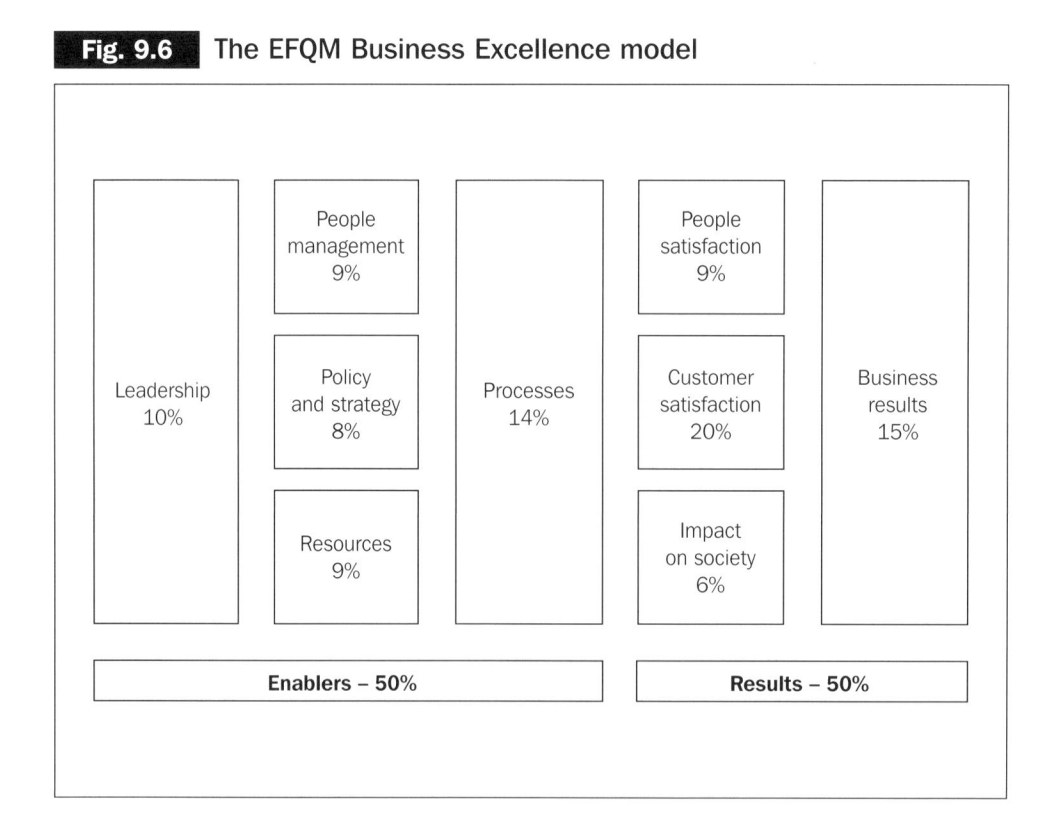

Fig. 9.6 The EFQM Business Excellence model

Enablers – 50%			Results – 50%	
Leadership 10%	People management 9%	Processes 14%	People satisfaction 9%	Business results 15%
	Policy and strategy 8%		Customer satisfaction 20%	
	Resources 9%		Impact on society 6%	

EFQM

Enablers

		Scoring (%)
(i)	Leadership	10
(ii)	People management	9
(iii)	Policy and strategy	8
(iv)	Resources	9
(v)	Processes	14
		50

Results

		Scoring (%)
(vi)	People satisfaction	9
(vii)	Customer satisfaction	20
(viii)	Impact on society	20
(ix)	Business results	15
		50

Fig 9.7 The Malcolm Baldrige National Quality Award

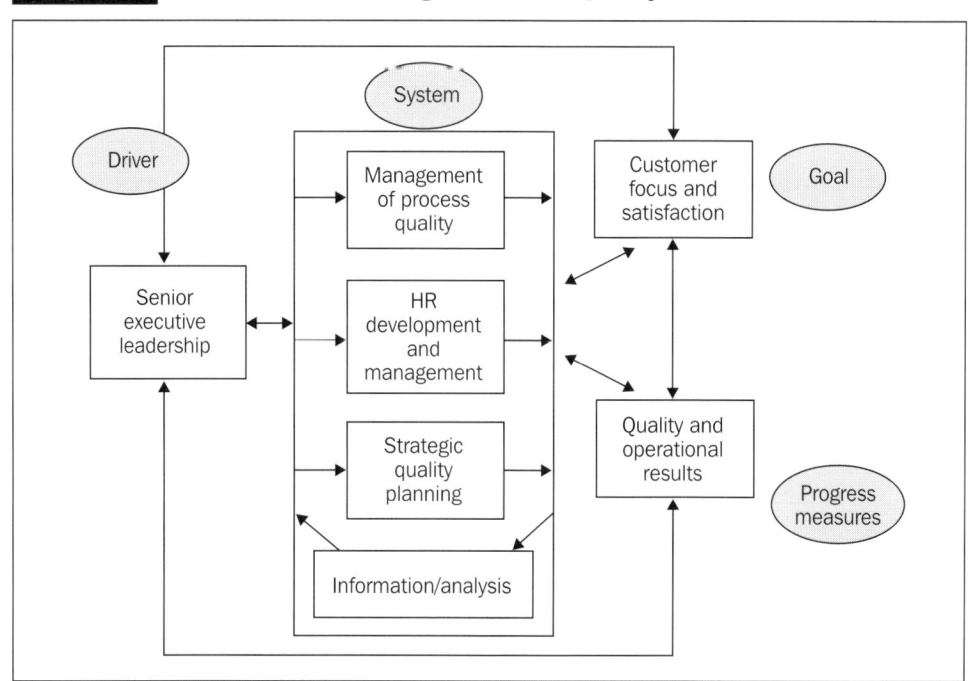

The key elements of each model are as follows:

Malcolm Baldrige

		Scoring (points)
i	Leadership	95
ii	Information analysis	75
iii	Strategic quality planning	60
iv	Human resource development and management	150
v	Management of the quality process	140
vi	Quality and operational results	180
vii	Customer focus and satisfaction	300
		1,000

Because of the detail and focus of these quality models, there is considerable merit in linking this detail to both BSCs and/or activity-based management systems. This has been successfully achieved in several companies, for example in British Telecom, and has become widespread under the auspices of Best Value, with many local authority organizations, like the police, already using EFQM.

9.7 Case studies

e-BSC

Cedric Read in *eCFO*[4] reveals that studies of internet companies have resulted in a number of e-metrics emerging to evaluate the seven dynamics of e-business:

- customer focus
- brand equity
- management capabilities
- business design
- content
- agility
- timing.

These need to be incorporated into a BSC.

Media and publishing business

A company with 90 different websites, which had sprung up independently across its magazine and radio holdings, faced some pivotal questions:

- How much is all this costing?
- Are we making any money?

- How can we channel all our scattered internet resources into a viable digital business and create new revenue streams?
- How can we apply e-metrics that link to the seven drivers of shareholder value and the business strategy?

It combined all the e-businesses into one and created a balanced e-BSC. It followed five steps:

- The strategy for the new e-business was described, together with critical success factors: 200 drivers were identified.
- A dynamic performance measurement model was created.
- Managers selected those KPIs that were thought to be strategically important; 45 emerged in the ten-cluster categories – advertising, marketing, content, e-commerce, technology, customer, staff, finance, business development and value delivered.
- Then each driver was defined by name, how it was to be measured, how often it would be reported, the time period reflected, who owned the data and the strategic goal.
- Finally, a scorecard visual format was designed for presentation purposes. It showed the 45 KPIs at the aggregate level and on a site-by-site level, showing both B2B and B2C perspectives.

KPIs selected included:

- Advertising:
  - forward ad bookings
  - click-through rates on banners sold
  - advertising revenue
  - inventory utilization
  - advertising ratings.
- Marketing:
  - user acquisition cost
  - value of PR
  - return rates of registered users
  - session per unique user
  - impression per session
  - session length
  - impressions
  - sessions
  - unique users
  - new users (net)
  - active registered users
  - total registered users.

Lastminute.com

Julian Culhane, CFO of Lastminute.com, explained[5] how he found it necessary to complement the traditional financial indicators – sales, profit and loss, cash position and spending on marketing and technology – with some e-business measures. These 'dash board' web metrics included:

- how many shoppers have visited the firm's sites across Europe;
- how many of them made purchases;
- how many are repeat customers;
- how many items are bought on average on each visit;
- how much it costs to draw a visitor to the lastminute.com site;
- what customer payback levels are.

By getting this data in real time, with a one-page flash report daily, decisions can be responsive. For example, special offers can be changed several times a day based on click-through rates. The web allows data to be collected on customers in a way that is not possible for off-line companies, making it easier to adopt a customer-centric culture.

ProXchange

Similarly, Michael Ogrinz, CFO of ProXchange, explains his 'seven-level waterfall', in which each level corresponds to a certain part of the website's transaction process.

- At the top level is the first-time visitor,
- level two is repeat visitors,
- level three registered users,
- level four registered users who interact with the site,
- level five bidders,
- level six accepted bidders and level seven commission from trades. This monitoring enables visibility of where visitors were getting stuck in the system and allows necessary corrective action to be taken.

NetValue

NetValue is an internet monitoring firm, which has panels of 3,000–5,000 people in each of seven European countries and can accurately predict traffic flows across the internet for benchmark purposes.

9.8 Case study
Manchester Housing's information strategy[6]

Manchester's vision and objectives

Manchester City Council's corporate aims and objectives give the city a clear, focused and realistic vision for the future. They are placed firmly in a Best Value framework to develop and deliver services and to define the city's role in the national and regional context. They describe how the city's future will be secured. Together, the corporate strategies deliver the vision of Manchester as:

- a European regional capital – a centre for investment and growth;
- an international city of outstanding commercial, cultural and creative potential;
- an area distinguished by the quality of life and sense of well-being enjoyed by its residents;
- an area where all residents have the opportunity to participate – making their communities truly sustainable.

The City Council's wider economic, environmental and social strategies consolidate the corporate housing strategy, ensuring responsiveness and adaptation to local needs. This approach is essential to deliver co-ordinated services and create places where people want to live. Manchester Housing manages about 70,000 council homes in addition to its corporate objectives of regeneration of the city. The 1998–2001 Corporate Housing Strategy defines Manchester Housing's objectives as follows:

1. To provide a choice of desirable and affordable housing to improve the quality of life for current residents and to encourage people to come and live in Manchester.
2. To make proper provision for people who are homeless or inadequately housed and for people being cared for in the community.
3. To offer tenants a wide choice of alternative management and ownership arrangements through empowerment, effective consultation and real participation.
4. To deliver a customer-oriented, locally based, Best Value housing service that is seen as a market leader.
5. To prevent homelessness by corporate intervention.
6. To use a comprehensive approach to improve housing conditions and help communities become more cohesive.
7. To deal with the problems of low demand evident in some areas of our housing.

Manchester Housing's information strategy: rationale

By using Business Objects (an Integrated Decision Support Tool) and its intranet, Manchester Housing is able to bring together all its various sources of information and present them in such a way that management can easily monitor and control all aspects of the plans. The introduction of a balanced scorecard allows all the necessary indicators that have to be controlled to be monitored by the Departmental Management Team (DMT), enabling its members to keep their 'finger on the pulse' at all times. Additionally, once defined, the performance indicators provide one of the ways for demonstrating Best Value by benchmarking them against similar organizations and facilitate focused performance reviews.

Methodology

With its three-year plan objectives clearly laid down, the DMT was able to identify the key outcomes to be monitored over the next year under the following headings:

- housing demand and rehousing
- estate management

- housing investment
- Best Value
- crime and disorder
- human resource issues
- finance issues.

1 Beneath each of these outcomes is a hierarchy of critical success factors and associated measures, each with differing levels of importance to the achievement of the desired outcome, the top level of which can be seen in Fig. 9.8.

Fig. 9.8 MH – Balanced scorecard outcomes

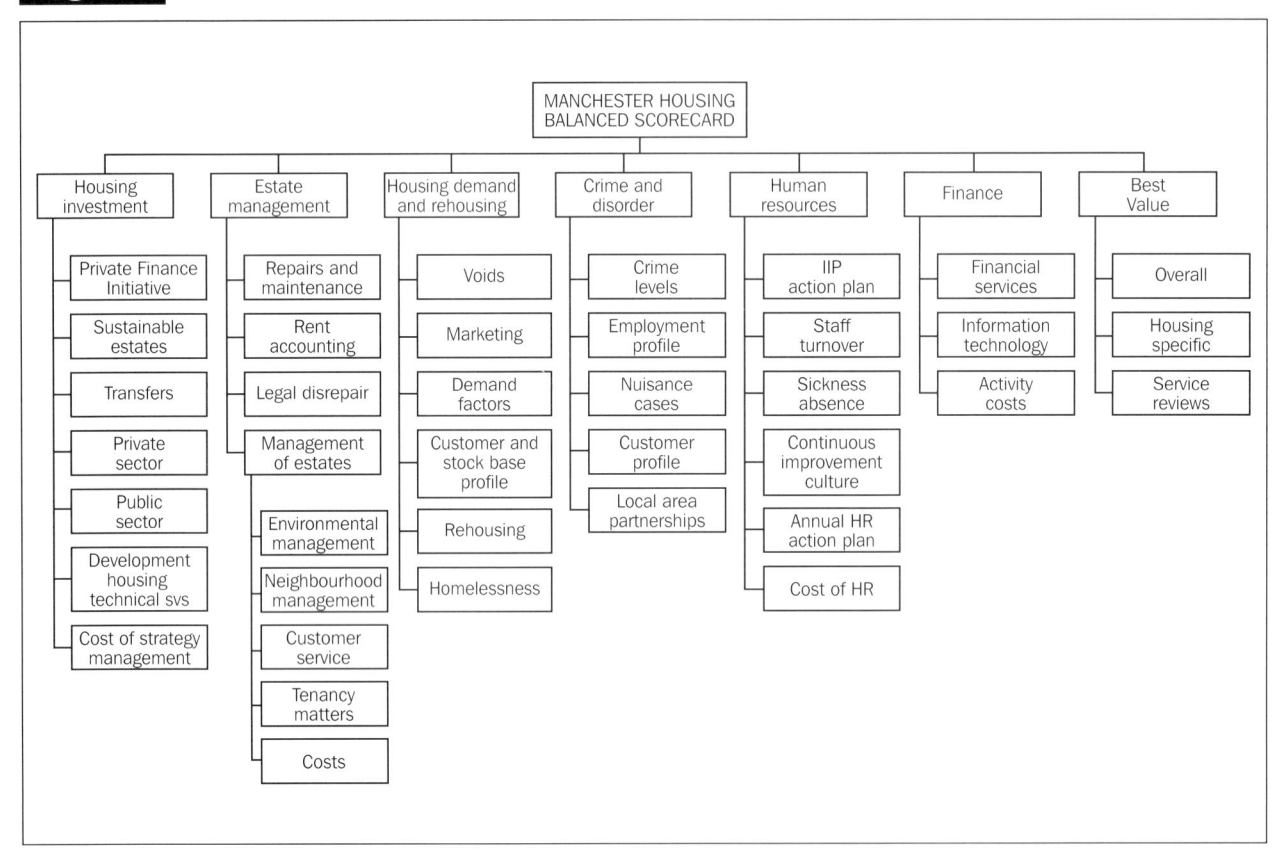

MANCHESTER HOUSING BALANCED SCORECARD

- Housing investment
  - Private Finance Initiative
  - Sustainable estates
  - Transfers
  - Private sector
  - Public sector
  - Development housing technical svs
  - Cost of strategy management
- Estate management
  - Repairs and maintenance
  - Rent accounting
  - Legal disrepair
  - Management of estates
    - Environmental management
    - Neighbourhood management
    - Customer service
    - Tenancy matters
    - Costs
- Housing demand and rehousing
  - Voids
  - Marketing
  - Demand factors
  - Customer and stock base profile
  - Rehousing
  - Homelessness
- Crime and disorder
  - Crime levels
  - Employment profile
  - Nuisance cases
  - Customer profile
  - Local area partnerships
- Human resources
  - IIP action plan
  - Staff turnover
  - Sickness absence
  - Continuous improvement culture
  - Annual HR action plan
  - Cost of HR
- Finance
  - Financial services
  - Information technology
  - Activity costs
- Best Value
  - Overall
  - Housing specific
  - Service reviews

2 The use of Business Objects enables each measure to be weighted. As performance indicators are not mutually exclusive to each outcome, the same indicators can occur under more than one outcome, for example customer profile, and can be given a different weighting in each outcome arm.

3 One of the detailed hierarchies beneath the outcomes can be seen in Fig. 9.9, which has been weighted to reflect significance.

4 By using alerts, exceptions and trend analysis (see Fig. 9.10) only those measures that are not on target will be highlighted throughout the hierarchy. This enables DMT to see at a glance if all outcomes are going according to plan (green), or give cause for concern (amber) or need immediate attention (red), and to 'drill down' and identify the root cause of the problem.

Fig. 9.9 MH – Housing demand and rehousing

Housing demand and rehousing

- **Rehousing** (property type and size) 15%
  - Applicants general/transfers/homeless supported housing 30%
  - Central register activity 15%
  - Offers/refusals/acceptances (types) (reasons for refusal) 20%
  - Cost of rehousing 15%
  - Offer/acceptance rate 20%

- **Voids** (property type and size) 30%
  - Number of voids 25%
  - Average time of void 10%
  - Frequency of void 10%
  - Reason for void 20%
  - Average length of tenure 15%
  - Cost of relet 15%
    - Rent loss 70%
    - Void repair costs 30%
      - Building 25%
      - Security 25%
      - Decorating 25%
      - Vandalism 25%
  - Cost of management of voids 5%

- **Marketing** 15%
  - Hotline promotions 15%
  - Specific/ongoing projects 15%
  - Poster campaigns
  - Lets (total compared to hotline/open days) 30%
  - Cost of marketing 25%
  - Open days (no. attended, lets, etc.) 15%

- **Demand factors** (property type and size) 25%
  - Support needs (disability, drugs) 10%
  - Estate management 25%
    - Chartermark measures 15%
    - Environmental (rubbish, cost) 70%
    - Tenant groups (TMOs/TAs) 15%
  - Demand levels (no, low, demand)
  - Crime and disorder 35%
    - Employment profile (levels, types) 10%
    - Crime levels (types, volume) 30%
    - Nuisance cases (mediations/no of voids) cost of nuisance 30%
    - Vandalism 30%
  - Social exclusion
    - City atlas (schools, etc.) 30%

- **Stock/customer base profile** 10%
  - Customer profile 40%
    - Waiting list profile (furnished/unfurnished) 30%
    - Other tenure 10%
    - Homelessness profile 15%
    - Hotline caller profile (reasons for rejection) 25%
    - Tenants profile 20%
  - Stock profile (property type and size) 60%
    - Local authority (includes stock condition) 60%
    - Private landlords/owner occupiers 10%
    - Registered social landlords 30%

- **Homelessness single/families** 5%
  - Presentations nos and profile
    - Representations nos/no of times/profile
  - Investigations
    - No duty nos/profile
    - Admissions nos/profile
      - Discretionary local connection/profile/nos
      - Legal five criteria/profiles
      - Length of time to complete (30 days requirement)
  - Permanent solution profile/no by SPT/length of tenure
    - Rehoused where and what type
      - Council
      - Other
        - Supported homes scheme
    - Length of time from presentation to permanent housing
    - Length of time offer to occupation reason for delay
  - Temporary accommodation profile/transfers length of tenure
    - Type of accommodation
      - Council
      - Homeless families temporary scheme (no of legal cases)
      - Other (B&B, private/hostels)
  - Costs singles/families, etc.
  - Quotas monitor targets by teams

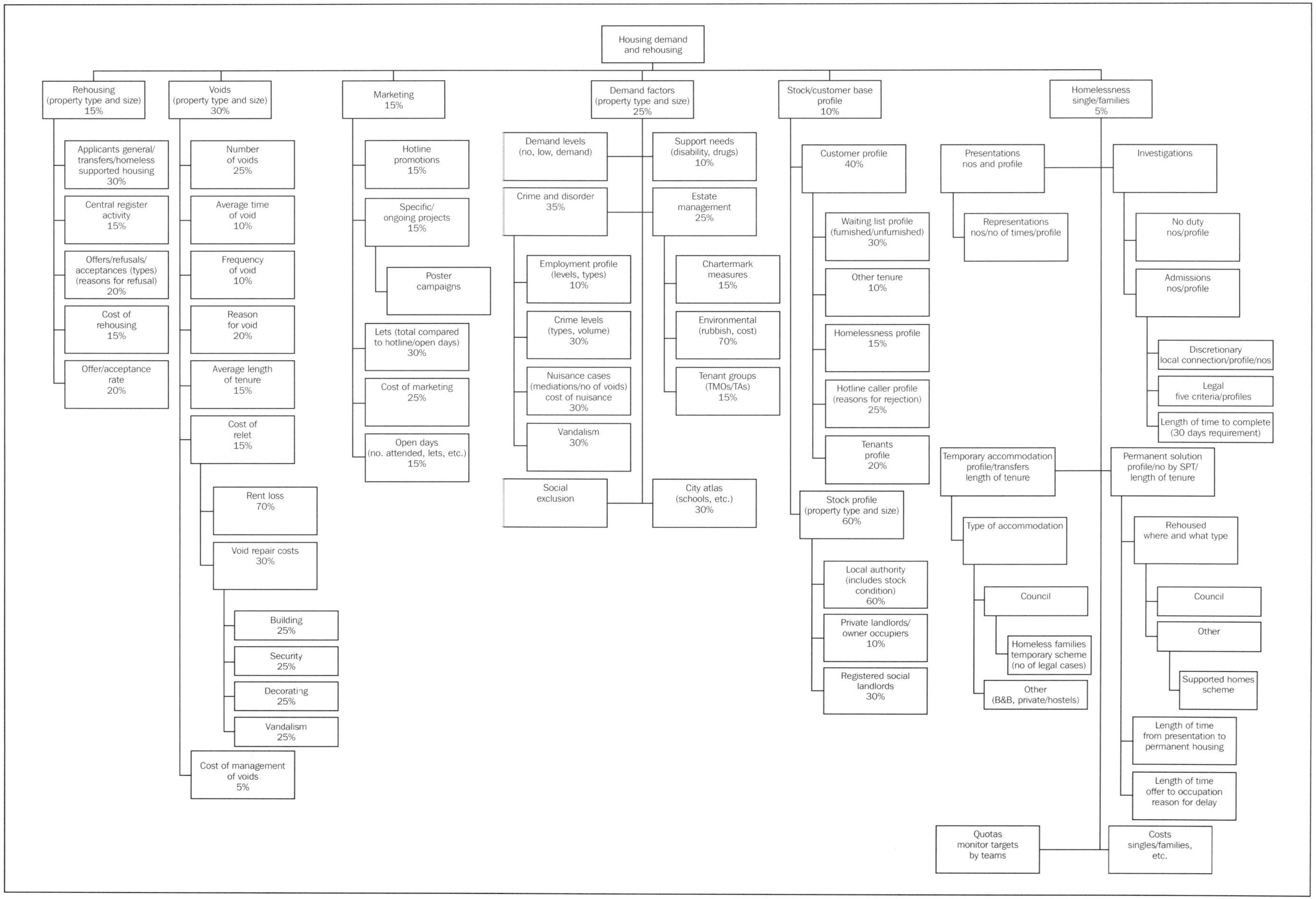

Fig. 9.10 MH – Graphical trends

XXX Housing team

16 Voids in week 11
+2 Since last week
+1 Over target

5 Beneath each hierarchy of measures it is possible to 'drill down' geographically to regions, areas and teams to see where problems have arisen and if there is variance from plan (see in Fig. 9.11). The weightings, alerts and trends are shown at all levels in the hierarchy and, in fact, 'drill up' from the lowest level.

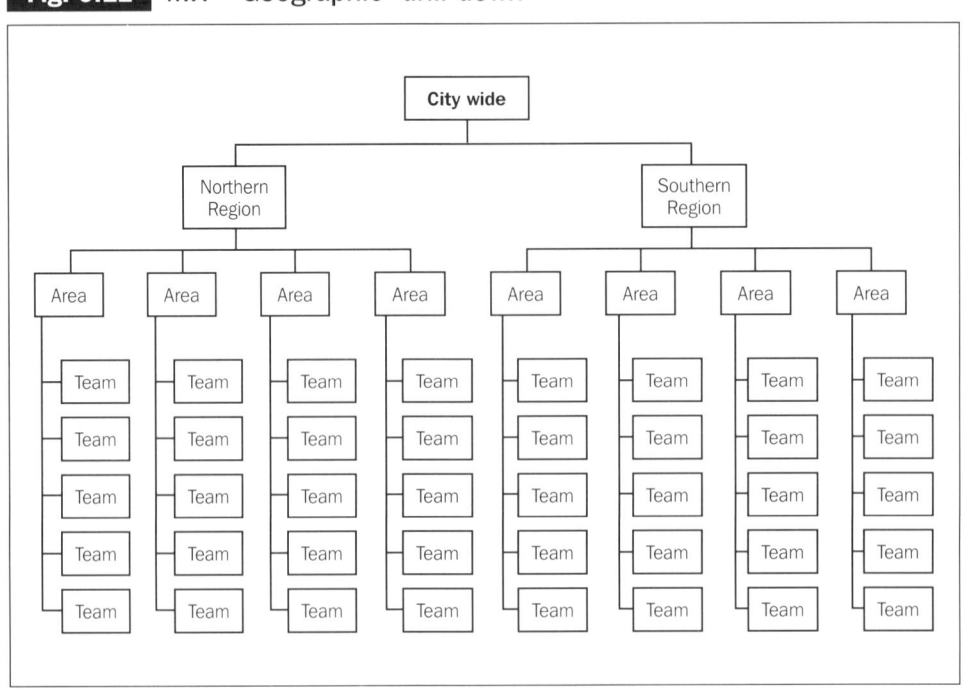

Fig. 9.11 MH – Geographic 'drill down'

The balanced scorecard

6 Other views allow each functional director to see all the measures that relate to their areas of responsibility in one hierarchy, with exceptions and alerts drawing attention to problems needing their immediate attention (see Fig. 9.12).

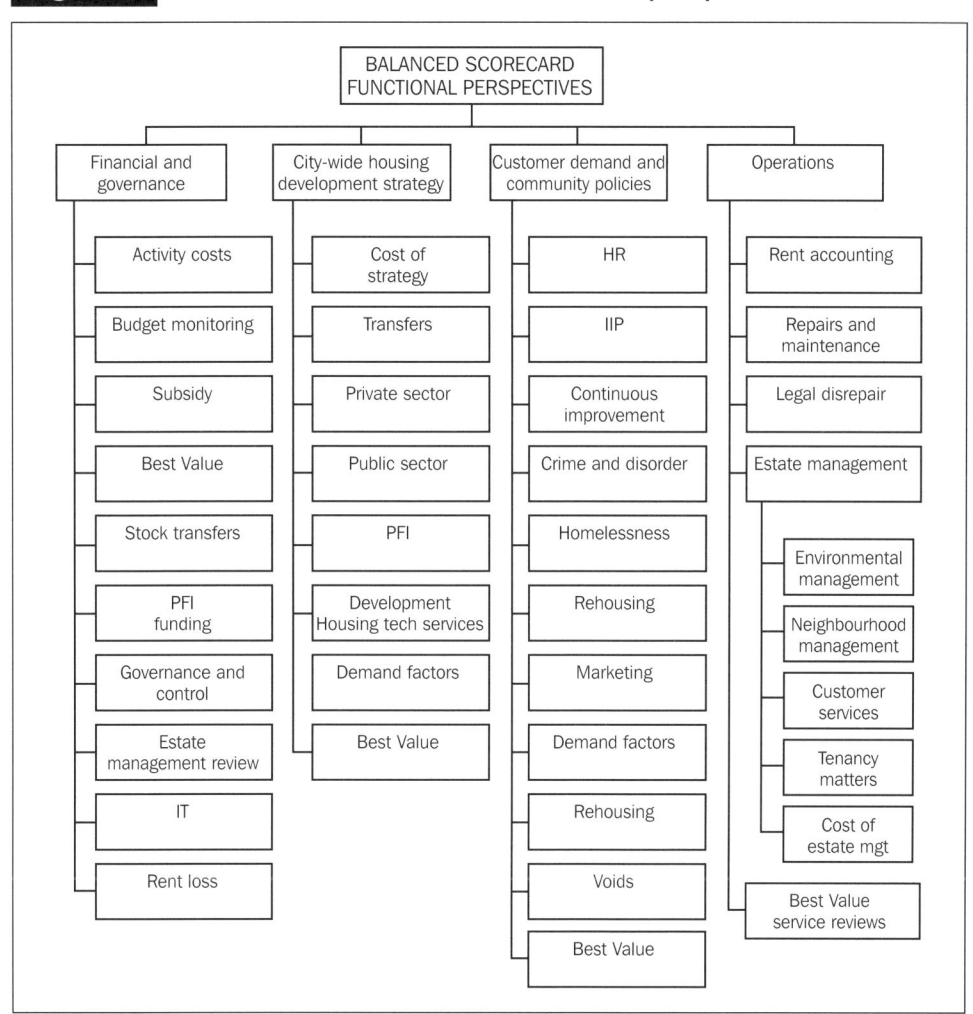

Fig. 9.12 MH – Balanced scorecard functional perspectives

```
                         BALANCED SCORECARD
                       FUNCTIONAL PERSPECTIVES
     ┌──────────────────────┬──────────────────────┬──────────────────────┐
  Financial and      City-wide housing     Customer demand and      Operations
  governance       development strategy    community policies
     │                      │                      │                      │
  Activity costs      Cost of strategy            HR                Rent accounting
  Budget monitoring   Transfers                   IIP               Repairs and maintenance
  Subsidy             Private sector     Continuous improvement     Legal disrepair
  Best Value          Public sector      Crime and disorder         Estate management
  Stock transfers     PFI                Homelessness                   │
  PFI funding         Development        Rehousing                  Environmental management
                      Housing tech services                         Neighbourhood management
  Governance and      Demand factors     Marketing                  Customer services
  control
  Estate              Best Value         Demand factors             Tenancy matters
  management review
  IT                                     Rehousing                  Cost of estate mgt
  Rent loss                              Voids                      Best Value service reviews
                                         Best Value
```

7 Equally, views can be defined that cut across at any level in the hierarchy, linking any specified measures, for example a statutory KPI view. The use of the intranet not only allows these hyperlink features to be used but enables focused access across the network to be given to dispersed staff, based on password controls.

Requirement

■ Prior to the purchase of Business Objects, information was held in many different sources, some of which were not under the control of Manchester Housing. This made access difficult. Transporting all the relevant information into a single data warehouse enabled information to be accessed. Business Objects can also access information held by individual departments (internal or external), as long as access is available to the server, so one of its most important roles was in pulling together information from diverse sources. However, without the balanced scorecard approach, Business Objects provided a data-rich information pool but was not sufficiently focused to enable the wood to be distinguished from the trees.

- Having brought all of the information together into one database, it was then necessary to translate this data, often held as spreadsheets at team level, into easily understood trend information. This would show, for example, the trend over a period and against target in a graph, 'drilling up' from team to organization level, using traffic lights to alert to any problems. This enabled all staff to be aware of problems without the need for each interested party to spend inordinate amounts of time calculating the necessary facts or having to 'spot' the issues in a mass of data or statistics. Having set in place the 'rules', Business Objects can carry out the calculations automatically on a weekly/monthly basis, reducing the need for 'routine' paper reports to be circulated.

- While the City Council's Service Plan is a very detailed and lengthy document, updated twice a year, it does not always hold the most pertinent information or insist on specific targets and measures. The Service Plan is related to Manchester's objectives by number, but it is not possible to weight the importance of any of the measures to contributing to the achievement of those goals. What this information strategy allows is for all the information currently held in the Service Plan to be linked directly to objectives, with clear targets and weightings indicating importance, and it ensures that all business perspectives, including finance, for example, are considered in respect of each planned outcome.

- The need to demonstrate Best Value is now a requirement and what this information strategy allows is a mechanism utilizing the techniques defined in the Best Value White Paper, including for example activity costing. It provides for the first stage of benchmark comparisons to be made against similar organizations, leaving the way clear for process mapping, and utilizing the full range of indicators identified under the balanced scorecard principles. This clear definition of performance indicators, at such an early stage, will allow Manchester to lead the way in influencing how Best Value NPIs should proceed within housing. In particular, it will facilitate the Compare element of the four Cs of Best Value, in addition to enabling a mechanism for Challenging, Consulting and demonstrating Competitiveness in service reviews.

- Finally, once built, the comprehensive set of hierarchical indicators, with associated targets and objectives, forms the basis of a business improvement model, enabling changes in measures, targets and objectives necessary to meet future years' Service Plans to be effected easily.

10

Benchmarking

- 10.1 Introduction 169
- 10.2 Types of benchmarking 169
- 10.3 Data-gathering methods 171
- 10.4 Phases of the benchmarking process 172
- 10.5 The Benchmarking Code of Conduct 175
- 10.6 Benefits of benchmarking 177
- 10.7 Case study – Tower Hamlets benchmarking project 177

Benchmarking

10.1 INTRODUCTION

Benchmarking is a tool used to establish processes, costs and performance indicators and compare them against similar organizations, with the aim of identifying and progressing towards 'best practice and best value' through continuous improvement. The importance of ensuring 'true comparability' cannot be stressed strongly enough. It is unlikely that any two products or services will be identical; the key is to identify all the relevant performance measures, ensuring that the level of service is clearly demonstrated. In this way similar services can be compared, with differences clearly understood.

No two organizations carrying out the same services will necessarily agree on the 'best' level of service to be provided in terms of quality, time and cost at all stages in the process. However, by making comparisons they each learn about the other's costs, methods, procedures, values and judgements. At the end of the process, providers will need to justify the 'value' in the service they are providing and it will be up to customers to decide what level of service they are willing to pay for. Benchmarking can be facilitated by utilizing the activity-based techniques described in *Business Process Management*,[1] particularly the definition and prioritization of service levels, whilst balanced scorecard techniques are discussed in Chapter 9 of this book.

10.2 TYPES OF BENCHMARKING

Internal

Depending on the type and size of organization, it is often possible to benchmark services internally. This can be because there are several operational units performing the same tasks or because there are numerous subsidiaries/divisions/SBUs all having their own support functions, including, for example, finance, personnel, training, purchasing, facilities management and payroll. Internal benchmarking, wherever possible, should precede external benchmarking.

External databases

There are now a vast number of external databases, provided mainly by firms of consultants, which make industry, functional, process and other specific comparisons. These are variable in nature and degrees of usefulness. The questions to ask when selecting a database include:

- How many organizations are taking part?

- Over what period have the comparisons been made? Beware of any over more than a two-year period.
- Are they divided into organization size, industry sector etc.?
- What information is analyzed and at what level? Be wary of those that deal at a superficial level and are unable to identify important differences in processes.
- What data are fed back and how often are they updated?
- Is access offered to other benchmark organizations?
- What does it cost?

Two such databases in the finance function are PwC's Global Benchmarks Alliance and Hackett Benchmark's ongoing study. The Global Benchmarks Alliance is reasonably priced, has many organizations participating, gives extensive feedback and offers contact with other benchmark organizations. However, it does operate at a high level of process.

Collaborative

Collaborative benchmarking falls into two categories:

In the sector

Again, large numbers of collaborative initiatives are now taking place, and numbers will grow considerably with the advent of Best Value in the public sector, where benchmarking is a condition of the philosophy. Collaborative initiatives also occur in the private sector, providing that the exchange of information is carefully controlled, often by a third party. One example, which has been under way for a number of years, is that of the London Boroughs Process Benchmarking facilitated by Tower Hamlets and detailed in the case study at the end of this chapter.

Outside the sector

Collaboration does not have to take place within the same industry sector, especially where competitive pressures make it impossible. The support processes discussed above in internal benchmarking lend themselves to benchmarking across a wide range of organizations within the public and private sectors. Equally, benchmarking partners can be identified who share similar operational problems but are in different business sectors. For example:

- British Airports Authority, Wembley Stadium and Ascot Racecourse all share the problems that come with managing large numbers of people and cars;
- McDonald's, banks and the Post Office (Consignia) all share the problems associated with customers queuing for service.

Competitive

Benchmarking in competitive situations is obviously more difficult. Sometimes information can be found in the public domain (discussed below), or a more unusual approach may be called for. A well-publicized example is Xerox, which:

- runs a competitive analysis laboratory to test and analyze competitors' products, testing after-sales service by calling out engineers and measuring their performance;
- bought ten Canon personal copiers when they were first introduced and gave them to its customers to analyze and test their reactions;
- studied Japanese inventory methods and as a result reduced the number of vendors from 5,000 to 300;
- compared itself to Kodak, IBM and Bell; one metric it used in comparisons was the median time from concept to product.

10.3 DATA-GATHERING METHODS

Data-gathering methods for benchmarking will vary in terms of cost, amount and accuracy of the data collected and must be driven by the purpose of the benchmarking. They include:

- clearing houses, exchange groups and benchmarking clubs (illustrated in the case study at the end of the chapter);
- consultant and academic research, frequently carried out for publication in conjunction with sponsors; for example, CIMA Research Foundation is sponsoring a project by the University of Leeds, comparing 500 UK implementations of the balanced scorecard;
- reverse engineering, as discussed above in the Xerox example;
- company visits, which if well planned can achieve a great deal or can become industrial tourism;
- questionnaires;
- mail or telephone surveys;
- internal sources, which include:
    - sales and technical representatives
    - buying officers and suppliers
    - delivery drivers
    - quotes
    - surveys

- customer and factory visits
- competitive analysis
- library databases;
- public domain sources, which include:
  - trade publications and shows
  - user groups
  - analysts' reports
  - annual reports
  - patent records
  - research papers
  - newspapers, newsletters
  - buyers' guides
  - government information
  - focus groups;
  - the world wide web.

10.4 PHASES OF THE BENCHMARKING PROCESS

Selecting and prioritizing benchmarking projects

While wishing to benchmark everything eventually, it is advisable to select those processes that are likely to yield the most benefit and prioritize them for action first.

Organizing benchmarking teams

When selecting a project team to conduct the benchmarking project, always involve people who are knowledgeable about the individual processes in addition to permanent members of the benchmarking team. Skills to consider in selection should include:

- functional/process knowledge
- credibility and respect
- communication skills
- teamwork skills
- interest/motivation
- project-management skills.

It is worth remembering that this benchmarking team will be representing the company externally and should project its culture and image.

Documenting own processes and measures

Before attempting to benchmark externally, it is essential that the company clearly documents its own processes using process-mapping techniques and identifies a balanced set of performance indicators, including time, quality and costs. Both techniques are explained in *Business Process Management*.[1]

Researching and identifying benchmarking partners

The selection of benchmarking partners for each process will be driven by the project objectives, but needs to be undertaken as early as possible in the process, since there can be a long lead-time.

Analyzing benchmarking data and choosing enablers

Analysis of the data collected is crucial to the success of the project, as is the use of tried and tested tools such as:

- Data stratification using the fishbone diagram – for root cause analysis (*see* Fig. 10.1).

Fig. 10.1 Fishbone diagram

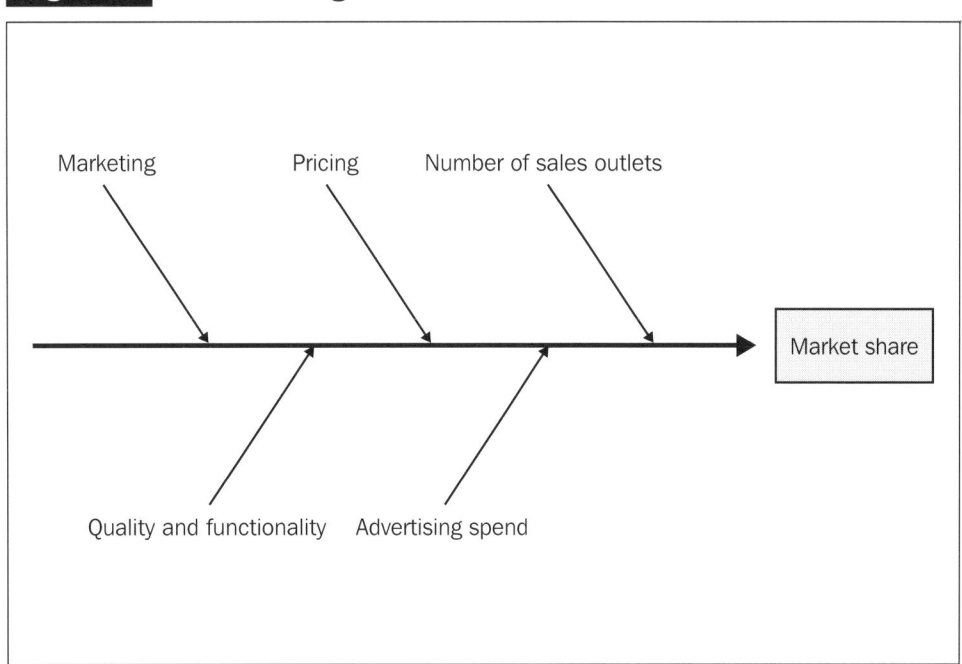

- Z chart – illustrating graphically the gap between the historical trend and the planned future trend (*see* Fig. 10.2).

Fig. 10.2 Z chart

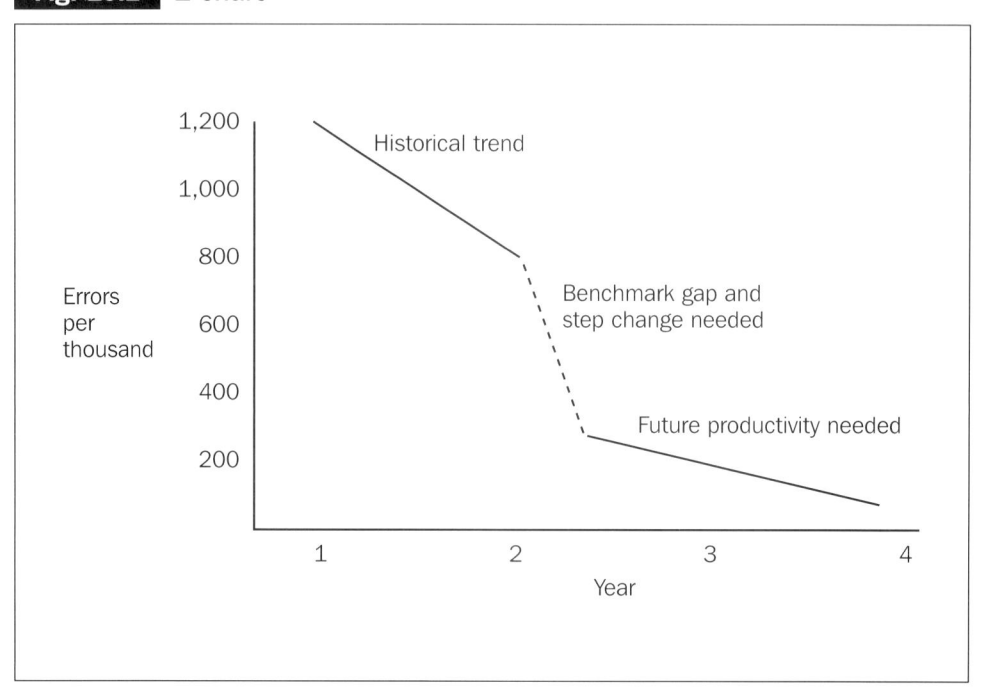

- Forcefield analysis – demonstrating the impact of helping and hindering forces (*see* Fig. 10.3).

Fig. 10.3 Forcefield analysis

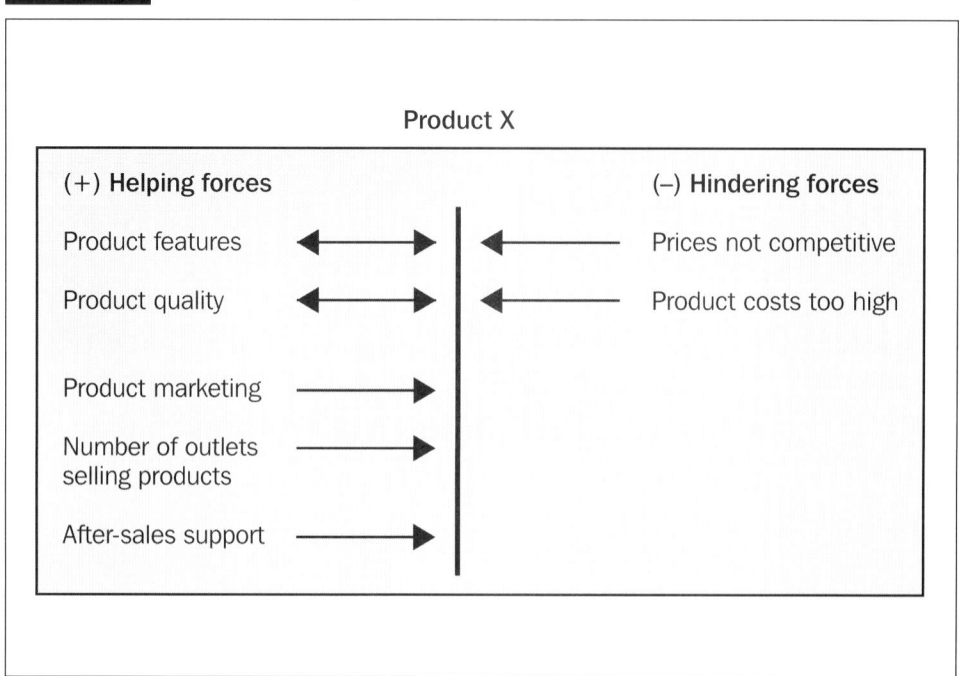

- Process enablers hierarchy – showing the path from goal to new practice via the enabler (*see* Fig. 10.4).

Fig. 10.4 Process enablers' hierarchy

```
Goal  ──────────▶  Reduced clerical
 │                  documentation workload
 ▼
Benchmark ──────▶  Use of bar codes for
practice           automatic data capture
 │
 ▼
Enabler  ───────▶  Training in use of scanners
```

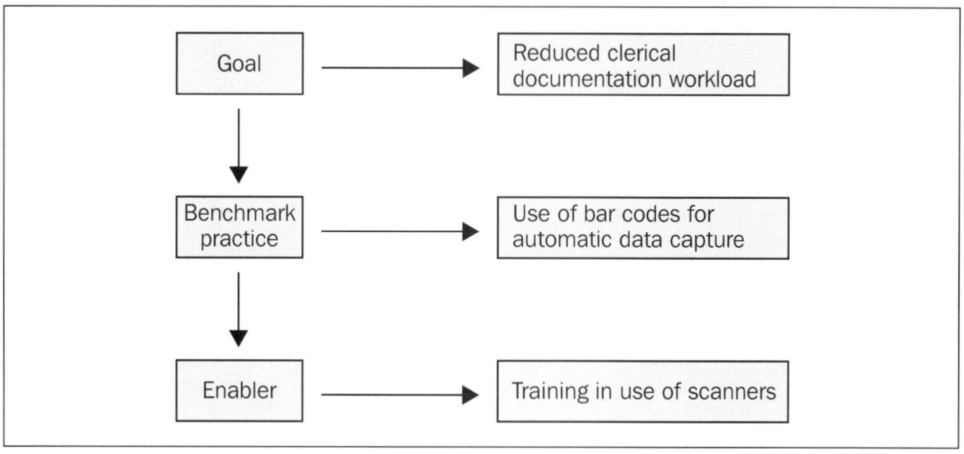

These and other tools are important in brainstorming and communicating the results in the most effective way possible to aid the success of the project.

Implementing benchmarking study recommendations

Once the desired practice has been agreed through a process of consultation, clear plans of implementation need to be drawn up with responsibilities identified.

Review benchmarks regularly

It is necessary to continue to monitor progress to ensure that gains against benchmarked partners are maintained. Although initial studies may reveal the organization to be competitive, it needs to be remembered that benchmarking partners and competitors could improve disproportionately. Recalibration should take place at least once a year.

10.5 THE BENCHMARKING CODE OF CONDUCT

This code has been drawn up by the Society of Management Accountants of Canada.[2]

Principles

- Legality – beware implied restraint of trade or price fixing.
- Exchange – be willing to provide same level of information.

- Confidentiality – maintain between benchmarking partners.
- Use – use only for purpose agreed.
- First-party contact – obtain mutual agreement on any hand-off.
- Preparation – demonstrate commitment by adequate preparation at each step.

Benchmarking etiquette and ethics

- Establish ground rules up-front.
- Do not ask for sensitive data.
- Use an ethical third party for competitive data.
- Treat information as internal and privileged.
- Do not:
    - disparage a competitor's business to a third party
    - limit competition or gain business through the relationship
    - misrepresent oneself as working for another employer.
- Emphasize openness and trust.

Benchmarking exchange protocol

- Abide by the Benchmarking Code of Conduct.
- Follow the benchmarking process.
- Determine what to benchmark and complete self-assessment.
- Develop a questionnaire and interview guide.
- Have the authority to share information.
- Work through a specified host and agree a meeting schedule.
- Follow good practice guidelines in face-to-face site visits:
    - provide meeting agenda in advance
    - be professional, honest, courteous and prompt
    - introduce all attendees and explain why they are present
    - adhere to agenda
    - do not use own 'jargon'
    - do not share proprietary information without prior approval
    - offer to set up a reciprocal visit
    - conclude meetings and visits on schedule.

10.6 BENEFITS OF BENCHMARKING

Once an organization has measured its own performance and made improvements through internal discussion, the next logical step is to make comparisons with similar external organizations, particularly those considered to be utilizing 'best practice' and 'best value'. Benefits of the technique include that it:

- provides a better understanding of exactly where the organization stands compared with best practice;
- focuses attention on those areas needing improvement;
- helps to cure tendencies toward self-satisfaction;
- encourages innovation;
- forces change;
- facilitates the demonstration of 'best value'.

10.7 Case study

Tower Hamlets benchmarking project[3]

Background

Following a change in political parties taking control of the London Borough of Tower Hamlets in 1994, the Council found itself needing to consolidate seven neighbourhoods – which had been decentralized since 1986, operating with mini town halls and policy agendas – back into one corporate unit. To facilitate this process Tower Hamlets had to undertake benchmarking between the neighbourhoods' council processes and decided to invite the other 32 London boroughs to participate in the project, which Tower Hamlets was offering to resource.

After research examining benchmarking initiatives elsewhere, both in the private and public sectors, Tower Hamlets London Borough Council found a tool that combines attention to current performance with preparation for a probable future. This tool was process benchmarking. In respect to current performance, process benchmarking identifies good practice to improve quality and/or value. Comparisons, as well as being odious, have been notoriously difficult to undertake successfully. Service providers can find a multitude of reasons for contesting that any given comparison has not been conducted on a like-for-like basis. Generally, the common denominator used to assess performance has been cost but this mechanism alone does not adequately reflect comparative quality, value and political priorities.

All local authority services, which are offered on a regular basis, operate via a process. Detailed mapping of processes and comparison of the time/effort involved in reaching various milestones can indicate which process is the most efficient and effective. Process analysis does not attempt a like-for-like contrast; rather, it is concerned with a like-for-best comparison. It does not judge whether the process is operated well or whether it is appropriate to the needs of the community. It does, however, find a 'best' way of organizing a service. Just as the medium was the message, the process is now the priority.

Methodology

The first phase of the Tower Hamlets benchmarking exercise involved 25 of the 32 London borough councils and covered 28 different activities. These ranged from high-volume, repetitive administrative tasks, such as benefit processing and development control, to operations incorporating a long chain of different professionals, such as identifying and satisfying the need for an adaptation to a property to allow continued occupation by a disabled person. A further category of study involved emerging services, such as responding to racial harassment where there is, as yet, an absence of accepted professional practice (see Fig. 10.5).

Fig. 10.5 Tower Hamlets – Phase 1 list of activities and published reports

1. Council tax collection*
2. Payments
3. Compulsory competitive tendering
4. Housing benefit application processing
5. Purchasing
6. Aids and adaptations*
7. Access to the under-8s service*
8. Social work caseload management system
9. Electoral registration*
10. Members support
11. Education statementing
12. Adult education enrolment
13. Student awards*
14. Youth service management and contract administration
15. Former tenants' arrears*
16. Housing allocations
17. Homelessness to Section 64 determination*
18. Development control
19. Building control
20. Markets administration*
21. Parking control penalty ticket processing
22. Sundry debt collection*
23. Contract monitoring
24. Racial harassment
25. Community safety (focusing particularly on domestic violence)
26. Noise nuisance enforcement*
27. Access to domiciliary care
28. Staff performance appraisal

* denotes published study

The Tower Hamlets approach began with the secondment of three officers to research benchmarking literature and devise a specific local authority methodology. The method developed involves careful selection of subjects for study, eliminating those that are too circumscribed by statutory procedures to yield substantial scope for process improvement, and obtaining an overview of the chosen activities by interviewing service managers. This leads to the production of a management and performance data questionnaire for circulation to the participating authorities.

Returned questionnaires are assessed on:

- the range of the service provided: that is, whether, in addition to the core elements of the service, activities such as an advice function are carried out;
- the level of the service provided: that is, the maximum number of service events per 1,000 head of relevant population;
- the quality of the service: that is, the mechanism for quality assurance, the accuracy, the adherence to statutory timescales, the internal performance targets and so on.

The services represented by the returned questionnaires are ranked by this assessment routine and the staffing input of those in the upper quartile is then assessed. In other words, the better services are assessed by their cost in terms of staff and that with the lowest staff cost is assumed to have the 'best' processes.

While the questionnaires are completed and assessed, a detailed map of the processes used by Tower Hamlets is drawn up. A similar exercise is then undertaken with the 'best' practice authority. The maps are compared at a benchmarking club meeting involving staff of all the participating authorities, where constructive criticism of the 'best' practice can identify improvements.

A benchmarking report details the 'best' practice identified and recommends the adoption of appropriate improvements. These are quantified and fed into the budget process, where they result in cost reductions, and into the performance-monitoring system, where new performance targets are required.

Results

The first study, about electoral registration, found sufficient ideas for improvement to give a slightly improved outcome with a reduction of about 50% in staffing. The study of housing benefits processing resulted in a potential saving of £1 million as a result of the following process changes identified:

- centralize the processing of claims;
- allow local access for queries through IT;
- streamline processing with DIP;
- separate public and private claimants;
- use patchwork systems;
- provide remote-access terminals.

Similarly, council tax collection yielded ten possible process changes, with a potential saving of £0.5 million from the following:

- send bills as soon as possible;
- delay benefit bills until correct;

- run billing twice a week;
- encourage direct debit;
- work closely with housing benefit staff;
- make council tax and housing benefits work alongside one another;
- outline repercussions with reminders;
- allow fax signatures on summons forms;
- make discounts simple to apply for;
- monitor discounts through sharing information, e.g. parking control;
- centralize council tax, incorporating it with NNDR.

Conclusions

Problems found from the project include:

- length of time (longer than anticipated)
- resource problems
- developing the methodology
- waiting/idle times
- confidentiality
- performance information
- names
- ownership.

Benchmarking has been defined by the Audit Commission as:

> *the process of comparing procedure and performance levels between and within organisations, in order to identify what improvements are possible, how they might be achieved and how much benefit might be delivered.*

Since the project began, the Labour Government has taken benchmarking a step further, adopting the Best Value initiative, which incorporates benchmarking with the following identified characteristics:

- continuous process of measuring services against others for improvement
- identifying and sharing good practice
- focus on proving 'Best Value'
- commitment to learning from others.

The second phase of the benchmarking project is now under way and has extended the club to outside London, to include the private sector and non-council processes, such as payroll, personnel and catering. Completed reports are available for purchase from Tower Hamlets for a modest fee to cover production costs.

Part 5

Executive summary

PART 1 THE TWENTY-FIRST-CENTURY FINANCE FUNCTION

1 Finance in the twenty-first-century organization

1. Finance, driven by technology, has developed from big box computers of 1970s, through devolved PCs and spreadsheets of the 1980s, to shared service centres (SSCs) and decision support delivered electronically in the 1990s. Full integration of business processes through web technology is delivering business intelligence in the 2000s, moving towards becoming completely 'lights out' (virtual finance, eliminating transaction-processing altogether) by 2010.

2. Over the last two decades organizations have experienced exceptional levels of change. These include the increase in shareholder power; growth in environmental, ethical and social awareness; legislation requiring the public sector to deliver value for money; changes in organizational culture and structure; globalization of business and financial centres; and government legislation, placing new challenges on organizations to become 'world class'.

3. The challenge for finance is to become more cost effective, value-adding, embedded within the business processes, customer focused and service oriented, adding company-wide value in a technology-driven environment, and reacting quickly when responding to ever-changing needs.

4. The cost of the finance function is falling dramatically as evidenced by the Hackett Benchmarking study and the opportunity is to retrain and re-deploy finance professionals to add company-wide value. These new roles contain a high-level of non-financial content with names like business consultants, analysts or commercial managers, all requiring an in-depth knowledge of the business.

5. In the words of Susan Jee of Magnox:

> *We have to earn the right to be taken seriously by the business generally. We have to prove that we can provide more than just the numbers while recognising that these numbers are still of critical importance.*

6. It is the role of the finance function to ensure that finances are used as efficiently and effectively as possible throughout the whole business. The implementation of value-adding tools and techniques should therefore be driven by finance.

7. While finance no longer owns the information it provides within the business, it has a clear role to fulfil as information facilitator. This includes training in the understanding of tools and techniques, collecting and analyzing information,

designing systems, acting as a catalyst for change across functions, assisting in the assessment of improvement ideas, assisting in planning, forecasting, performance measurement and monitoring, and validating information.

8 Case studies of leading twenty-first-century organizations (including finance functions) illustrate the way forward and, not surprisingly are dominated by technology-driven electronics giants like Dell Computer, Microsoft UK, Intel and Cisco.

2 The process of transforming the finance function

9 This chapter provides a practical blueprint for re-engineering the finance function to ensure that the warning of Hugh Collum, CFO of SmithKline Beecham, does not become reality for your organization:

Accountants could go the way of coal miners! A mighty industry that once employed three-quarters of a million and helped bring down a government today employs fewer than SmithKline Beecham. I believe that accountants in industry could go the same way if they do not realise the fundamental changes they need to make.

10 Instead, consider the words and vision of Stephen Hodge, Director of Finance at the Shell Group:

Shell recognised that the concept of a finance function with the right to exist was obsolete – finance would need to earn and maintain its standing as a supplier to the business leading Shell's digitisation by enabling e-business process design across the whole value chain. The goal was to become the 'top performer of first choice' through Shell Financial Services, whose mission is to provide specialist finance management and decision support skills to the operating businesses, organised as a virtual business in a few global locations and in competition with external providers.

11 Steps in establishing the transformation project include putting together the business case, appointing a steering group and project team, identifying customers and suppliers of the finance function to consult, identifying benchmarking partners and setting up communication media.

12 The next stage is to analyze the present finance function activities and processes; then develop the vision for the future of the finance function; create the change strategy; align staff skills and competencies; implement; monitor continuously; and communicate results.

Executive summary

13 Case studies illustrate leading-edge examples: Adidas-Salomon affected change through trust-building measures, which result from when members of the finance function provide value-added analysis before it is requested. Dell Computer combines a clear understanding of its business model, a company-wide determination to boost return on invested capital, a fierce appetite for information and a rigorous analysis of both financial and operating performance.

PART 2 THE TECHNOLOGY-DRIVEN FINANCE FUNCTION

3 Shared service centres

14 Shared service centres (SSCs) are a type of 'internal outsourcing', the focus being to provide non-core services to strategic business units (SBUs), and often they are set up and run in conjunction with an external outsourcing partner. SSCs can contain one or several support processes, from high-volume, transaction-based, like purchase order processing, to specialist services like legal.

15 In the 1990s organizations implementing enterprise resource planning (ERP) systems found it cost effective to locate an SSC in a geographically beneficial country, like India. Initially, this would handle high-volume transaction-based activities, then whole processes and now, in the web-enabled environment end-to-end 'lights out' processes, it links customers, suppliers, partners and employees.

16 The move towards profit/value-accountable SBU trading internally with other SBUs, including finance, has forced the adoption of a more customer-focused, service-oriented culture.

17 According to a PwC five-year SSC benchmarking survey, cost savings from SSCs in Europe are reported to be as high as 30% in procurement, 40% in invoicing, 60% in accounts payable, 100% in processing accounts payable and 50% in general accounting staffing levels.

18 Technical considerations to be taken into account when establishing an SSC include which processes should be incorporated, accounting and legal differences between countries, taxation problems and opportunities, IT challenges, cost and availability, and language skills of staff.

4 Outsourcing

19 Organizations have recognized that many of their non-core activities and processes can be operated more efficiently by an outside company that specializes in added-value outsourcing. Traditionally, service functions such as security and catering have been outsourced, but over the last 18 years IT and

other services, driven by compulsory competitive tendering in the public sector, have been widely outsourced. Mainstream finance outsourcing began in the early 1990s, with 50% of companies now outsourcing some part of their finance function.

20 Steps in outsourcing, which can take about two years, include gathering basic information; beginning dialogue with providers; preparing the invitation to tender (ITT); providing assistance to outsourcers during the bid process; evaluating the bids; making a decision; implementing, managing and monitoring the outsourcer.

21 In recent years outsourcing deals have moved into a second generation. The inevitable conflict of interests and lack of incentives to save money and add value, inherent in old-style deals, have been addressed. No longer is the emphasis on highly prescriptive contracts, but instead on risk-sharing partnerships and joint ventures.

22 Application service provision (ASP) is the delivering of computing resources via a one-to-many model. Users rent software applications through on-line links with a service provider, avoiding the initial costs of purchasing and the problems associated with implementing.

23 The BBC case study is a good example of the way joint ventures are being formed to run outsourced SSC. It describes the 18-month process of negotiation and the considerable amount of commitment that is required from both sides for the arrangements to be successful.

5 Information management delivering business intelligence

24 The role of the information manager is pivotal within the organization. The challenge is to replace or integrate the myriad of unconnected legacy systems to make an enterprise-wide system that can deliver the information that the company needs to ensure that it continues to add value year on year.

25 Great care must be taken to define the business requirement for the company's information system – to provide an integrated understanding of the financial and operational position of the company in a dynamic business environment, using the latest web-enabled technological developments. Its success is not important merely to ensure value for money but to maintain the company's competitive position.

26 When formulating the company-wide information strategy, the following steps need to be taken – understand the latest technological options including ERP, SCM, CRM, EAI middleware, web-enabled technology, data warehousing, decision-support systems, business intelligence tools and collaborative computing; set up a project team; analyze existing company, supplier and

customer systems; analyze future business needs; and gain consensus from the whole organization for the recommended solution.

27 Chief knowledge officers tend to be technologists – understanding capturing, storing, exploring and sharing knowledge. They are also environmentalists – facilitating knowledge creation. Cap Gemini Ernst & Young's KWeb is one of the largest knowledge infrastructures in the world.

28 Modern business intelligence and decision support tools are simpler to use for both query and drill-down and no longer need specialists. Data warehousing, on-line analytical processing, enterprise information portals, website and customer relationship management (CRM) analytics are examined.

29 Activity/process-based analysis is now fundamental to the way organizations are managed and are an integral part of the design of any enterprise-wide system. Decision-support systems (DSS) and ERP alliances are now in place for most leading software vendors.

30 The Nationwide case study explains how a data warehousing solution was applied to the set-up of a new operation at a greenfield site in Swindon. Delivery of the system was a small but key part of the development of the management reporting solution. It involved addressing cultural and educational issues around implementation, data and information ownership, development of critical success factors (CSF) and key performance indicators (KPIs) and a monitoring basis for all business areas.

PART 3 VALUE-BASED MANAGEMENT

6 Delivering shareholder/Best Value

31 Research carried out by Price Waterhouse in 1997 revealed that chief finance officers worldwide placed maximizing shareholder value as their number one priority.

32 A gulf has opened up between profit used by the company as a measure and cash generation used by investors to judge company performance. Adoption of common measures based on cash was first put forward by Rappaport in 1986, based on seven value drivers.

33 Following Rappaport, a number of different shareholder value calculation models have been developed, falling into three main categories: economic value added (EVA™), cashflow return on investment (CFROI) and cash value added (CVA).

34 Shareholder value analysis needs not only to drive strategic decision making but to become embedded in the behaviour of all levels in the organization, integrating the various management processes, including remuneration.

35 A Best Value authority must make arrangements to secure continuous improvement in the way in which its functions are exercised, having regard to a combination of economy, efficiency and effectiveness. Best Value requires local authorities to review their services, set new and demanding targets for each service, publish local performance plans and be externally inspected.

36 The rest of the public sector is undergoing similar initiatives, which are forcing a reappraisal of the role of the finance function. The Highways Agency finance function has been at the heart of a new management plan and performance system, which covers external service delivery and internal performance. The improved focus on delivery has seen half of the 70 management accountants devolved to local operations.

37 In organizations adopting value-based management (VBM), the creation of autonomous SBUs, trading with each other, utilizing service level agreements (SLAs) and inter-SBU charging, is now becoming the norm. This encourages the behaviour of a third-party supplier, eager to please its customers.

38 The case study of VBM at British Aerospace (BAe) explains how the success of the pilot projects carried out at Regional Aircraft is now being mirrored across the whole company. VBM is a priority action for BAe in helping to deliver long-term sustainable growth in value for its customers, employees and shareholders.

7 Valuing intangible assets/intellectual capital

39 In 1978 the book value of financial and physical assets on average equalled 95% of market value. In 2001 it was nearer 20%. The other 80% derived from intangible assets/intellectual capital, such as knowledge, brands, research and development (R&D), intellectual property, reputation, and relationships with employees, customers, suppliers and business partners.

40 Only a few companies manage, measure and monitor intangibles. Some intangibles, like brands, are assigned value if they are acquired but not internally generated. Techniques for valuing intangibles are still developing; they are currently underreported and undervalued, and lack of transparency and consistency adds to share price volatility. Internally, an understanding of intangibles is essential to aid resource allocation decisions.

41 The role of the finance function is to apply its skills in encouraging the creation and integration of knowledge in their organizations; to direct and control the intellectual capital formation process; and to evaluate, report and audit the results of these processes on an ongoing basis.

42 Intellectual capital can be categorized into three main types; first, customer (relational) capital – customer and brand value; second, organizational (structural) capital – R&D, intellectual property and infrastructure assets; third,

human capital. They are all interrelated and link with the financial capital to form the market value of the organization and its corporate reputation.

43 The importance of a clear and well-communicated enterprise risk strategy cannot be overemphasized. The requirement is to develop comprehensive company-wide processes and policies for identifying, understanding, assessing and mitigating risk, which give assurances that controls are in place to assess significant risk and highlight strategic opportunity. It is fundamental to maximizing shareholder value.

44 Businesses are considering the ways in which environmental issues can secure competitive advantage. They need to link expenditure on good environmental management to improved performance and reputation. Fund managers now expect organizations to anticipate possible future legislation by investing wisely in environmental issues.

PART 4 BEYOND TRADITIONAL BUDGETING

8 Scenario planning, forecasting and resource allocation

45 Investors put their funds where the best opportunities for maximizing shareholder value occur. Allocation/attraction of funds within the organization must therefore be approached in a similar way – by viewing strategy as a series of options offering different opportunities, with different costs, values and outcomes.

46 The traditional planning and budgeting process was primarily concerned with how to manage the limited capital available for investments, often making allocations at operating company level based on history. The modern organization finds no shortage of capital available for the right investments, but other – often intangible – resources are becoming more scarce.

47 Although most organizations have switched to a bottom-up empowered culture, finance functions have lagged behind in 'binning the budget', which still supports the command-and-control culture of a top-down organization and stifles innovation.

48 A definition of budgeting is an annual process that sets the performance agenda for the year ahead. It has wide behavioural implications because it is a performance contract. The purpose is to commit people to achieving a certain result. Once set, this process demands adherence to the plan. Despite the time invested there is no evidence that the budget adds any value to the business.

49 There is now a sense of urgency about the need to replace traditional budgeting techniques. New methods of planning, control and allocating resources are

being introduced before permanent, long-term damage is done to the health of many businesses. These tools and techniques include enterprise-wide business intelligence, VBM, rolling forecasts, balanced scorecards (BSCs), benchmarking and process-based management.

50 The *CAM-I Beyond Budgeting Round Table White Paper* sets out 12 principles that will provide managers with a robust framework for implementing the new model, split into two categories: creating a devolutionary framework and adaptive management processes.

51 Traditionally, companies used accounting tools like the profit and loss and balance sheet to plan the company's future, resulting in an internally focused illusion of numerical precision. Organizations are now recognizing that they need to examine all possible and relevant futures, not just one – hence the move to scenario planning.

52 The technique works best when it is used to answer specific questions about the future that have commercial significance to the organization. Continual reassessments of plans, giving short, medium and long-term perspectives, are essential to an organization's success.

53 With the latest technological developments, forecasting can be more sophisticated and more frequent, and – unlike the annual budgeting process – much more accurate. More attention to forecasting must make sense when research shows that companies issuing profits warnings suffer an average 21.5% fall in their share price.

54 Researchers from Tennessee have produced a guide to world-class forecasting processes including who does the forecasting; what is forecast and how; which IT tools are used; and how accurate the forecast is.

55 A continuous planning process should be followed, which involves formulation (scenario planning, options review, resource attraction to value-adding investment and resource allocation to support services, forecasting and target setting) and execution (action planning and implementation, measuring, reporting and rewarding performance and taking corrective actions), before starting the continuous cycle again.

56 Published case studies of companies that have gone beyond traditional budgeting include Volvo, Borealis, Diageo, HP Bulmers and Jabil Circuit.

9 The balanced scorecard

57 The BSC shows how to link the corporate vision to CSFs or outcomes and KPIs, representing all perspectives of the business – customer, internal process, innovation and learning and financial. It encourages the senior management

to operate as a unified team, balancing competing objectives to achieve the optimum result for the company as a whole.

58 When setting KPIs it is important to appreciate cause and effect relationships between measures and perspectives. For example, improvements in the learning perspective will help improve business processes, which will in turn benefit customers and ultimately result in better financial results.

59 Kaplan and Norton examine the impact of the BSC at some of the 200 companies that have implemented it and are able to demonstrate its success in operation. Bain & Company research shows that it is now used by about half of North America's top companies; in Europe the estimate is 45% and in Australia 35%.

60 Although every organization had its own way of working, Kaplan and Norton found that there were five principles that ran through the strategy-focused organizations – mobilize change; translate strategy into operational terms using the BSC and strategy maps; align the organization to the strategy by cascading; make strategy everyone's everyday job; and make strategy a continual process.

61 The strategy map describes the process for transforming intangible assets into tangible customer and financial outcomes. It provides executives with a framework for describing and managing strategy in a knowledge economy. This generic architecture has four strategic themes – build the franchise; increase customer value; achieve operational excellence; and be a good corporate citizen.

62 By weighting the different measures within the BSC, scores may be varied according to importance, within the overall vision and achievement of specified outcomes.

63 The ten commandments of BSC implementation, researched by KPMG in Europe in 1996, lays out the dos and don'ts to be followed for success. This is advice that would hold good for any project.

64 Because of the focus and detail of quality frameworks (such as EFQM and Baldrige), there is considerable merit in linking this detail to both BSC and activity/process-based management systems.

65 Case studies of e-BSC reveal e-metrics used in internet companies, including a focus on customers, advertising and marketing. ProXchange has a system that corresponds to the seven levels in the website transaction process.

66 In the Manchester Housing case study an information strategy utilizing Business Objects and the intranet is used to bring together information contained in disparate systems and provide a corporate traffic-light BSC – utilizing alerts, exceptions and trends – for the Departmental Management Team. In addition,

it replaced the service plan with a tree of measures, drilling down beneath the BSC to service the information needs of all employees.

10 Benchmarking

67 Benchmarking is a tool used to establish processes, costs and performance indicators and compare them against other similar organizations, with the aim of identifying and progressing towards best practice and best value through continuous improvement. Care must be taken to ensure true comparability.

68 Types of benchmarking include internal; external databases; collaborative, within and outside the sector; and competitive. When benchmarking outside the organization, the accepted code of conduct should be followed.

69 Methods of gathering data vary in terms of cost, accuracy and amount of data collected and must be driven by the purpose of the project. Methods include clubs; research; reverse engineering; company visits; surveys; questionnaires; internal sources; and public domain sources.

70 Phases of the benchmarking process include selection and prioritization of processes; forming project teams; documenting processes; researching and identifying partners; analyzing data collected; determining best practice; implementation; and review.

71 Once an organization has measured its own performance and taken steps to improve, the next logical step is to make comparisons with outside organizations to demonstrate efficiency and effectiveness.

72 The benefits of benchmarking include its ability to focus attention on areas needing improvement, driving innovation and change where necessary.

73 The London Borough of Tower Hamlets case study explains the process benchmarking project that it has been running for the last five years, involving 25 London boroughs and 28 different council processes in the first phase. The second phase has been extended outside London and the public sector and covers non-council processes common to most organizations.

References

Introduction

1 Cedric Read et al., *eCFO*, Wiley, 2001.

PART 1 THE TWENTY-FIRST-CENTURY FINANCE FUNCTION

1 Finance in the twenty-first-century organization

1 Margaret May, *Business Process Management: Integration in a web-enabled environment*, Pearson FT Executive Briefing, 2002.

2 Margaret May, 'An activity-based approach to resource accounting and budgeting in government', *Management Accounting*, July/August 1996.

3 Hackett Group, *Ongoing Benchmarking Survey*, 2000.

4 The Society of Management Accountants of Canada, *Redesigning the Finance Function*, 1997.

5 James Creelman, *Creating the Value-Adding Finance Function*, Business Intelligence, 1998.

6 R.M.S. Wilson and W.F. Chua, *Managerial Accounting: Method and meaning*, Chapman and Hall, 1993.

7 Steve Harvey, Microsoft's UK director of people, profit and loyalty, *Accountancy Age*, October 2001.

8 Shani Raja, 'Intel', *CFO Europe*, May 2000.

9 Andrew Sawers, 'Cisco Systems, I'm not worried about our share price', *Financial Director*, April 2001.

10 PwC Case Studies, 'IT portfolio', *Management Consultancy*, February 2000.

2 The process of transforming the finance function

1 KPMG Management Consulting, *Finance of the Future*, 1998.

2 Cedric Read et al., *eCFO*, Wiley, 2001.

3 Margaret May, *Business Process Management: Integration in a web-enabled environment*, Pearson FT Executive Briefing, 2002.

4 James Creelman, *Creating the Value-Adding Finance Function*, Business Intelligence, 1998.

5 The Hackett Group, *Best Practices Benchmark Study of Finance*, 1997.

6 Price Waterhouse, *CFO, Architect of the Corporation's Future*, John Wiley, 1997.

7 *Changing Work Patterns*, CIMA Research, 1996.

8 *Excellence in Finance*, written in co-operation with Arthur Andersen, Economist Intelligence Unit, 1998. There are extracts here from two of the 12 case studies contained in this book.

PART 2 THE TECHNOLOGY-DRIVEN FINANCE FUNCTION

3 Shared service centres

1 John Barnsley, PwC, 'How to stay on top of the world', *Accountancy Age*, 11 February 1999.

2 Cedric Read et al., *eCFO*, Wiley, 2001.

3 Information in this section is drawn from a series of four articles in *Management Accounting* in 1998, written by KPMG staff and entitled 'Shared service centres'.

4 Michael Jocobi, CFO Ciba Speciality Chemicals, *CFO Europe*, March 2000.

4 Outsourcing and shared service centres

1 Richard Holway Limited, *The Holway Report*, 2001.

2 L. Wilcocks and G. Fitzgerald, *A Business Guide to Outsourcing IT*, Business Intelligence, 1995.

3 J. Brian Heywood, *Outsourcing the Finance Function*, Accountancy Books, 1996.

4 James Creelman, *Creating the Value-Adding Finance Function*, Business Intelligence, 1998.

5 Matthew May, 'Stepping up the pace of change', *CFO Europe*, April 1999.

6 BBC case study contributed by Richard Hartt, Quality Manager, MedAS and Penny Lawson, APOLLO Communications Manager, BBC.

5 Information management delivering business intelligence

1 CIMA Technical Services, *Information Management – the Fundamentals*, CIMA, 2000.

2 Kevin G. Dilton-Hill, 'Management information to support a world-class company', *Accountancy SA*, May 1993.

3 Margaret May, *Business Process Management: Integration in a web-enabled environment*, Pearson FT Executive Briefing, 2002.

4 'Chief Knowledge Officers', *Sloan Management Review*, 2000.

5 Guy Matthews, article in *Management Consultancy*, December 2000.

6 Rod Newing, 'Data warehousing', *Management Accounting*, March 1996.

7 David Longworth, 'High standards', *Computers and Finance*, April 2000.

8 'Top 18 accounting software vendors review', *CFO Europe*, May 2000.

9 Nationwide case study contributed by Abhai Rajguru, former Nationwide Management Information Controller, published in *Management Accounting* and by IFAC in 1997, as part of research by Margaret May entitled *Preparing Organisations to Manage the Future*.

PART 3 VALUE-BASED MANAGEMENT

6 Delivering shareholder value/Best Value

1 Price Waterhouse, *CFO, Architect of the Corporation's Future*, John Wiley 1997.

2 Alfred Rappaport, *Creating Shareholder Value*, Free Press, 1986.

3 EVA™ is a trademark of Stern Stewart & Co, USA.

4 Paul Nichols, 'Unlocking shareholder value', *Management Accounting*, October 1998.

5 Stern Stewart, cover story in *Financial Director*, April 2000.

6 CVA™ is a trademark of FWC AB, Sweden.

7 CIPFA, *Accounting for Best Value Consultation Paper*, CIPFA, 1999.

8 Peter Bartram, 'Special delivery', *Financial Director*, September 2001.

9 Margaret May, *Business Process Management: Integration in a web-enabled environment*, Pearson FT Executive Briefing, 2002.

10 James Arnold, 'Value judgements', *CFO Europe*, October 1999.

11 British Aerospace case study contributed by Tony Bryan, former VBM Executive, Regional Aircraft Woodford, and Rogan Dixon, VBM Champion, BAe Head Office, Farnborough.

7 Valuing intangible assets/intellectual capital

1 Andrew Sawers, 'Cisco Systems, I'm not worried about our share price', *Financial Director*, April 2001

References

2 Cedric Read et al., *eCFO*, Wiley, 2001.

3 Stern Stewart, 'FT500 MVA ranking based on 1998', *CFO Europe*, 2001.

4 Real Options Valuation (ROV) is the trademark of Applied Decision Analysis, a subsidiary of PwC.

5 KPMG's IP Services, 'IP Days are here again', *Real Finance*, June 2001.

6 Ben McLannahan, 'Good teamwork', *CFO Europe*, November 2001.

7 A study undertaken by the Institute of Internal Auditors Research Foundation and consultants Tillinghurst-Towers Perrin in 2001.

8 Steve Toms, 'Eco-logical', *Financial Management*, January 2001.

PART 4 BEYOND TRADITIONAL BUDGETING

8 Scenario planning, forecasting and resource allocation

1 H.T. Johnson, *Relevance Regained*, Free Press, 1992.

2 CAM-I, Consortium for Advanced Manufacturing International, is a not-for-profit group of companies, consultants and academics from around the world, undertaking research in the area of management accounting. Its UK base is in Poole, Dorset.

3 Robin Fraser and Jeremy Hope, *The CAM-I Beyond Budgeting Round Table White Paper*, CAM-I, 2000 (www.bbrt.org).

4 Margaret May, *Business Process Management: Integration in a web-enabled environment*, Pearson FT Executive Briefing, 2002.

5 Gill Ringland, *Scenario Planning: Managing for the future*, Wiley, 2000, reviewed by *Financial Director*, September 2000.

6 Justin Wood, 'Scenario Planning at Amerada Hess', *CFO Europe*, January 2000.

7 Janet Kersnar, 'Forecasting', *CFO Europe*, October 2001.

8 John Mentzer, Carol Bienstock and Kenneth Kahn, paper published in *International Journal of Forecasting*, 2001.

9 Janet Kersnar, 'Time to bin the budget', *CFO Europe*, May 1999.

10 Peter Bartram, 'HP Bulmer', *Financial Director*, November 2001.

11 Stephen Barr, 'Circuit training', *CFO Europe*, November 2001.

9 The balanced scorecard

1 R.S. Kaplan and D.P. Norton, 'The balanced scorecard: measures that drive performance', *Harvard Business Review*, January/February 1992.

2 R.S. Kaplan and D.P. Norton, *The Strategy-Focused Organisation*, Harvard Business School Press, 2001.

3 Professor Lewy and Lex du Mee, *Management Control and Accounting*, KPMG Management Consultants, 1996.

4 Cedric Read et al., *eCFO*, Wiley, 2001

5 Justin Wood, 'Dash board web metrics', *CFO Europe*, February 2001.

6 Manchester City Council Housing Department's case study written by Margaret May, with kind permission from Hilary Vaughan, Assistant Director (Finance), and the DMT at Manchester Housing.

10 Benchmarking

1 Margaret May, *Business Process Management: Integration in a web-enabled environment*, Pearson FT Executive Briefing, 2002.

2 The Society of Management Accountants of Canada, *Implementing Benchmarking*, 1993. The Code of Conduct was co-authored by The American Productivity and Quality Center's International Benchmarking Clearinghouse and The Strategic Planning Council on Benchmarking, January 1992.

3 Tower Hamlets case study contributed by Mike Howes, former Head of Benchmarking, and updated with information from Keith Luck, former Head of Finance, published in *Management Accounting* and by IFAC in 1997, as part of research by Margaret May entitled *Preparing Organisations to Manage the Future*.

Index

Accenture (formerly Andersen Consulting) 59
accounting operations 11
activity analysis 23–4, 79
activity-based budgeting (ABB) 80
activity-based costing 79, 134
activity-based management (ABM) 79, 158
activity-based techniques (ABT) 101, 169
Adaytum e Planning 80
Adidas-Salomon 34, 185
alternate service levels 134
application service provider (ASP) 58
audits, for Best Value 98

balanced scorecard 9, 12, 28, 30, 34, 46, 55, 59, 71, 73, 74, 79, 84, 120, 121, 134, 144, 142, 145–6, 171, 190–2, 196–7
  cause and effect relationship 149, 150, 152, 191
  customer perspective 84, 148, 150, 154
  financial perspective 147, 148, 154
  innovation perspective 147, 148, 149, 154
  internal perspective 148
  implementation 149, 151, 153, 155–156, 171, 175. 191
  measures driving performance 148–9
  strategy focused organisations 149–153
  strategy maps 149–153
  ten commandments of implementation 155
  quality frameworks 156–8
  weighted scorecard 153–155
Baldridge 158
Barings Bank 118
Barnsley, John 194
BBC 13, 58, 60–66, 186
Beebe, Michael 59

benchmarking 9, 11, 12, 23, 28, 30, 42, 74, 85, 124, 133, 134, 142, 161, 167–180, 192
  benefits 177
  case study 177
  code of conduct 175–6
  collaborative 170
  competitive 171
  data analysis 173
  data collection 171–2
  documenting own processes 173
  ethics and etiquette 176
  external databases 169
  Hackett Group study 11
  implementing recommendations 175
  internal 169
  partners 23, 26, 170, 173, 175, 176, 184, 192
  reviewing 175
  team organisation 172
Best Practice 12, 15, 26, 33, 35, 46, 47, 48, 56, 64, 85, 156, 169, 177, 192
Best Value 8, 10, 28, 33, 89, 97–99, 158, 160, 161, 166, 169, 170, 177, 180, 187–8, 192
  Audit and inspection 98
  Local Government (Best Value and Capping) Bill 1998 97
  Fundamental Performance Reviews (FPRs) 98
  Local Performance Plans (LPPs) 98, 188
  National Performance indicators (NPIs) 98, 166
beyond budgeting round table 135–6, 141–2
Boston Consulting Group 94
bottom-up empowerment cycle 8, 100, 132, 139, 148, 189
BP Exploration 53
BPR (business process re-engineering) 12, 15, 16, 28, 134
brainstorming 26, 175

Index

brand value   113–4
Brassington, Keith   26
British Aerospace   103–9, 188
budgeting   8, 9, 15, 28, 43, 74, 80, 81, 100, 108, 127, 129, 132–6, 140, 141, 142, 151, 189–190
   beyond budgeting round table   135–6, 141–2
   beyond traditional   132–136
   case studies   140–143
   priority-based budgeting (PBB)   9, 12, 28, 79, 134
business analysts   12, 13, 29, 32
business consultants   12, 13, 29, 32
business intelligence tools   6, 29, 71, 73, 77–82, 186
Business Objects   73, 77, 79, 161, 162, 165, 166
business process management   xvii, 7, 12, 15, 23, 28, 29, 73, 101, 134, 169
business planning tools   80, 181
business process re-engineering (BPR)   12, 15, 16, 28, 134

case studies
   Adidas-Salomon   34
   BBC   60–66
   Black Country Housing   124
   British Aerospace   103–9
   Body Shop   123
   Borealis   141
   BP   124
   CIBA Speciality Chemicals   47
   CISCO   16
   Dell Computer   34
   Diagio   124, 141
   HP Bulmer   142
   Intel   124
   Manchester Council Housing   160–6
   Microsoft   15
   MOD   16
   Monsanto   123
   Nationwide   82–7
   Nike   123
   Railtrack   123
   Scandia   124
   Shell International   124
   SmithKline Beecham   35
   Tower Hamlets   177–180
   Unipol   124
   Volvo   140
cash drivers   92
cash value added (CVA™)   94, 187
cashflow return on investment (CFROI)   94, 187
cause and effect relationships between perspectives 149, 150, 152, 191
CAM-I   132, 135, 190
CCT (Compulsory Competitive Tendering)   8, 186
change,
   facilitators of   14, 15
   finance function   11, 19–34
   impact of   46
   organisational culture   8
   organisational structure   9, 13
   public sector legislation   8
   roles   10–15
   skills   10, 29
   technology-driven   5
   transformation process   19–34
Chua, W.F.   14
CIMA   69, 122
CIMA Research   32, 171
CIPFA   99
CISCO   16
Citizens' Charter   8
Coca Cola   101
collaborative benchmarking   170
collaborative computing   6, 29, 73, 186
Collum, Hugh   21, 184
Common data model   35, 147
communication   23, 32, 57, 139, 155, 172, 184
competencies   22, 29, 31, 32, 64, 75, 117, 184
competitive benchmarking   171
competitive environment   60
Compulsory Competitive Tendering (CCT) 8, 186
computer and telephone integration (CTI)   29
Comshare   81
Conoco   53
continuous improvement   12, 28, 57, 75, 85, 97, 98, 123, 169, 188, 192

contract management 53
corporate reputation 8, 92, 113, 117–118, 189
costs,
 of the finance function 11, 26
 reducing 21, 25, 78
Creating Shareholder Value (Rappaport) 92, 120
Creelman, James 57
critical success factors (CSF) 83, 147, 162, 187
customer relationship management (CRM) 69, 72–3
CFO magazine 133
CSC 47, 48, 59
CTI (computer and telephone integration) 29
culture
 empowered organisation 129–132
 top down control cycle 8, 17, 130, 136, 139, 155,189
customer
 balanced scorecard perspective 84, 148, 150, 154
 capital (relational) 113–115, 188
 focused 9, 30, 41, 47, 57, 156, 183, 185
 profitability 28, 79
 satisfaction 30, 33, 47, 84, 85, 140, 157
customer (relational) capital 113
 customer value 113
 brand value 113–4
CVA™ (cash value added) 94, 187

data collection 82
data warehousing 29, 77, 78, 82–5, 186
decision support 10, 21, 28, 77–82, 183, 184, 187
decision support systems (DSS) 29, 78–80, 187
Dell Computer 34, 185
desktop information management tools 29, 72, 78, 79
Diageo 124, 141, 190
discounted cash-flow (DCF) 100, 129
document management 6, 29, 73, 76, 81

drivers 7, 79, 91, 92, 93, 99, 104, 115, 137, 142, 148, 151, 159, 187
DSS (decision support systems) 29, 78–80, 187

e-commerce 81, 159
Ernst Young 76, 187
Eastman Kodak 51
economic value added (EVA™) 93–6, 187
EDS 27, 61
EFQM Business Excellence Model 26, 30, 156–8, 191
electronic commerce 73
Elf Oil 59
EIS (enterprise information system) 6, 79
embedded VBM system 99–101
empowered organisation 129–132
enterprise information portal 81
enterprise information system (EIS) 6, 79
enterprise resource planning (ERP) 6, 72
enterprise risk management (ERM) 28, 118–122
environmental reporting 8, 122–124
ERM (enterprise risk management) 28, 118–122
ERP (enterprise resource planning) 6, 72
ethical reporting 8, 122–124
EVA™ (economic value added) 93–6, 187

facilitating change 14, 33, 91
finance function 1–34
 challenges 7–10
 changing roles 10–13
 changing structures 10–13
 facilitator of change 14–15
 lights out 5
 technology-driven 5
 transformation process 19–34
 web-enabled 6
finance professionals 10–14, 27, 69, 183
 business analysts 12, 13, 29, 32
 business consultants 12, 13, 29, 32

competencies 29, 31, 32, 64, 75, 117, 184
  job roles 10–14
  job specifications 29, 32
  people specifications 29, 32
  retraining 11, 12
  technical specialists 12, 13, 29, 32
Financial Perspective (balanced scorecard) 147, 148, 154
financing activities 10, 12, 28
force field analysis 174
forecast, rolling 9, 134, 140, 143, 190
forecasting 15, 28, 74, 81, 138–140, 184, 189–190
fundamental performance reviews (FPRs) 98

Gartner Group 58, 77
Gattenio, Christine 27
General Electric 136, 141
Giozueta, Roberto 93
Global Benchmarks Alliance 23
groupware 29, 73

Hackett Group 11, 27
Harris Research 51
Hawkins, Dean 34
Heywood, J Brian 53
HOLT Value Associates 94
Hoover 118, 120
human capital 116–117, 189
Hyperian Planning and Modelling 81

IBM 51, 82, 116, 171
impact of change 46
impact of technology 7,
information management 28, 60, 67–85, 186–7
  activity/process software 79–80
  client/server 77, 83
  computer and telephone integration (CTI) 29
  continuous improvement 12, 28, 57, 75, 95, 97, 98, 123, 169, 188, 192
  data warehousing 29, 77, 78, 82–85, 186
  decision support systems (DSS) 29, 78–80, 187
  desktop tools 29, 72, 78, 79

document management 6, 29, 73, 76, 81
electronic commerce (e-commerce) 81, 159
enterprise information system (EIS) 6, 79
enterprise resource planning (ERP) 6, 72
existing system analysis 22, 23–26,
future needs analysis 74
groupware 29, 73
impact of technology 7
legacy systems 62, 71, 74, 186
management information systems (MIS) 79
middleware 6, 29, 72, 186
on-line analytical processing (OLAP) 29, 69, 77, 78, 79, 187
project teams 192
role of 70
strategy 73–5, 82, 85, 186, 191
web-enabled 69, 72
workflow systems 29
information overload 69, 71
infrastructure assets 116
innovation 101, 129, 133, 134
  balanced scorecard perspective 147, 148, 149, 154
  stifling 131
integrated performance management 9, 28, 30, 147
integrated risk management 120
intellectual capital 8, 28, 92, 113–124, 188–189
intellectual property 115
intangible assets 8, 91, 113–124, 129, 151, 188–9
  corporate reputation 117
  customer (relational) capital 113
  human capital 116–8, 189
  organisational (structural) capital 115
  valuing 111–7
Intel 15, 184
inter-business unit charging 101–102
internal audit 28, 43, 54
internal benchmarking 169, 170
internal business perspective (balanced scorecard) 148
internal rate of return (IIR) 91, 94

International Accounting Standards
(IASC) 44
Internet 6, 15, 51, 71, 72, 76, 77, 82,
114, 119, 136, 158, 160, 191
portals 6, 21, 29, 69, 71, 72, 81, 82,
187
standards 6
intranets 6, 16, 71, 73, 76, 161, 164,
191
invitation to tender (ITT) 53, 54–5
invoicing process 25

Jee, Susan 14
job roles 12
job specifications 29, 32
Johnson, H.T. 130–132

Kaplan, R.S. 147, 148, 149, 151, 191
Kersnar, Janet 141
key performance indicators (KPIs) 24,
83, 103, 104, 121, 140, 142, 147,
149, 152, 159, 164, 187, 190
knowledge management 75–76
KPMG 101, 116, 133, 191

Lastminute.com 159
legacy systems 62, 71, 74, 186
local performance plans (LPPs) 98, 188

Malcolm Baldrige National Quality
Awards 156, 157
management information systems (MIS)
79
managing intangibles, case studies
123–124
Manchester Business School 53
Manchester City Council 160
market value added (MVA) 93–4, 115
May, Matthew 59
measures of performance 6, 24, 46,
71, 84, 102, 104, 148–149, 169
MedAS 61, 62, 66
Meredith, Tom 34, 35
Microsoft 15
middleware 6, 29, 72, 186
mission statements 27
Mobil 42, 149, 153

MOD 16
MVA (market value added) 93–4, 115

national performance indicators (NPIs)
98, 166
Nationwide 82–5
net present value (NPV) 91
Norton, D.P. 147, 148, 149, 151, 191
on-line analytical processing (OLAP)
29, 69, 77, 78, 79, 187
Oracle 17, 25
organisational (structural) capital
115–116, 188
infrastructure assets 116
intellectual property 115
research and development 115
organisation structure 9, 29, 101
outsourcing 9, 30, 41, 51–66, 82, 153,
185, 186
ASP 58
BBC 60–6
benefits 56, 63
bid evaluation 55
contract management 53
information gathering 54
invitation to tender (ITT) 53, 54–5
partnerships 54
problems of 51, 52
rejecting 52
risks in 51, 52, 57
second generation 54

PBB (priority-based budgeting) 9, 12,
28, 79, 134
people specifications 32
Peoplesoft 79, 81
performance improvement 14, 28, 134
business process re-engineering (BPR)
12, 15, 16, 28, 134
performance management 9, 15, 28,
30, 37, 99–100, 115, 134, 148
activity analysis 23–4, 79
activity-based budgeting (ABB) 80
activity-based costing 79, 134
activity-based management (ABM)
79, 158

activity-based techniques (ABT)   101, 169
alternate service levels   134
balanced scorecard   9, 12, 28, 30, 34, 46, 55, 59, 71, 73, 74, 79, 84, 120, 121, 134, 144, 142, 145–6, 171, 190–2, 196–7
business process management   xvii, 7, 12, 15, 23, 28, 29, 73, 101, 134, 169
critical success factors (CSF)   83, 147, 162, 187
key performance indicators (KPIs)   24, 83, 103, 104, 121, 140, 142, 147, 149, 152, 159, 164, 187, 190
integrated   147
priority-based budgeting (PBB)   9, 12, 28, 79, 134
planning process, continuous   140
price/earnings ratio (P/E)   91
pricing   28, 44, 63, 93
PriceWaterhouseCoopers (PwC)   16, 23, 42, 59, 170, 185, 187
priority-based budgeting (PBB)   9, 12, 28, 79, 134
process-based techniques   69, 134, 190
activity-based budgeting (ABB)   80
activity-based costing   79, 134
activity-based management (ABM)   79, 158
activity-based techniques (ABT)   101, 169
alternate service levels   134
business process management   xvii, 7, 12, 15, 23, 28, 29, 73, 101, 134, 169
BPR (business process re-engineering)   12, 15, 16, 28, 134
priority-based budgeting (PBB)   9, 12, 28, 79, 134
public sector
Best Value audits   98
Citizens' Charter   12
compulsory competitive tendering (CCT)   8, 51, 101, 186
Best Value fundamental performance reviews (FPRs)   98

Best Value local performance plans (LPPs)   98, 188
Best Value national performance indicators (NPIs)   98, 166
Highways Department
Local Government (Best Value and Capping) Bill 1998   97
legislation   8
Manchester City Council (Housing)   160
MOD   16
Tower Hamlets   177–180

quality frameworks   26, 147, 156–8, 191
Baldridge   158
EFQM Business Excellence Model   26, 30, 156–8, 191

Rappaport, Alfred, shareholder value formula   92, 187
reducing costs   21, 25, 78
Regional Aircraft (BAe)   104, 109, 188
Relevance Regained (Kaplan & Johnson)   130,
reporting   5, 6, 12, 43, 54, 79, 80, 81, 82
ethical, environmental and social   122–123
research and development   115
resource allocation   28, 74, 113, 129, 134, 140, 188, 189, 190
risk management   8, 9, 21, 28, 92, 118–122, 123
enterprise risk management (ERM)   28, 118–122
ERM (enterprise risk management)   28, 118–122
environmental reporting   8, 122–124
ethical reporting   8, 122–124
integrated risk management   120
social reporting   8, 122–124
Turnbull   122
rolling forecast   9, 134, 140, 143, 190

sales invoicing process   25
SAP   60, 61, 62, 79

SAS CFOVision   80
Scandia   124
scenario planning   9, 12, 28, 136–138, 140, 180
Sears   53
service levels   28, 52, 134, 169
service-level agreements (SLAs)   6, 9, 24, 101–2
service-oriented   47, 101
shared service centre (SSC)   5, 10, 13, 16, 28, 30, 32, 39–48, 153, 185, 186
   accounting and legal differences   43, 185
   benefits of approach   47
   BBC   60
   Ciba Speciality Chemicals   47
   implementation stages   45–7
   Medas
   suitable processes   42
   taxation   43, 44, 185
   web enabled   6, 30, 41
shareholder value   7, 59, 89–109, 115, 116, 117, 118, 120, 121, 129, 159, 187–188, 189
   British Aerospace   103–9
   cash value added (CVA™)   94, 187
   cashflow return on investment (CFROI)   94, 187
   characteristics of VBM organisations   101
   economic value added (EVA™)   93–6, 187
   embedded VBM system   99–101
   inter-business unit charging   101–2
   market value added (MVA)   93, 94, 115
   Rappaport's theory   92, 187
   SVA options matrix   97
SMAC   12
Shell   21, 119, 123, 124, 137, 184
skills requirements   12, 13, 31–33
Smith, John   61, 66
SmithKline Beecham   21, 35, 184
social reporting   8, 122–124
software   77–81
   activity/process   79, 80
   Activa   80
   Adaytum e Planning   80

Brio   77
Business Objects   73, 77, 79, 161, 162, 165, 166
Cognos   77, 82
Comshare   81
Corvu   80
ERP   44
Excel   78
Hyperion   78, 80, 81, 82
IBM   82
Interbiz   77
IManage   76
iTM1   78
Lotus Notes   76
Lotus Smartsuite   72
Metify   80
Microsoft Office   72
Microsoft SQL   78
NetScore/Prophet   80
Oracle   80
OROS   80
Panoramic Business View   80
Peoplesoft   79, 80, 81
Plumtree   81
Questor   82
SAP/R3   60, 62, 79, 80
SAS CFOVision   80
spreadsheet   5, 72, 78, 104, 165, 183
Verity   76
steering group   22, 33, 184
stewardship activities   10, 12
stifling innovation   131
strategy   73–5, 82, 85, 186, 191
   continuous planning process   140
   integrated performance management   9, 28, 30, 147
   maps   149–153
   scenario planning   9, 12, 28, 136–138, 140, 180
   strategy focused organisations   149–153, 191
strategy-focused organisation   150–153, 191
supply chain management (SCM)   69, 72–3

targets   41, 91, 98, 99, 100, 104, 122, 123, 134, 135, 136, 140, 141, 142, 153, 166, 179, 188

taxation   43, 44, 185
teams   13, 24, 74, 108, 138, 151, 162, 172, 192
technical specialists   12, 13, 29, 32
technological advances   29, 45, 69,
technological developments   7, 47, 69, 72–73, 138, 186, 190
top down control cycle   8, 17, 130, 136, 139, 155,189
Tower Hamlets   170, 177–180, 192
training   10, 29, 30, 32, 33, 51, 64, 83, 93, 108, 139, 155, 169, 183
transaction processing   21, 35, 45, 53, 60, 71
transformation project
  benchmarking partners   23, 26, 170, 173, 175, 176, 184, 192
  brainstorming sessions   26
  business case   31
  communication   23
  customer identification   23
  data collection   26
  develop the vision   26–30
  implementation   33
  monitoring   33–34
  process map   23–4
  project plan   30
  skills requirements   31–33
  specification definition   28–30
  steering group   22, 33, 184
  team appointment   22
  training and development plans   32
  vision statements   27
transfer pricing   44
transition planning   33
treasury   13, 43, 119
TUPE   61, 65
Turnbull   122

University of Leeds   171

value drivers   92, 93, 104, 187
value statements   27
value-based management (VBM)   12, 28, 89–124, 129, 153, 187–8, 190
  British Aerospace   103–9
  cash value added (CVA™)   94, 187
  cashflow return on investment (CFROI)   94, 187

characteristics of VBM organisations   101
  economic value added (EVA™)   93–6, 187
  embedded VBM system   99–101
  environmental reporting   8, 122–124
  ethical reporting   8, 122–124
  inter-business unit charging   101–2
  market value added (MVA)   93, 94, 115
  Rappaport's theory   92, 187
  risk management   8, 9, 21, 28, 92, 118–122, 123
  social reporting   8, 122–124
  SVA options matrix   97
  Valuing intangible assets/intellectual capital   111–7
VAT   44, 45
VBM (value-based management)   12, 28, 89–124, 129, 153, 187–8, 190
vision statements   27

web-enabled
  environment   7, 41, 129, 185
  finance function   30
  information management   72
  organisations   7, 13, 15, 72
  processes   14, 15, 28, 72
  self service applications   6
  solutions   16
  SSC   6, 30, 41
  systems   10, 72
  technology   21, 58, 69, 186
  virtual finance function   11
web tools   82
weighted average cost of capital (WACC)   92, 94
weighted scorecard   153–155
Welch, Jack   141
Wilson, R.M.S.   14
workflow systems   29
world wide web   172

Xansa   59
Xerox   171

Yea, Phillip   141

Z charts   173, 174